WHITENESS IN PLAIN VIEW

MINNESOTA
HISTORICAL
SOCIETY PRESS

WHITENESS IN PLAIN VIEW

A History of Racial Exclusion in Minnesota

CHAD MONTRIE

Unless otherwise credited, all images are from the collections of the Minnesota Historical Society.

Portions of this book have appeared in different form in the following publications:

"A Bigoted, Prejudiced, Hateful Little Area: The Making of an All-White Suburb in the Deep North." *Journal of Urban History* 45, no. 2 (March 2019): 300–320.

"'In That Very Northern City': Recovering the Forgotten Struggle for Racial Integration in Duluth, Minnesota." *Minnesota History* 67, no. 2 (Summer 2020): 70–80.

mnhspress.org

The Minnesota Historical Society Press is a member of the Association of University Presses.

Manufactured in the United States of America.

10 9 8 7 6 5 4 3 2 1

♾ The paper used in this publication meets the minimum requirements of the American National Standard for Information Sciences—Permanence for Printed Library Materials, ANSI Z39.48-1984.

International Standard Book Number
ISBN: 978-1-68134-210-8 (paperback)
ISBN: 978-1-68134-211-5 (e-book)

Library of Congress Control Number: 2021950245

This and other Minnesota Historical Society Press books are available from popular e-book vendors.

CONTENTS

INTRODUCTION

In the context of the Negro problem neither whites nor blacks, for excellent reasons of their own, have the faintest desire to look back; but I think that the past is all that makes the present coherent, and further, that the past will remain horrible for exactly as long as we refuse to assess it honestly.

JAMES BALDWIN
"Autobiographical Notes," *Notes of a Native Son*

THIS BOOK, as sociologist Avery Gordon might say, is a ghost story. Its primary aim, the purpose of acknowledging ghosts in our midst, is to fathom how we came to be haunted in the first place. Its secondary aim, what follows after we start seeing ghosts, is to use that awareness to put them to rest. Of course, by ghosts I do not mean actual spectral apparitions. Being haunted, in the sense that Gordon suggests and that I intend, is "the animated state in which a repressed or unresolved social violence is making itself known." This unsettled state can and does take sundry forms, "those singular yet repetitive instances when home becomes unfamiliar, when your bearings on the world lose direction, when the over-and-done-with comes alive, when what's been your blind spot comes into view." Still, Gordon insists, a haunting is not merely a newly roused sense, a feeling or perception of a historical wrong. When discernment finally begins to dawn, leaving us unmoored, it also transforms into "something to be done," forcing a confrontation with the truth and "forking the future and the past."¹

Whiteness in Plain View attempts to recover a particular occurrence of unresolved social violence, one chapter in the long and varied history of White Americans' purposeful efforts to exclude African Americans from their midst. This shameful past left a fossilized geography of Whiteness in its wake, something that is both a presence and an absence at the same time. For many Whites living in the current moment, that history is unknown, or mistakenly known, or known but checked, and the racial uniformity they encounter daily in their neighborhoods, schools, government, and elsewhere remains, as another sociologist, Jim Loewen, has put it, "hidden in plain view." It is impossible for them to see it, or to see its numerous facets and dimensions, until it is seen, and then it appears everywhere and in multiplicity. Confessing that the overwhelming Whiteness exists, and explaining how that Whiteness came to be, is the beginning of reckoning with what it means and, possibly, realizing the economic, political, and social reparations it requires.²

Even more specifically, this book focuses on the practice of racial exclusion of African Americans in the state of Minnesota during the nineteenth and twentieth centuries. It details the ways White residents in towns, cities, and suburbs across the state acted to intimidate, control, remove, and keep out Black residents. Their methods ranged from anonymous threats, vandalism, and mob violence to restrictive housing covenants, realtor deceit, and mortgage discrimination. These actions were aided by support from local, state, and federal government agencies as well as openly complicit public officials. What they did was not a lapse or aberration, an isolated flare of hatred in a single place or a minor blemish on a largely clean record of welcome and acceptance. It was conventional and common, and the efforts at exclusion enjoyed shifting legal license from decade to decade. Additionally, the all-White communities that resulted became their own justification and propagating agent, demonstrating (to Whites) that Blacks wanted to live only among their own race, confirming (to Whites) that African Americans did not have the economic means to integrate, and supporting the notion (among Whites) that Blacks' supposed racial failings must be what kept them out.

Whiteness centers on racial exclusion in Minnesota because for many Whites, at least until very recently, the pairing of the two is counterintuitive, and the state's history speaks to a larger conversation about how race, or more exactly the attempted exercise of "White supremacy," figures in standard regional distinctions. The popular rendering of the American South, as historians Matthew D. Lassiter and Joseph Crespino observe, often emphasizes how it is racially exceptional, attributing "episodes of racism and racial violence" there to the region's social and political structures, "while portraying similar events elsewhere as anomalous." The corollary to this "southern exceptionalism" is "northern exceptionalism," which, as another historian, Jeanne Theoharis, explains, frames manifestations of racism in the North as "flaws in an otherwise liberal land of opportunity," rather than as a constitutive element of the region's culture, politics, and economy. And, at first glance, that does seem to describe Minnesota. Located in the upper reaches of the Great Lakes region, the midwestern state has always had a relatively small Black population, one that posed little threat in terms of competition with Whites for housing and jobs, suggesting there was never any material basis for significant racial animosity. Likewise, the state has a reputation for putting forward racially progressive White political leaders, such as Hubert Humphrey, and nationally recognized Black race advocates, such as Roy Wilkins, which hints at a general racial tolerance. On the contrary, however, neither fact allowed Minnesota to avoid a sordid racist past, stained by formal restrictions on rights, recurrent racial violence, and other calculated efforts to remove and exclude African Americans from whole neighborhoods and towns—all of that grounds for challenging the "exceptionalism" mythology.[3]

To be sure, there were fractures in what was generally a White consensus about racial exclusion in the Great Lakes state, and African Americans themselves mustered resistance to their marginalization and segregation. Whites proposed farming colonies for Blacks newly freed from slavery in the 1860s and 1870s, supported judicial intervention to punish other Whites for participating in a lynching during the 1920s, lobbied for city and state fair housing legislation in the 1950s and 1960s, and organized human relations councils to encourage African American families to move to their neighborhoods in the latter decade as well. Likewise, Blacks in central city neighborhoods, outlying suburbs, and distant towns stood fast in the face of White intimidation, organized civil rights groups chapters, and engaged in acts of nonviolent civil disobedience. *Whiteness* also explores these various disjunctures, assessing how they came to be, tracing how they evolved, and weighing their impact. The resistance and activism were part of a dialectic, responding to manifestations of White racism and at the same time altering the context for its continued expression in housing and employment discrimination, besides inequality and disparity in education, health care, and other facets of life.[4]

By looking at what was happening throughout Minnesota, this book has another purpose too, which is to unmask the class dimension of racial exclusion. Moving from industrial blue-collar towns to genteel streetcar suburbs, it becomes clear that vulgar prejudice and violent attacks were more often associated with laboring Whites while "polite" pretext and realtor subterfuge were more typical among the affluent. In some cases, there were even public disagreements between working-class and middle-class residents living in the same place about how their racism might be expressed. Yet despite the differences in manner and method, and outside the flashes of class discordance, it is equally evident that Whites had the same purpose in mind: keeping African Americans out of their communities, or at least keeping them pacified and confined to a delimited area. When pressed, they were quite capable of mobilizing and acting as a race, from an organized campaign to embed White supremacy in the state constitution to steadfast opposition to fair housing legislation. In fact, assessing this simply in terms of demographics, by the mid-twentieth century the results of White people's efforts to achieve racial homogeneity were largely indistinguishable from one community to another.

As *Whiteness* takes stock of the mix of White historical actors involved in exclusion it also adds to a growing literature about the role that local, state, and federal policy played in enabling, accomplishing, and protecting residential segregation across the country. That work identifies an assortment of exclusionary zoning practices, racial covenants, discriminatory mortgage lending programs, and officially recognized color lines in public housing projects, all intended to forcibly separate Whites and African Americans. As evidence of the US government's full culpability accumulates, however, there is some risk of understating or overlooking the extent to which policy and law reflected, sustained, and reinforced popular White will and its more complex and evolving extralegal exercise. In terms of crafting a historical interpretation as well as assigning moral blame, it matters whether we emphasize government enacting and enforcing policy that required White citizens to honor the color line or White citizens demanding that their government give them the license and tools to establish and defend it. Focusing on the variations in cities, towns, and neighborhoods in one select state, over more than two centuries, provides an opportunity both to capture the full range of methods Whites used and to attempt an unusual version of looking at the past "from the bottom up," a perspective typically associated with recovering the lost history of the marginalized and disenfranchised.[5]

Examining the multiplicity of ways Whites accomplished racial exclusion in Minnesota raises another important question as well, about the validity of James Loewen's "sundown towns" concept. His book by the same title is an impressively commanding survey of White efforts to prevent African Americans from living among them or to remove and keep them away, showing how pervasive that was. Yet Loewen's now widely adopted claim that Whites did this in many places by posting signs or blasting sirens from water towers to tell African Americans they had to leave at sundown greatly oversimplifies what happened and, just as importantly, does not stand very well on evidence. We have no former signs or pictures of signs and no city council or town records directing sirens to be used to signal Black exclusion, only anecdotal recollections. For Minnesota, though, we have plenty of evidence of legislative efforts to make the state inhospitable to Black migration, violent removal of African Americans by White mobs, standard use of racial covenants by White housing developers, concerted obstruction by White realtors to prospective Black renters and homeowners, and organized neighborhood opposition by White families to racial integration, all of which were as much or more important than signs or sirens might have been. And, in some cases, we have perplexing incongruities. White working-class residents ran most of the few dozen Black residents out of Austin in the 1920s, for example, and Loewen claims it was thereafter a "sundown town" with a sign posted at the city limits, but the local Fox Hotel is listed in the 1962 *Negro Motorist Greenbook*.[6]

While some of the history told here may be familiar to scholars working in various fields or laypeople with certain interests, *Whiteness in Plain View* seeks to link together those stories and many other lesser acknowledged facets of Minnesota's past and fold them into a more expansive interpretation. That is, the book's wider historical perspective allows recognition of connections and meanings that more narrowly focused studies cannot see or understand. In a few cases, like the lynchings in Duluth during the summer of 1920, newly found archival material also allows for recasting and extending received or traditional accounts of events, further illuminating their place in a larger narrative. That atrocity was not an unforeseen violent outburst but rather the culmination of long-simmering racial tensions, stoked by White concern about porous racial boundaries in the city's vice underworld. Likewise, it was a foundational moment in a longer story of a hardening color line during the decades to follow—and eventually diligent efforts by Black and White residents to dissolve and break it—with resonant parallels to what was happening elsewhere. Examining racial exclusion in this manner, stretching between the parts to reveal a whole, and with a more methodical and meticulous use of available primary sources toward that end, lends a nuanced significance to each chapter.

It should be noted at the outset, however, what *Whiteness in Plain View* is not. The book is not a comparative history, illuminating racial exclusion in Minnesota by showing how it was similar to or different from racial exclusion in a nearby state or several states scattered around the country. That would require another mammoth amount of archival labor, and it would hinder chronological and topical coherence in ways that might make the study less rather than more accessible to a range of readers. *Whiteness* is also not African American history, at least not by most definitions. Black Americans are neither the main actors nor the principal subjects, although, because the lives of Blacks and Whites are intertwined in the United States, and it is the "why" and "how" of their absence that is in question, they are prominent in the narrative. Moreover, despite the book's title, it falls outside of "Whiteness studies." It employs the concept of "Whiteness" and the idea of "White supremacy," but it is not meant to be a cultural or intellectual history of those ideas. The story the individual chapters trace is about what White people did to impose White supremacy on the landscape as well as how they fashioned an erroneous and dishonest memory of what they did in order to perpetuate a racist social order in their own present, a memory that allowed them to deny or shirk responsibility for it. Where their notions of race and racial hierarchy came from, or how they changed over time, and why Whites believed in them, are subjects for another kind of investigation altogether.

Whiteness in Plain View is not Native American history either, yet it begins by explaining Whites' removal of the Dakota (and Ho-Chunk) tribes from Minnesota during the nineteenth century. Most of the African Americans who initially came to the territory were enslaved, and they worked for Whites as the latter extracted wealth through trade with different tribes, converted Indigenous people to Christianity, and dispossessed Native Americans of their land. Consequently, the racial histories of each group were tightly linked. For a few decades, in fact, this was sometimes literal. Numerous territorial residents were bi- or triracial as well as multilingual and multicultural, the sons and daughters and grandchildren of White, Black, and Native parents and grandparents. The various forms of common interaction did not last, however, and the color line hardened as Whites' land- and bloodlust reached their conclusion in the US–Dakota War, which ended with the Dakota's removal, at the very same moment the United States was plunged into a Civil War over racial slavery. Especially for readers unfamiliar with Minnesota history, chronicling the shift from racial entanglement to Whites' first act of wholesale racial exclusion is critical for putting subsequent White efforts to hinder postbellum Black migration to the state in their proper context. What's more, the need many Whites felt to shore up White supremacy in the wake of the two concurrent wars, each of which was driven by conflict over that very thing, was a key dimension of Minnesota Whites' racism against African Americans into the next century.

Finally, as a historical account, *Whiteness in Plain View* is first and foremost about the past, but it is about the present as well. Chapter by chapter, the book establishes a record of intentional and widespread racial exclusion that is the foundation for a legacy of privilege Whites as a group enjoy today. Barring African Americans from neighborhoods and even whole towns reserved certain amenities for Whites, from political power and union jobs to select social networks and well-funded schools, and it gave White families a chance to build up modest if not significant wealth through federally subsidized home equity. They then leveraged their privilege and wealth in generations to follow, many enjoying a considerable amount of financial stability or even experiencing a leap of economic mobility as a result, and that widened contemporary racial disparities. This fact underlies Blacks' comparatively poor health, low life expectancy, lagging educational achievement, high rates of incarceration, and persistent poverty into the present day. Whites from the past and in the current moment are very much implicated in this, and the book not only makes clear their role in creating and maintaining inequality but also points to the responsibility they have for undoing it.

There is, of course, an ongoing struggle to address racial inequality in Minnesota and elsewhere in the United States, rooted in tireless past efforts by people of color and allied Whites and injected with new militancy by the advent of Black Lives Matter (BLM) organizing and protests. BLM started in 2013, after George Zimmerman was acquitted in the shooting death of African American teen Trayvon Martin, and seven years later, when White police officer Derek Chauvin murdered African American George Floyd in Minneapolis—on land that once belonged to the Dakota, and in a section of the city that was once nearly all White—activists became even more determined to force a public reckoning with racism and its many manifestations. This contemporary struggle is reflected in two edited collections, *A Good Time for the Truth: Race in Minnesota*, published in 2016, four months after a Minnesota police officer killed Jamar Clark and three months before another killed Philando Castile, and *Sparked: George Floyd, Racism, and the Progressive Illusion*, published a year after Floyd's death. "Our hope," Walter R. Jacobs writes in the preface to the latter, "is that the essays in this volume will spark conversations among friends and family about race, racism, and racial inequality in Minnesota and beyond, and that they spark progressive action and radical change." *Whiteness in Plain View* is meant to complement the written personal testimonies in these and other books, as well as those voiced at street protests and public forums, and also aid honest conversations and transformative action. As an accounting of one critical part of the long and complicated history of White supremacy in Minnesota, it seeks to make a measurable contribution to the historical consciousness necessary for altering the present.[7]

Keeping in mind the past's potency, and the lasting pain it exerts on people now, readers should be forewarned that *Whiteness in Plain View* often allows racist Whites to speak for themselves. It does this in order to more effectively bring their racism into plain view. Whites' regular, casual, and public use of the "n" word and other hateful speech lent a linguistic dimension to how they accomplished, maintained, and defended racial exclusion, and that needs to be made explicit. Additionally, in the matter of language, it should be noted that this book capitalizes Black, Indigenous, and White (when not in a direct quote where usage was otherwise). It does this because "race" is not a natural category but rather an artificial one, a social and historical construction. To be sure, some style guides capitalize Black and Indigenous yet still do not capitalize White. The *Star Tribune* follows this usage, insisting that "Black describes a shared experience in a way that White does not." Likewise, Minnesota Public Radio follows selective capitalization for the print versions of its stories, asserting that White "doesn't represent a collective identity and history in the same way that Black does." As *Whiteness in Plain View* demonstrates, however, this is simply not true. Racial exclusion could not have happened if White people did not think of themselves and act as a race persistently over time (people can have a shared history and culture by being the oppressing group as well as by being the group oppressed). Claiming otherwise also treats "white" as a fact and leaves it as a normative category, which dances dangerously on the margins of a different kind of racist thinking.[8]

The first chapter of this book is titled "'The Master Race of the World Is Caucasian': Punitive Expeditions, Mass Hanging, and Forced Removal." It traces the entangled history of Native people, White colonists, and African Americans (both enslaved and free) living together along the Minnesota and Mississippi Rivers during the first half of the nineteenth century. It begins in the 1820s, with the American government's establishment of Fort Snelling and the first Christian missionary projects and concludes with the US–Dakota War of 1862 and its aftermath. The chapter also notes how the military tribunal leading to the mass execution of captured Dakota men largely rested on evidence acquired through formerly enslaved African American and tribal member Joseph Godfrey, who survived the ordeal and was himself subsequently moved to a distant reservation with remaining Dakota. This forced removal brought an abrupt end to the few missionaries' hopes for integrating Native people into Euro-American society and to many Whites, like Minnesota State Supreme Court justice Daniel Buck, it followed logically from the belief that "the master race of the world is Caucasian." What's more, as noted above, war and removal established the context for African Americans' post–Civil War migration to the newly formed state, and the possibility of that migration in turn provoked determined White efforts to prevent it, albeit alongside some Whites' deliberate endeavors to welcome it.[9]

The second chapter, "'They All Must Be Taught Their Duty': Barbers, Porters, Washerwomen, and Inmates," records the arrival and fate of early Black migrants in Minnesota, looking primarily at the area where the US–Dakota War took place. It starts with the story of White St. Peter resident Thomas Montgomery, who joined the military expedition against Dakota people in 1862 and soon after left to command a regiment of "colored" troops in Louisiana during the Civil War. Taking an interest in the future and well-being of the emancipated slaves, at one point the lieutenant sent the wife of one of his soldiers to live with Montgomery's ailing mother. Later, he entertained the idea of organizing a larger Black "colony" on available farmland in Minnesota. "They all must be taught their duty," Montgomery wrote in a letter home, describing the newly freed people he daily encountered, and he pledged to be an instrumental part of that by overseeing their resettlement. Like other such plans, though, this one did not come to fruition. Over the following decades, African American migration to St. Peter and Nicollet County, as well as other counties throughout greater Minnesota, slightly expanded and then drastically contracted. Black residents typically left for St. Paul and Minneapolis, while those who stayed were limited to just a few occupations and socially marginalized. What increase there was in their numbers after the turn of the twentieth century was due to the dozens of Black patients and inmates sent to newly established state-run "insane" asylums, prisons, and orphanages, and most if not all of those patients were transfers from other institutions or residents from the Twin Cities.[10]

The next chapter, "Not 'a Negro Town': Packinghouse Workers and Whiteness in Austin," examines a community in southern Minnesota where a small number of African American migrants moved following the Civil War and, like those in St. Peter, did not experience anything like social equality. In fact, in 1922, after a group of enraged Whites violently expelled a group of Black strikebreakers during a railroad shopmen's strike—marching down the main street asking cheering spectators if they wanted Austin to be "a Negro town"—nearly all the Black residents left. The next decade, some of the men who were part of the mob helped to organize a union at the local Hormel meatpacking plant, greatly improving wages and benefits for the thousands of workers there, every one of whom was White. Ironically, their union, the United Packinghouse Workers of America (UPWA), was known throughout the country for its commitment to racial integration. Moreover, the Hormel local's newspaper, *The Unionist*, faithfully reported on the civil rights movement in the South, linking White southern political leaders' support for segregation to their equally determined opposition to organized labor. In the

1950s, however, when Austin's UPWA leadership organized a Human Rights and Fair Employment Practices Committee and made an investigation of the city's housing, jobs, and schools, they found no apparent racial problems there.[11]

From racial violence and its legacy in industrial Austin, the book turns to a story in a Minnesota steel town and port city. This next chapter, "'In That Very Northern City': Making the Color Line in Duluth," begins by exploring the background, details, and aftermath of a lynching during the summer of 1920, when Whites pulled three Black circus workers accused of raping a White woman from the downtown jail and hanged them on a utility pole in front of thousands of onlookers. Chief of police John Murphy, who was criticized for not adequately protecting the murdered men, later said that he and other colleagues "didn't think anything would happen in this part of the country, that if it were down South it might." But the *New York Times* countered this common claim, observing that the extralegal violence in "that very northern city" showed "human nature" was much the same in both regions. Subsequently, some city leaders feared that Whites might attempt to run Black residents out of the city altogether, a threat averted only by the mustering of National Guard troops and the relatively formidable size of the African American population. Instead, Whites redoubled their efforts to define and maintain a rigid color line, excluding Blacks from all but a few places to live and limiting them to only a handful of menial occupations. Later, at mid-century, a small group of activists came together to challenge Duluth's residential segregation, with an attempt to move African Americans Matt and Helen Carter and their children into an all-White area, but they did this in the face of obstinate and persistent opposition, ranging from specious petitions at public zoning meetings to repeated acts of covert nighttime violence.[12]

Chapter 5, "'A Bigoted, Prejudiced, Hateful Little Area': Racial Exclusion in Edina," shifts the focus back to the western outskirts of Minneapolis, chronicling the history of a community that underwent a transformation from an interracial farming village in the late nineteenth century to an all-White "streetcar" suburb by the late 1930s. Although several African American families were welcomed to Edina following the Civil War and participated in a range of community activities and public roles, after two generations they were gone. Houses in the Country Club District that replaced the farmland were saddled with restrictive racial covenants, and the few Black residents who remained in the district were live-in maids and yard-hands. Moreover, local churches and schools regularly hosted blackface minstrel shows for fundraising. Those shows were fixed on an imagined, "traditional," rural South, and they associated African Americans—or rather, Blackness and Black inferiority—with an era, place, and culture profoundly not the "modern" urban North. Unwittingly or not, the performances helped wipe clean Whites' collective memory of the area's earlier interracial era and, at the same time, marshaled racist caricature to justify racial exclusion. Later, in 1960, when the African American Taylor family attempted to move to Edina's Morningside neighborhood, racist Whites were challenged to stop them without overstepping the pretense of proper social etiquette. Other Whites organized to help, in an effort to transform what mayor Ken Joyce described as "a bigoted, prejudiced, hateful little area," but even after the Taylors settled in, it was a decade and a half before another (interracial) Black family followed.

The next chapter, "'This Vicious Vice': Black Removal in St. Paul," moves across the Twin Cities to examine several adjacent neighborhoods where African American residents were forced out by planning and clearing for highway expansion and "urban renewal" projects. Those sorts of projects were happening all over the country in the decades after World War II, funded by local, state, and federal governments as part of a range of official programs, ostensibly to bring needed improvements to metropolitan areas. Some of the Black families in the St. Paul neighborhoods had originally settled there after leaving small industrial and agricultural towns in various parts of the state. Making the best of social forces compelling racial separation, over decades they built up a cohesive and thriving African American community, albeit one that made room for interracial neighborliness, friendships, and even marriages with the many White residents who lived there too. As (White) public officials began drawing up plans as well as appraising, acquiring, and demolishing homes during the mid-1950s—effectively dismantling the only truly interracial part of St. Paul—the projects sparked protest. The indignity and turmoil did not end there, however, because unlike displaced Whites, Blacks were caught in a "vicious vice," St. Paul National Association for the Advancement of Colored People (NAACP) president Leonard Carter explained, forced to leave but challenged to find other affordable housing in the racist local housing market. Subsequently, demands for city and state "open-occupancy" legislation intensified, culminating in a limited yet useful state fair housing law in 1962.[13]

Following the narrative arc of *Whiteness,* chapter 7, "'The First Negro Family on Our Block': A Housing Integration Campaign in Blooming-ton," examines residents' organizing efforts in another suburb south of Minneapolis and originally the site of the first Christian missions among the Dakota. It uses Bloomington as a window on the local and state-wide fair housing movement as well as fair housing efforts nationally. The campaign there was pushed by a human relations council, founded in 1964, and included civil rights activist Josie Johnson as well as Greater Minneapolis Interfaith Fair Housing Program executive director James Tillman, the two of them among the mere handful of the suburb's Black residents. With their guidance, the council took a varied approach to its task, ranging from themed house meetings like "The First Negro Fam-ily on Our Block" to legislative lobbying for stronger housing legisla-tion, which was achieved in 1967. The next year, their work was helped by passage of the federal Fair Housing Act, and at the beginning of the 1970s, the Minnesota legislature passed the Metropolitan Land Use Plan-ning Act, requiring all suburban communities to provide "a fair share" of moderate- and low-income housing, an indirect way to undo racial exclu-sion. Within another decade, though, it was clear that legal remedies, undermined by continued White resistance, were failing to bring about significant change.

Lastly, the epilogue for *Whiteness in Plain View* addresses racial exclu-sion's persistence in Minnesota and throughout the United States in the twenty-first century. As Bloomington and other communities demonstrate, many suburbs in the Twin Cities metropolitan region have remained more or less racially homogenous, while many cities and towns beyond still have only a small population of Black residents and more than a few have none at all. As a corollary to this, the number of racially segregated, high-poverty neighborhoods in Minneapolis and St. Paul has increased. Still, there are important qualifications in all these respects, as some sub-urbs have become significantly less White, others hold rings or pockets of segregation within their boundaries, and certain towns and cities have seen a notable influx of immigrants who are not White. One of the most evident demographic variations during the last few decades has been the steep rise in local Latino populations, largely Mexican, in many places now considerably surpassing the number of African Americans. Not far behind are those counted by the federal census as "Asian," mostly Hmong families who began to arrive at the end of the US war in Vietnam. The latter group also showed marked increase relative to Blacks but not yet enough to exceed them as a group overall. And Minnesota has the largest Somali population in the country, about 80,000 in 2018. Although these other "non-White" minorities face their own particular challenges with racism, the fact of their growing presence, set against more meager growth in the Black population, suggests that the long history of racial exclusion by Whites against African Americans has had a singular effect on where they live to the present day.[14]

As the content and organization of the book shows, it is not meant to be a fully comprehensive or final account of racial exclusion in Minnesota but rather an episodic history revealing interrelated events in a variety of different places over a long span of time. Each chapter begins with an illustrative anecdote that establishes a topical, geographical, and temporal focus for what follows, and individually they add to a cubist-like portrait of a larger subject. From one to another, the separate installments examine features of White efforts at preventing African Americans from moving to their communities, removing the individuals and families who were already there, or segregating Blacks in certain areas and neighborhoods, and they incrementally make connections between those efforts. Other books and articles have done much to explore various dimensions of the story, and particular sections of *Whiteness in Plain View* add new observations and interpretations to that existing literature. This includes the fluidity and hardening of race relations during White settlement, the periodization as well as serial progression of the Great Migration, the role of industrial labor unions in promoting and challenging racism, the regional and class dimensions of lynching, the modern history of blackface minstrel shows, the differential impact of urban renewal on Whites and Blacks, as well as the invariable Whiteness of suburbs over the twentieth century.

Most importantly, however, this book is meant to demonstrate that Minnesota's overwhelming Whiteness is neither accidental nor incidental and that racial exclusion's legacy is very much interwoven in the state's contemporary politics, economy, and culture. Over the (many) years that I have been writing *Whiteness*, friends, colleagues, and strangers have asked me what I was working on. When I told them, their next question, invariably, was "Why Minnesota?" A few were asking why I would study that state instead of any other. Most of the White people, though, were asking (even if they did not fully understand what they were doing), "Why are you studying a state that—because it's so far North, because it's associated with baked-in cultural pleasantry like 'Minnesota Nice,' because there are so few people of color there (a paradox)—has no real history of racism?" Even now, after George Floyd's murder and the public protests it ignited, many readers will be surprised that racial hatred and racial inequality have been such a fundamental part of Minnesota's past. But *Whiteness in Plain View* is its own answer to the hidden question, and the larger significance of the book is grounded in that fact. It reveals the way long-standing assumptions about regional distinctions based on race are off the mark (if not a lie), and that raises fundamental questions about the country as a whole. The ghosts, to return to Avery Gordon's metaphor, are all around us. If they are in Minnesota, they are everywhere, wherever we are.

Joseph Godfrey, hand-drawn image by Robert O. Sweeny, 1862.

CHAPTER 1

"The Master Race of the World Is Caucasian": Punitive Expeditions, Mass Hanging, and Forced Removal

WHEN DANIEL BUCK CAME TO MANKATO, in the heart of the Minnesota Territory, in May of 1857, he was nearly thirty years old and a bar-certified lawyer. Following his arrival, Whites in several southern states provoked a national civil war to protect Black slavery in the spring of 1861, and Native Americans from reservations along the Minnesota River began their own war against White settler-colonists in the summer of 1862. Volunteers and federal troops brought a relatively quick end to the US–Dakota War, after which the military put hundreds of men on trial, hanged thirty-eight in Mankato's central square (in the largest mass execution in the nation's history), and expelled all but a few Dakota people to distant reservations in Nebraska and South Dakota. Buck was a personal witness to these events and carried vivid memories of them as he launched a celebrated political career, always a stalwart Democrat, just as the other war, the Civil War, concluded. Initially, he served in the state house of representatives, then moved over to the state senate, and finally, at the close of the century, took a seat on the state supreme court. In

1904, the year before he died, he wrote a book as well, an impassioned defense of racial purity and White supremacy titled *Indian Outbreaks*. Although focused specifically on the causes of the US–Dakota War, the book was also meant to address turn-of-the-century Minnesota race relations generally, making a case against what he believed had been too-fluid boundaries between Whites, Native Americans, and African Americans and explaining the need for the removal or exclusion (or at least the separation and subordination) of all those who were not White.

"The master race of the world is Caucasian," Buck declared in his polemic's opening lines, and that dominance was sustained, he claimed, by a singular devotion to both "Civilization and Christianity." The "Indian," however, was "wild" and would "forever remain so," and he was "fully aware of the impending fate hanging over his nation and dooming it to eventual extermination." The fault line in this otherwise elementary truth, Buck believed, was race mixing. Decade after decade, a group of "White outcasts"—horse thieves, dishonest interpreters, and unprincipled traders—had "wormed themselves into the confidence and lives of these wild tribes" and violated "nature's purest laws." The progeny of the "unholy and shocking" acts "disgraced the Anglo-Saxon blood" and fell "below that of the Indian himself." Equally outrageous, if not more so, was the mixing that included enslaved Blacks. In particular, Buck made a point to mention "mulatto" Joseph Godfrey, born of a French Canadian fur trader father and enslaved African American mother. Godfrey had escaped his own bondage, married a Dakota woman, and raised a family with her on the Lower Sioux Agency. The Native people called him "Atakle," or "one who kills many," and according to the jurist he was "one of the blackest-hearted villains that disgraced humanity at the time of the Indian massacre."[1]

Carefully parsed, Buck's interpretation of early Minnesota history placed at least some blame for Indigenous anger and violence on "renegade White men" and the "cross breeds" they produced with Native women. If not for those among his own race who apparently had no respect for "nature's purest laws," he suggested, the meeting of different groups of people in the western territory could have been more peaceable. Yet his account still insisted that Whites were destined to displace the presumably inferior Indigenous populations. That allowed Buck (and sympathetic readers) to dismiss or even justify the sordid wrongs the latter experienced at the hands of the United States government, Christian missionaries, and invading settler-colonists. In his view, the loss of millions of acres of land through partial treaties and outright theft, confinement to small reservations away from traditional hunting and gathering places, starvation caused by overdue and mishandled annuity payments, manipulative attempts at cultural and religious conversion, and regular White encroachment on the few areas left for Native use were all steps in the fated and divinely sanctioned Indigenous disappearance.

Indian Outbreaks also showed how Buck's thinking about Native Americans was intertwined with his thinking about people of African ancestry. In his mind, there was a distinction to be made between the races, but he and other Whites saw themselves at the top of a larger racial order, though one in which they only falteringly exercised mastery over everyone else. As Buck well knew, most of the earliest Black inhabitants came to Minnesota as enslaved people accompanying army officers and territorial officials posted to Fort Snelling. In the company of these officers and officials, or hired out to traders, many Blacks had regular interactions with Ojibwe and Dakota tribes, and some became fluent in native language and culture. Later, during the Civil War, the first large groups of free Blacks came to Minnesota as "contrabands," fugitive enslaved people shipped north from military camps in Missouri and Illinois. This included more than one hundred men (along with their families) recruited on request of former governor and Brigadier General Henry H. Sibley to serve as teamsters and cooks for a punitive expedition against Dakota in the summer of 1863. Tellingly, the general himself had once been a fur trader, during which time he briefly lived with another trader who had purchased Godfrey's mother, and he personally had owned a Black slave named Joe Robinson. Sibley also had a daughter by a Dakota named Red Blanket Woman, a member of the Native band he was preparing to hunt down.[2]

Just as Buck and many Whites rejected the idea that Native Americans could be "civilized," however, they roundly dismissed the idea that Blacks could ever be their social or political equals, and to ensure that they tried to keep African Americans away from Minnesota. They received legal cover for their racism in 1857, the year the young lawyer arrived in the state, when the US Supreme Court decided the *Dred Scott* case, which had its origins at Fort Snelling. Dred Scott and his wife, Harriet, had been enslaved while at the fort, in ostensibly free territory, and sued for their freedom on that basis, but Chief Justice Roger Taney declared that persons "of the African race" were "so far inferior, that they had no rights which the White man was bound to respect." Subsequently, for a second time (the first was in 1854), Minnesota lawmakers considered though did not act on a petition to bar African American settlement by requiring an exorbitant personal bond from would-be migrants. Several years later, hoping to maintain the state's Whiteness by other means, outraged Irish dockworkers met the first steamer delivering its load of "contrabands," forcing it to land farther upstream, even knowing some of the passengers were there to assist Sibley. "The *Northerner* brought up a cargo of 125 niggers and 150 mules on Government account," the *Saint Paul Pioneer* explained, and it removed "eight or nine hundred Indians" whom Whites had forcibly interned at Fort Snelling in the wake of the US–Dakota War. "If we [Whites] had our choice," the newspaper mused, "we would send both niggers and Indians to Massachusetts, and keep the mules here."[3]

After the Civil War, as Buck's book suggests, Minnesota Whites felt newly challenged to advance their goals of racial purity and shore up their assumed racial superiority, and their notions about race and racial separation became even more uncompromising. The US–Dakota War and forced removal that followed had effectively made outlaws of

Dred and Harriet Scott, engravings from *Frank Leslie's Illustrated Newspaper*, June 27, 1857.

remaining Dakota people who were not members of the missionaries' churches. Meanwhile, Rochester resident John Stevens began touring the state with his 222-foot panorama about the "frontier tragedy," including a panel showing Joseph Godfrey tomahawking a pleading White woman as well as another featuring buffoonish Black teamsters chasing misbehaving expedition mules. The popular tableau memorialized White innocence and Indian savagery, besides Black ineptitude and gratuitous violence, and helped to reinforce a cautionary racial narrative. Meanwhile, as emancipation began to release more freed people for northward settlement, Whites stepped up their efforts to keep Minnesota inhospitable to African Americans, twice rejecting Black male suffrage before a third referendum finally prevailed. Rhetoric against the suffrage measures made clear the perceived threat they posed. Extending the vote, fumed the editor of the *Chatfield Democrat*, was "but a step[p]ing stone to universal equality in everything, even to the detestable and God-forbidden principle of miscegenation," and that "putridity" would eventually "blot from earth the white race of this continent." In the eyes of some White Minnesotans, Blacks were quickly becoming the new threat to the "master race of the world."[4]

"We Cannot Breathe the Same Air"

In the early part of 1819, writing to Lieutenant Colonel Henry Leavenworth, Secretary of War John Calhoun made a point to unambiguously affirm the US government's purpose in building fortifications throughout the "Northwest Territory," and he put this in a way that seemed meant for a figurative reader in posterity as much as for anyone particular in his present. "The military movement which has been made up the Mississippi under your command was ordered for the establishment of posts to effect two great objects," he explained, "the enlargement and protection of the fur trade, and permanent peace of our north western frontier by securing a decided control over the various tribes of Indians in that quarter." Later that fall, Colonel Josiah Snelling arrived to relieve Leavenworth and oversee final construction of the fort that would eventually bear his name, perched on a bluff above the confluence of the Mississippi and Minnesota Rivers, and occupied by four companies of the First Regiment of US Infantry. Major Lawrence Taliaferro also arrived to serve as the local agent for the federal Office of Indian Affairs, working out of

Major Lawrence
Taliaferro, oil
on canvas by
unknown artist,
about 1830.

the St. Peter's Indian Agency, two stone buildings adjacent to the fort. At
the time, the area was populated by the Mdewakanton band of Dakota,
who stretched throughout the southern half of the territory from Fort
Snelling to Fort Crawford in present-day Prairie du Chien, Wisconsin.
Beyond that expanse were other Dakota bands (Wahpekute, Sisseton,
and Wahpeton) and various other tribes, including Ojibwe, Ho-Chunk
(Winnebago), Sauk (Sac), Meskwaki (Fox), Menominee, Báxoje (Iowa),
Odawa (Ottawa), Potawatomi, and Illinois.[5]

Despite his role as Indian agent, Taliaferro never learned any native
languages and he employed several interpreters over the course of his
career. The most constant among them was Scott Campbell, the son of
Scottish trader Archibald Campbell and a Dakota mother, and fluent
in Dakota, Ojibwe, French, and English. While living near the agency
Campbell married Marguerite Menager, who was either part Dakota or
part Menominee, and their sons later gained notoriety for their roles (on
the Indigenous side) in the US–Dakota War. Taliaferro married as well, in
1827, on a furlough trip back to Bedford, Pennsylvania, and he returned

with his wife, Elizabeth Dillon, although he already had a "country marriage" (*à la façon du pays*) with The Day Sets (Anpetu Inajinwin), the niece of the Mdewakanton chief Cloud Man (Mahpiya Wicasta), whose village was located several miles west of Fort Snelling. During the summer of 1828, while the Indian agent was still in Pennsylvania, she gave birth to their child, Mary, who afterward was educated and lived at two of the Christian missions in the area, one at nearby Lake Harriet and the other at Bde Maka Ska.[6]

It was also probably during the trip to Bedford that Taliaferro acquired Harriet Robinson, whom he brought back to Fort Snelling, and who later married Dred Scott. Elizabeth Dillon's father, Humphrey, was an innkeeper in the mountain spa town, and although heritable perpetual slavery was no longer legal in Pennsylvania, he recorded three enslaved people in the county register, allowed under a gradual emancipation law. Evidence suggests that seven-year-old Harriet was one of those enslaved and worked as a chambermaid or housekeeper at the hotel, and following common practice Humphrey Dillon gave her away as part of his daughter's dowry. At the time, Taliaferro already owned two or three other enslaved people, including a boy named William and an adolescent girl named Eliza, and in the course of his life he had a property claim over at least twenty-one different individuals. He justified this in his journals by pointing out the scarcity of manual laborers on the frontier and often referred to his enslaved people as "servants," revealing an awareness of the fact that slavery was banned from the territory by the Northwest Ordinance of 1787 as well as the Missouri Compromise of 1820.[7]

During the first few years after Fort Snelling was established, slaveholding among army officers and administrative personnel posted there was rare, but by the mid-1820s it was increasingly common. Likewise, while the first enslaved people simply traveled with their enslavers to continue serving them on the "frontier," eventually more and more enslavers purchased men, women, and children in southern markets for the express purpose of bringing them north. The turning point was when the Boston-born commander Josiah Snelling bought a woman named Mary and her daughter Louisa in St. Louis, using a designated allowance provided by the army. That established official sanction for slaveholding among his subordinates, who received a similar allowance. By 1828, when the Fifth Infantry replaced the First Infantry at Fort Snelling, making Kentucky-born plantation owner and enslaver Zachary

Taylor the fort commander, officers who did not personally possess or hire enslaved people were becoming the exception. The trend began to abate somewhat after 1836, following the Missouri Supreme Court's decision granting freedom to an enslaved woman named Rachel, who argued that her brief residence in Minnesota in the possession of Lieutenant J. B. W. Stockton nullified her subsequent owner's property claim, but the judgment did not entirely end slaveholding there or in other parts of the territory.[8]

Just outside Fort Snelling, on the other side of the Minnesota River, was a large settlement known as Mendota, a diverse yet inegalitarian community composed of White and métis traders as well as enslaved Blacks and other mixed-race residents. Living among the residents was Courtney, who had originally come to the area in 1826 with her Virginia enslaver, Captain John Garland, after which he sold her to Alexis Bailly, who was one-quarter Ottawa and the principal representative for John Jacob Astor's American Fur Company. In 1830, Courtney had a son by a French Canadian fur trader. She named the boy Joseph Godfrey, after his father, and five years later she had another son named William. The next year, Bailly hired out Courtney and William in St. Louis and took young Godfrey with him to Prairie du Chien, Wisconsin, and then back to southern Minnesota, at Wabasha, to set up a trading post there among Dakota and Ho-Chunk. Meanwhile, Courtney filed a freedom suit, and when Rachel won her case in 1836, Bailly agreed to emancipate William and his mother. Two years after that, Courtney moved with her son to Prairie du Chien, aided by Maria Fasnacht, a Black woman who had been an indentured servant at Fort Snelling but had acquired her freedom and married former army private Jacob Fasnacht. Courtney herself later married a Canadian-born White man, Benjamin Boudre, and ran a bakery with him until he died in the Mexican-American War, after which she remarried to local baker and German immigrant Charles Weidimer.[9]

Another enslaved person brought to Minnesota by an army officer, who later secured his freedom, was James Thompson. Born into slavery in Virginia, the child of a White father and Black mother, he was originally owned by George Monroe, a nephew to future president James Monroe. The nephew sold Thompson to settle gambling debts, and New Yorker Lieutenant William Day eventually purchased him in St. Louis. Day belonged to the First Infantry, and in 1828 he brought Thompson to Fort Snelling. In Minnesota, the African American man married a Dakota woman, after which, in 1836, Day took him to Fort Crawford, near Prairie du Chien, forcing Thompson to leave his wife behind. Worried that he had a strong case for freedom, however, Day sold Thompson to Reverend Alfred Brunson, who had raised money from among Methodists back east to emancipate and employ him as an interpreter for missionary work among the Dakota. The next year, in April 1837, Thompson went with another minister to establish a new mission on the Mississippi River, ten miles downstream from Fort Snelling, near the Mdewakanton village where Little Crow was chief. This allowed him to reunite with his wife, who had taken the English name Mary, and together they had a daughter and son, Sarah and George.[10]

Missionaries like the ones Thompson associated with understood that the fur trade was coming to an end, and that the Dakota and Ojibwe would soon face the full-scale land dispossession and forced removal (racial exclusion) that otherwise characterized Jacksonian-era Indian policy. Presuming that supposed racial traits were not fixed (most Whites believed that they were), they hoped to transform Indigenous people, converting them to Christianity and turning them into settled farmers, thus saving them from obliteration. Among others in the region who were part of this multifaceted endeavor were the brothers Samuel and Gideon Pond, who left their Connecticut home after a religious revival and arrived at Fort Snelling in the spring of 1834. Major Taliaferro promptly hired them to be farming instructors at Cloud Man's village on the shores of Bde Maka Ska, where the Indian agent had been trying to establish an agricultural colony. The chief showed the brothers a spot on the lake that was ideal for building a cabin, and in return they assisted the band in plowing and planting their land. The next year, Samuel and Gideon joined Reverend Jedediah Stevens and Dr. John Williamson at their mission at Lake Harriet, but when Cloud Man's band moved down to the Minnesota River in 1839, the Ponds moved with them and built a new mission and school at Oak Grove (the center of what would become Bloomington).[11]

By this point, the Dakota had reluctantly signed a treaty that relinquished all their lands east of the Mississippi River in exchange for regular annuities, as well as funding for agricultural programs, to be overseen by White farmers. Samuel believed that the annuity payments worked contrary to his attempts to indoctrinate the Dakota people in Euro-American ways, however, and he acknowledged that the agricultural programs were mostly failures. Although Gideon remained at Oak Grove for the rest of his life, Samuel left in 1847 when a new Indian agent, Colonel Amos Bruce, asked him to establish a mission and school in Shakopee, a few miles to the west, supposedly on invitation from the chief there. Samuel was suspicious of this proposal because the chief was known for opposing such work, and his wariness proved well founded, as the Dakota band constantly thwarted his entreaties. "Children were dragged from school, cattle killed, potatoes stolen," a Pond family record later claimed, "and peril and annoyance encountered on every side."[12]

In the months Samuel Pond and his family were getting settled in Shakopee, Joseph Godfrey made a brief appearance there too, accompanying Alexis Bailly's brother-in-law, fur trader Oliver Faribault, aiding him at the trading post and consequently further improving his knowledge of Dakota language and culture. Pond described Faribault as a man possessed with "wickedness," and after Godfrey talked with Alexander Huggins, a militant abolitionist who happened to pass through, he ran away and followed Huggins to Traverse des Sioux. His owner routinely abused and beat him, he said, and he could not take it any longer. The abolitionist then wrote a letter to Faribault, letting him know that he was harboring Godfrey, and the fur trader replied that he had no more use for him anyway, by which point the self-emancipated man had fled to live with nearby Native people. Although surely aware that his own mother as well as others had been able to negotiate their freedom, he also probably knew that the federal government had since passed the Fugitive Slave Act, in 1850. This law greatly enhanced the power enslavers had to recover runaways, with assistance from local authorities and without a jury trial, and he was not taking any chances.[13]

At midcentury, in fact, Godfrey and other African Americans had much to fear from Minnesota Whites, even if they were "free." As established White residents were joined by increasing numbers of White newcomers, and a shift from fur trade to land speculation intensified, what had been a relatively fluid racial order began to become much less so. Although many newcomers were abolitionists, and a few of those abolitionists advocated for Black civil rights, Democrats and even some Republicans stood in the way of meaningful emancipation for African Americans. At the first territorial legislature in 1849, representatives explicitly barred Black men from voting, which meant they were barred from serving on juries as well. Two years later, in order to increase the population count and speed the prospect of statehood, another legislature passed a law granting voting rights to "all persons of mixed white and Indian blood who have adopted the customs and habits of civilization." They retained, however, the restriction on Black suffrage and enacted legislation excluding African Americans from running in village elections. Then, in 1853, legislators banned Blacks from participating in town meetings. The following year, they considered although did not pass a bill "to provide for the good conduct of Negro and mulatto persons" with a personal bond of $300 to $500, a requirement that would have effectively choked off African American settlement in the territory. And three years after this, not many months after the US Supreme Court decided the *Dred Scott* case, Minnesota Republicans agreed to Democrats' language in the new state constitution that limited voting to Whites and "civilized Indians." The Democrats had insisted that upcoming elections for the state legislature, Congressional seats, and the next presidential race would be contests between "White supremacy" and "negro [*sic*] equality" and enfranchising African American voters would give Republicans an unfair advantage.[14]

In general, these attempts to codify racial inequality were less about restricting the rights of resident African Americans and more about ensuring that Minnesota was an unwelcome place for prospective Black migrants. For the moment, African Americans constituted only a miniscule part of the population, and as a group they were wholly marginalized. In 1850, the territorial census recorded six thousand Whites, a sizable increase from five hundred in 1835, but it registered only thirty-nine Blacks and "mulattoes," just a slight increase over the same period. Some of those African Americans were formerly enslaved or the children of Blacks who had been enslaved at Fort Snelling or elsewhere. Others were newly arrived families, with free male heads of household, many originally from Virginia or Kentucky. Slavery was not yet unknown in the region, however, as army officers continued to bring bondsmen and bondswomen with them to their postings. Pennsylvania-born Lieutenant Colonel Henry Wilson, for example, who commanded Fort Snelling on the eve of the Mexican-American War in 1846, arrived with two long-enslaved men, Dan and Abe, whom he took with him when he was reassigned to Fort Crawford in Prairie du Chien. Likewise, Wilson's replacement, Lieutenant Colonel Francis Lee, had enslaved four people— Jenny, Joe, Hetty, and Lucy—and he brought them with him when he

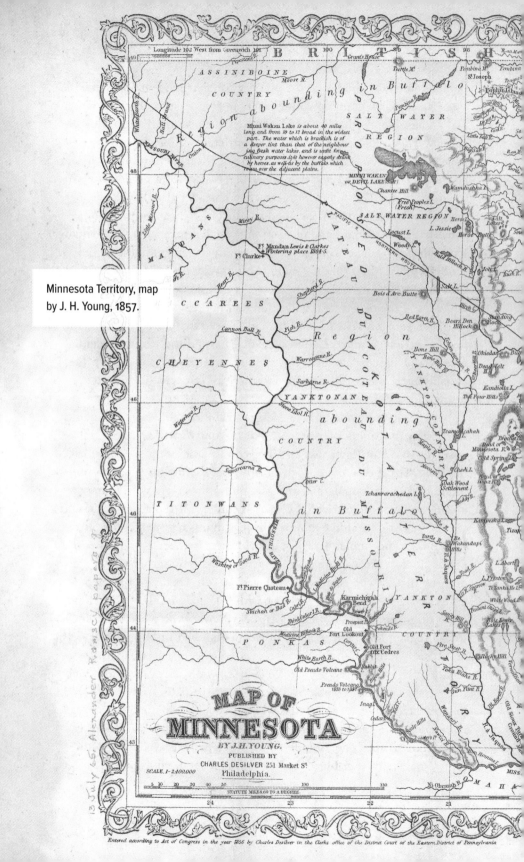

Minnesota Territory, map by J. H. Young, 1857.

LANDS OF THE DAKOTA OR SIOUX INDIANS.

By the treaties of Traverse des Sioux, and Mendota concluded in the year 1851. the Dakota or Sioux Indians ceded all their lands to the United States lying in Minnesota, and Iowa between the Mississippi and Sioux rivers, and between Lat. 42° 37′ N. and Lat. 47° 10′ N. extending N. and S. 338 miles and E. and W. from 100 to 250 miles. Area about 59,100 square miles or 38 million acres, comprising a region fully equal in extent to the States of Pennsylvania. and New Jersey. The Dakota Reserve, a tract of land on the head waters of the Minnesota river 120 miles in length, and 20 miles wide, has been appropriated by treaty for the use of said Indians.

The red line is the boundary of the Dakota cession.

Longitude 91 West from Greenwich 90

Longitude West 17 from Washington 16

established Fort Ridgley, southwest of Minneapolis, in 1853, part of a growing military presence in the area.[15]

Just as they were actively working to deny civil rights to African Americans, Whites in the Minnesota Territory were also eager to draw a prospective population of settler-colonists by expropriating more Indigenous land. Although so-called "civilized Indians" had received voting rights in 1851, that same year two more treaties ceded (or seized) twenty-four million acres of Dakota territory, west of the Mississippi River, and all six thousand members of the Mdewakanton, Wahpekute, Sisseton, and Wahpeton bands were forced onto two small reservations along the Minnesota River. A few years later, political leaders negotiated additional treaties that took Ojibwe land along Lake Superior's western shore as well as in the interior, extinguishing the remaining Indigenous title to much of the territory. The impact of these treaties and others that followed, including the failure on the part of the United States to uphold its end of compensation in the agreements, proved devastating to Native Americans. The promised annuity payments that would have at least kept them from starvation were delayed from year to year while their hunting grounds were dramatically reduced by the expanding Euro-American settlement. Not surprisingly, the suffering this entailed, compounded by faltering attempts at food distribution, provoked growing resentment and open defiance.[16]

In late 1862, Dakota anger came to a head with the outbreak of the US–Dakota War. On August 17, four Dakota men on a hunt forty miles north of the Lower Sioux Agency killed Robinson Jones and several members of his family in retaliation for an insult. They returned to the reservation and spent the night in a lodge meeting with other Mdewakanton. The next morning, the group went to Chief Little Crow and asked him to lead a war against the White settler-colonists. He reluctantly agreed, and the Dakota attacked the Redwood Agency, killing government employees and traders—sparing most of those who were mixed-blood—while taking other men, women, and children captive. From the reservation, groups of Dakota warriors extended their attacks to White farms and settlements throughout the area. By the time it was over, nearly six hundred Whites were dead, including one hundred children. As other settler-colonists fled, twenty-three southwestern Minnesota counties—between one-third and one-half of the state's populated regions—were virtually emptied of their White inhabitants.[17]

One group of fleeing settler-colonists had made their way to New Ulm, located at the confluence of the Minnesota and Cottonwood Rivers, just below the lower reservation and not far from Mankato. Dakota warriors followed them, however, and launched two attacks on the town. Among the fighters involved in the second attack was Joseph Godfrey, who had moved to the lower Dakota reservation in 1857, married a Dakota woman named Takanheca, and had a son with her. Later, Godfrey recounted that the day after the war started, he was helping a neighbor load hay when a Dakota man came to the farm on a horse, gun in hand, and told him to go home and "put on a breech-clout." At first, Godfrey tried to convince his wife that they should run away, but her uncle disabused them of that notion, insisting they would be killed with the Whites if they left and that they would be safe among the tribe. At that point, Godfrey joined a small war party, willingly or unwillingly, and the men began killing White residents in the area. Although he sometimes later claimed to be only a witness to the violence, as the warriors got close to New Ulm he rushed with them into a home where a family was having dinner. Godfrey alternatively admitted he struck a man with the flat side of his hatchet there, before he was pushed aside by others who came in and shot everyone to death.[18]

The difficult choice Godfrey faced also confronted James Thompson, who had given up missionary work and had gone into business as a whiskey trader. Both Thompson and Godfrey had been born to a White father and enslaved Black mother, both lived on the lower reservation near the Redwood Agency, both were married to Dakota women, both had triracial children, and both spoke fluent Dakota. Yet Thompson decided to flee rather than fight. He left his family behind for refuge at Fort Ridgley, and when warriors came to his home looking for him, they burned all his possessions and took his wife and children captive. Even less fortunate was William Taylor, a Black man who had come to Minnesota from Galena, Illinois, married an African American woman, opened a barbershop in St. Paul, and became a key figure in the Underground Railroad there. By mid-August of 1862, he had been at the lower reservation for several weeks, cutting hair and performing music. When the fighting broke out, he tried desperately to escape, believing that he would be treated no better than Whites, though as it turned out he suffered a worse fate. Missionary Emily J. West, who had to make her own frightening escape from the reservation, recalled meeting Taylor in the company of a dozen White men, women, and children wandering across the prairie. "Changing our course a little we soon separated," she said, and "after they left us they met a party of Indians who killed the black man and took the rest prisoners."[19]

Once alerted to what was taking place, Governor Alexander Ramsey appointed Henry Sibley to lead state militia forces against the Dakota, and his thousand-man army was soon engaged with them on the plains. The campaign continued for six weeks, but members of other bands did not join the fight, and the warriors were outmatched. A "peace party" among the Sisseton, Wahpeton, and Mdewakanton bands secured control over the White and mixed-blood captives, including James Thompson's family, and negotiated their return with Sibley at what he called "Camp Release." At the end of September, after a final battle at Wood Lake, several hundred Dakota among the war party also surrendered. A few days later the colonel caught up with Joseph Godfrey and his group and arrested them, and in mid-October, Sibley ordered mass arrests of Dakota men at Camp Release as well. Following that, he moved all of the prisoners to the lower reservation and formed a military commission to begin trials.[20]

Drawing on his connections with political leaders, Minnesota's first Episcopal bishop, Henry Benjamin Whipple, stepped up to plead the Indians' case to those who might intercede and administer leniency. Toward that end he went to Washington, DC, and met with President Abraham Lincoln, insisting that corrupt government agents and greedy traders deserved most of the blame for creating the circumstances that led to the war. The president ordered his secretary of interior to look into the matter, and he found evidence of mispaid annuities. Pressing the point, Whipple followed up with a formal letter to Lincoln, signed by two dozen other Episcopal bishops, reasserting the government's role and calling for an official investigation. "The history of our dealings with the Indians has been marked by gross acts of injustice and robbery, such as could not be prevented under the present system of management," the bishop wrote, and "these wrongs have often proved the prolific cause of war and bloodshed." Whipple's letter went on, however, to describe the Dakota people as a "helpless race," degraded by the terms and implementation of past treaties, incapable of organizing themselves into an "independent nation," and needing the US government to deal with them as "wards." Saving a more purposeful paternalism, he concluded, there would never be "permanent peace and tranquility on our western border."[21]

For most Whites, though, the bloody US–Dakota War ended any concern for the welfare of Native people, including those who previously had pleaded their case. Jane Grey Swisshelm, for example, was a Republican firebrand who came to St. Cloud in 1857, and as editor of the local newspaper, she had not hesitated to voice her various "open-minded" political ideas. When she arrived, Swisshelm later recalled, she regarded Indians as "noble yet uncivilized, virtuous and uncorrupted, but heathen and savage," and wronged much in the same way as enslaved Blacks. "Our government," she wrote in one early column, is "permitting them to be robbed and demoralized by the brutal Whites who seek their ruin." During the war, however, her views dramatically changed. "It is folly to fight Indians as we would European soldiers," she declared. "Let our present Legislature offer a bounty of $10 for every Sioux [Dakota] scalp, outlaw the tribe and so let the matter rest." Hoping to put her case before President Lincoln, as Bishop Whipple had done, Swisshelm traveled to Washington and, while biding her time for a meeting that never came, she gave lectures about the "demon" Native peoples of Minnesota. If the Dakota were not brought to justice, she told one audience, "our people will hunt them, shoot them, set traps for them, put out poisoned bait for them. . . . We cannot breathe the same air with those demon violators of women, crucifiers of infants."[22]

As the calls for White revenge against the Dakota intensified, the military commission established by Sibley began to hold trials, and the first prisoner to give testimony was Joseph Godfrey, who found himself once again in a perilous position. Among the three men serving on the commission was Stephen Fowler, who was married to Emily Faribault, the daughter of Jean Baptiste Faribault, whose family had once enslaved Godfrey. Additionally, the soldiers charged with guarding the prisoners harbored a special enmity for Godfrey and, as Sibley reported, their "statements favor the natural prejudice against his color, to a White heart." Because he was fluent in both Dakota and English, though, the commission employed him as an interpreter and, in that capacity, he also effectively served as an interrogator, sometimes helping the Dakota prisoners to defend themselves and sometimes orchestrating their confessions. In his own trial, the commission found no evidence that Godfrey was personally guilty of murdering anyone, contrary to his own frequent boasts and to the testimony of White witnesses, but it did find that he was present at many killings. For his complicity, they sentenced him to be hanged, though as a reward for his service, the judges recommended that be reduced to ten years' imprisonment. By early November, the commission had tried and convicted more than three hundred others as well, sentencing every one of them to be hanged.[23]

When the trials concluded, the military forcibly moved all the captured Dakota eastward to one of two places. The largest group, including all women and children, some mixed-bloods, and mostly elderly men who had not been accused of any crime, moved their camp to Fort Snelling, most of them walking the 110 miles, over five days in November's cold. Although an armed guard accompanied them, their line was more than four miles long, and at several points along the way Whites violently attacked the vulnerable families, in one incident pulling a baby from its mother and bashing it on the ground, although nobody was arrested or punished for these acts. Likewise, a smaller group of captives, the Dakota warriors who had been convicted of murder and condemned to death, were shackled together and sent to a camp about a mile and a half outside Mankato, newly christened Camp Lincoln. As they passed New Ulm, Whites harassed them as well, viciously attacking the defenseless men with sticks and stones, clubs, axes, pitchforks, and knives, seriously injuring fifteen of the prisoners and killing two. In this case, soldiers arrested more than a dozen of the town residents and took them along to the camp but let them go free once they arrived there.[24]

Struck by the haste of the trials and the large number of warriors sentenced to be hanged, President Lincoln (who was now fully engaged in leading the country in war against White southerners determined to protect Black slavery) delayed the executions for several weeks while he and his aides reviewed the commission's full transcripts. After finding many errors in the trial records, including several cases of mistaken identity, Lincoln concluded that he could sign death warrants for thirty-nine of the Dakota fighters, singling out those who directly participated in killing civilians, rather than just battles with volunteers and enlisted soldiers. So, on December 26, 1862, thousands of White spectators gathered in Mankato's main square, buffered from the rows of gallows by more than 1,400 federal troops, and the US government executed thirty-eight Dakota men, one less than the number of warrants since there had been one more reprieve.[25]

In January, Whites made clear what they thought should happen next. "The Sioux [Dakota] Indians of Minnesota," Governor Ramsey declared to the legislature, "must be exterminated or driven forever beyond the borders of the State." The legislators agreed and sent a message to President Lincoln and members of Congress to say they would not rest until all Native people, not just the Dakota, were gone. "Indian removal, immediate and total," they insisted, "is the universal prayer of the people of Minnesota." Subsequently, while General Sibley prepared to lead one of several punitive expeditions against the Dakota who had fled, soldiers removed the men interned at Camp Lincoln to a prison camp in Iowa. On May 4, they also packed 770 of the prisoners at Fort Snelling onto the *Davenport*, bound for a bleak reservation at Crow Creek, South Dakota. The next day the *Northerner* delivered a load of "contraband" Blacks (who had run away from White enslavers) and took on 540 more Dakota, bound for Crow Creek as well. More than two thousand Ho-Chunk people who had not participated in warfare—but whose reservation near Mankato occupied prime farming land—were also expelled. Hundreds of people of both nations died on the crowded steamboats, and three years later, after hundreds more died of starvation and disease, most of the remaining Dakota moved to the Santee Sioux Reservation, and the Ho-Chunk moved to the Omaha reservation, both in Nebraska. Among the Dakota tribal members reassembled there was African American Joseph Godfrey, who had parted ways with his first Dakota wife after he testified against her father and got him hanged. He survived constant harassment and violent retaliation, married another Dakota woman (and another when she died), returned to farming, and lived several more decades until his death on the reservation in 1909.[26]

As an expression of their supposed claim to racial supremacy, Minnesota Whites' regard for Native Americans following the US–Dakota War was entwined with their regard for African Americans as the Civil War came to an end too. St. Paul teacher Harriet Bishop, who personally witnessed the expulsion of the Dakota and Ho-Chunk and the Black fugitives' arrival, bluntly compared those embarking and disembarking the steamboat. "It was a novel sight, quite amusing to the beholder," she recalled. "The blacks had thought that no mortals were as degraded as themselves, but had found themselves outdone," while "the Indians had thought themselves the blackest of the human race, but now looked upon those of a deeper dye." Another White observer, describing the

African Americans once they were encamped at Fort Snelling, characterized them as objects of amusement and suited for little more than servile labor. Camp guard Robert McLaren wrote to his wife about seeing "slaves" for the first time, reporting how "we made them dance, sing, & c," and promising "to get a Contraband and after the war is over take him home." In fact, while about one hundred freedmen were quickly recruited as cooks and teamsters for Sibley's expeditionary force on the plains, the army also attempted to find work for the more than 150 family members left behind by placing advertisements in local newspapers. "A number of persons in our city have been desirous of procuring colored house servants," the advertisements read, "as it is almost impossible to get respectable white servants now at any price." In light of this "problem," the quartermaster at Fort Snelling announced "that there are 64 women, 70 children, and 30 young men who can be hired by applying at his office."[27]

To be sure, some of the state's White political leaders were increasingly more open to extending civil rights to African Americans than they had been before the war, mostly because they recognized that Blacks could be wooed as voters, but Whites were far from united on the matter. In the spring of 1865, with full control of the state legislature, and backed by a vigorous petition campaign in Anoka, Hastings, Rochester, and Winona, Republicans passed a bill calling for a referendum to strike the word "white" from the state's suffrage provisions. In the run-up to the November vote, however, Democrats did what they could to stoke White prejudice and fear, notably by raising the specter of what they called "mongrelism," prefiguring one of Daniel Buck's main concerns later in *Indian Outbreaks*. "[The intent] is to place them with you in the jury box, beside you at the table, along with you in bed, to make them your father-in-law, your brother-in-law, your son-in-law, your uncle, your aunt, your niece, your nephew, your equal in everything and your superior in patriotism, blackness and flavor," the Chatfield *Democrat* warned its readers. "It don't mean that the privileges of Sambo are to cease when he shall march to the polls and offset your vote with his, but you must take him to your home, have your wife wait on him, let him kiss your sister, set up with your daughter, marry her if he wants her, and raise any number of tan-color grandchildren." In light of this warning, the referendum failed on a vote of 14,651 to 12,138, although the Republican candidate for governor and the rest of the party's slate easily won their elections, indicating that a significant number of Republican voters were also part of the suffrage opposition.[28]

For a few years, it seemed, African Americans fared much better at the federal level, when the Civil Rights Act of 1866 reversed the *Dred Scott* decision and sanctioned Black citizenship, the Reconstruction Act of 1867 enfranchised Black men in the former Confederate states, and the Fourteenth Amendment (ratified in 1868) prohibited states from adopting laws that discriminated on the basis of race. Meanwhile, in 1867, a majority of White male voters in Minnesota again denied the vote to African American men. Yet a year later, in a stunning reversal, voters finally enfranchised them, and did it with broad approval, 39,493 to 30,121, as well as two years before ratification of the Fifteenth Amendment, which likewise protected the right to vote for all men regardless of "race, color, or previous condition of servitude." Better tactics by the Republicans, plus the greater turnout for the presidential election, made the difference. The next year, in 1869, the state legislature outlawed segregation in public schools, and that spring the first African Americans served on a jury. A decade and a half later, in 1885, Minnesota also enacted a civil rights law providing that all citizens "of every race and color" were entitled to equal access to "inns, public conveyances on land and water, theaters and places of public amusement, [and] restaurants and barbershops," with modest fines and jail terms imposed for violators.[29]

While the semblance of racial equality for African Americans began to take shape in the state constitution and legal code, however, segregation and discrimination filled the breach between the declaration of rights and actual enforcement, and many Whites continued to prefer to be rid of Blacks altogether. To address this, and sustain the gathering momentum toward realizing full citizenship, Minnesota's African Americans began to organize. Among the most prominent Black leaders was John Quincy Adams, who came to St. Paul from Louisville, Kentucky, in 1887 to be editor of the *Western Appeal* newspaper and, that same year, established the Minnesota Protective and Industrial League. His paper also influenced the son of formerly enslaved parents and newly credentialed lawyer Fredrick McGhee to move to the city from Chicago. Together, in 1889 the pair formed the Afro-American League of St. Paul, anticipating the founding of T. Thomas Fortune's National Afro-American League the next year, with other local affiliate leagues formed in Minneapolis, Duluth, Anoka, Stillwater, and Faribault. To raise the group's profile,

McGhee put together a celebration on Emancipation Day, January 1, 1891, and opened the event with hopeful words. "The sun of our perfect freedom is rising in this Northwest," he said, and "we are creating a sentiment which will spread throughout the country." To McGhee and other African Americans in Minnesota, the moment seemed to be a beginning filled with at least some prospect of advancement.[30]

"The Secret of Right Race Relations"

In 1935, on the one-hundredth anniversary of the Pond brothers' arrival at Bde Maka Ska, members of the Pond Family Association met at Oak Grove, in Bloomington, on a farm owned by Gideon's son Hine. There they took the opportunity to consider the meaning and legacy of missionary efforts among the Dakota people and, in doing that, to resurrect a mythology that separated the religious work from the cruelty it helped to facilitate. In a program titled "The Secret of Right Race Relations," participants acknowledged that there was little to show for all the missionary labors by the time of the US–Dakota War, but apologetically pointed to the "courageous" acts of the few Christian-inclined Dakota to save White captives during the fighting as well as the mass "conversion" among the Mankato prisoners shortly after. Demonstrating what was and would remain a familiar practice of misremembering history to dodge culpability and escape responsibility for past and present racism, the gathered Whites rewrote what had happened. "The way of greed and prejudice in this case led to wholesale massacre and destruction," the program explained, "while the way of service and friendship led to the healing of wounds and the opening of a new chapter of hope."[31]

Similarly, when a White audience gathered to mark the installation of a US–Dakota War memorial window at the Fort Snelling chapel, they bemoaned the errors of conquest and the failure of past "uplift" endeavors among the Native Americans. They soothed their collective conscience, though, by disassociating themselves from the greatest wrongs and insisting that particular aspects of their "civilized" racial superiority eased the eventual terrible outcome. "The advance of the white man was too often ruthless," one speaker acknowledged, "he encroached relentlessly on the rights of the red man whose hunting grounds this continent had been for untold centuries." It was difficult to read the record of this, he said, "without a blush of shame." Yet while nothing could have averted "the inevitable racial clash," thankfully both "the missionary and the military" were present "to soften the blow." Working in tandem they sought "to teach the Indian the white man's law and language and to instill in him new ideals and new purpose of life." The "fruits of their labors may have been discouraging," the speaker concluded, "but surely the lot of the American Indian was far less tragic than it would have been had not the followers of the cross and the flag stood between him and those who dispossessed him of his land and the only means of gaining subsistence that he knew."[32]

CHAPTER 2

"They All Must Be Taught Their Duty":
Barbers, Porters, Washerwomen, and Inmates

AMONG THE MEN WHO JOINED General Henry H. Sibley's expedition to sub-
due the Dakota in the summer of 1863 was twenty-two-year-old Thomas
Montgomery, who originally had come to the United States from Ireland
with his family in the mid-1850s and settled on a farm with them in
Cleveland, Minnesota. That town was among a cluster of others just north
of Mankato and east of New Ulm and close to the Lower Sioux Agency.
Coincidentally, only days before fighting began there, area residents held
a public meeting in response to President Lincoln's call for troops to
defend the Union, and Montgomery enlisted in the newly formed Company K of the Seventh Minnesota Volunteer Regiment, which was soon
put to duty on the nearby "frontier." After the initial battle against the
Dakota was over, the condemned prisoners were hanged, and many
Dakota families fled to the Dakota Territory and Canada, the regiment
joined the expedition to follow. On May 4, they set off from Mankato and
marched sixteen miles, finally camping three miles west of New Ulm,
where the "scene of great desolation" unsettled the young Montgomery. "I walked around amid the ruins," he wrote in a letter home to his

mother, "& seen where several were killed, seen several human skeletons." There were houses burned to the ground, animal carcasses strewn about, as well as pieces of dress, furniture, glass, and china cluttering the roadsides, and one member of the company found his dead brother's body half-buried in manure.[1]

In early June, Sibley assembled the rest of the full mile-long "wagon train" that would venture farther west, a varied assortment of men (and some women), ominously simmering with racial tension. "There are between 200 & 300 wagons in camp and we expect 100 more shortly," Montgomery wrote in another letter home, along with "a heavy squad of niggers for teamsters ... [and] a score of Indian scouts from Ft Snelling with their squaws & papooses." In early July, he reported, as the train made its way across the prairie, a cavalry lieutenant mounted on his horse shot one of the scouts walking beside him, "apparently unprovoked." This violent act also disturbed Montgomery, who "saw the poor fellow shortly after ... lying on the ground in his blood." It was the first person he had ever seen shot, he noted, "but it may not be the last." There was a trial and the lieutenant was acquitted, and the expedition carried on toward the Missouri River. Eventually, the US soldiers encountered groups of fleeing Dakota in the hills—as well as Yankton, Yanktonai, and Lakota groups who had not been part of the war—and they engaged them in several battles. The battles at Whitestone Hill and Kildeer Mountains were in fact attacks on peaceful Lakota hunting camps, and those massacres left more than three hundred dead. By the fall of 1864, the fleeing Dakota also either were captured and moved to reservations or found safe haven with western tribes and on ancestral territory in Canada.[2]

Soon after returning to Mankato, Montgomery was commissioned a first lieutenant in the Seventy-Sixth US Colored Regiment and, in the early part of 1864, posted to the Benton Barracks in Missouri. "I presume you have heard ere this that I have left the old 7th Minn and am now associated with the colored population," he wrote to his parents and brothers, "those of dusky hue and who all their lives have been slaves but are now thanks to the war & old Abe, free men." When the freedmen came to camp, he explained, they were usually "destitute of clothing and look pretty hard," bearing scars from bad treatment by their enslavers, and mostly "dull" and illiterate. In March, twenty of his nearly one hundred soldiers were hospitalized and thirteen died, and later, when they moved to New Orleans, the sickness and death continued, which

Montgomery insisted was due to "the change of food and manner of living and that lack of vitality characteristic of whites." Observing their presumed frailty, he concluded "that the present race of black men will not be of any account." Yet the lieutenant had a high regard for his own command and the responsibility that entailed, and he aspired to make the best of the situation. "They all must be taught their duty," he wrote, "and we must join the example."[3]

Montgomery thought he might directly help one of his men by sending the soldier's wife north to Minnesota, where she would be away from the war and could work as the lieutenant's widowed mother's servant. The couple, William and Elizabeth Estell, had first met the young officer at the Missouri camp, where "Lizzie" was his cook and laundress and played a critical role in nursing him through his own serious illness, and he felt obligated to make special arrangements for her. She was in Cleveland, Minnesota, by the fall of 1864 but intensely missed her husband and their two children, whom she had left behind. As she pondered returning to the South, Montgomery wrote to his mother to do all she could to keep her there. "One thing is certain," he wrote, "if she leave[s] you now it will be her ruin as she has no means to take care of herself any more than she can with you and it will be running great risks of life and liberty." He told her to tell Lizzie that William wanted her to stay put as well and that the children had been moved from New Orleans back to St. Louis, where they were safer. Montgomery recognized, however, that it was ultimately Lizzie's decision to make. "I want her to be contented & fulfill her promises to me but if she is bound to leave I would let her go," he concluded. "Perhaps she is [the] best judge of her own feelings."[4]

Persuaded by the pleading, Elizabeth decided to stay in Minnesota, where she remained for the next three years. Meanwhile, Montgomery (brevetted major in 1865) continued to command different "colored" regiments in Louisiana, where his commitment to the war's higher ideals germinated and his respect for the Black soldiers grew. "When I entered the service," he explained in a letter to his brother, "it was solely to aid in putting down the Rebellion which was undertaken and carried on by Slaveholders, whose character as such I detested." After a long stint in the South his sentiments about slaveholders remained unchanged, but now he felt especially honored to have had the chance "to give my services and life if necessary to aid the glorious cause of constitutional liberty, the abolition of Slavery, and the consequent future prosperity of this Republic." Montgomery also wanted to aid the practical uplift of his troops after the war and, when his father wrote to tell him that their close family friend and General Land Office agent Abner Tibbets had suggested the idea of forming "a settlement of colored families" in the nearby St. Peter Land District, he jumped at the chance. "I have no doubt but I could form a good colony," the son replied. "All of my men are without homes and are desirous of procuring them and they could each bring their friends," he wrote, and "all of them I have no doubt would make good industrious citizens."[5]

By the early part of 1867, though, when Montgomery was finally mustered out of the army, the colony plan had faltered. This was due in part to the auspicious prospects that seemed to be taking shape for African Americans in the South (at least the section under federal military control) and in part to the obstacles to migration and settlement elsewhere (including Minnesota). "The colored people are becoming a power in the land," the major wrote in one of his last letters from Louisiana, "and [they] are far more respected in their rights as citizens &c by the sensible people here than they are by their would be friends at the North." So, Montgomery returned home alone, promptly established a real estate and insurance business in St. Peter with another war veteran, Captain T. G. Carter, and married Sarah Ann Purnell, the daughter of an English immigrant family near Mankato. During the next two decades, Montgomery held a range of civic positions in town, until he moved his family to St. Paul in 1891. There, he served on the board of aldermen for two terms, from 1892 to 1896, and lived in Hamline Village until his death in 1907.[6]

William Estell probably did not survive the war (he was gravely sick during the summer of 1865, again at the beginning of 1866, and once more later that year), and Elizabeth did not tarry long enough in Cleveland, Minnesota, to be counted in the 1870 census (she had been listed in the Montgomery household in 1865). After she left, no Black residents remained in the town or moved there, and only a few others moved to any of the other towns in Le Sueur County. In fact, there was only insubstantial Black migration to the same general area of south-central Minnesota through the next several decades, and no African American migrants became landowning farm families there. Instead, they made do as hotel porters, household servants, farmhands, and occasionally barbers. By 1880, nearly twenty Black residents lived in nearby Mankato, in

Blue Earth County, but during the decades to follow, even this small population began to shrink. At the same time, an increasing number of Black patients were committed at the St. Peter State Hospital for the Insane, in Nicollet County, following a building expansion overseen by the Carter & Montgomery company. Fifty years later, in 1930, there were just four African Americans in all of Blue Earth, among a total population of 33,847, and three of those Black residents were inmates at the county jail, while the fourth was a porter at a bakery. Also by then, Nicollet County had a total population of 16,550, including forty-two "Negro" residents, although forty of those were St. Peter hospital patients and one was a transient member of a traveling circus.[7]

The same failed racial reordering that happened in Thomas Montgomery's part of Minnesota happened in other regions as well. During the second half of the nineteenth century, a small number of African American migrants settled in nearly every outlying southern and eastern county in the state, yet they were always greatly overwhelmed by the thousands of Whites moving in, and for the most part, they were limited to servile occupations. The transformation of the prairie into cultivated farmland and industrial towns after the Civil War was not accompanied by anything close to racially egalitarian opportunity. Moreover, by the first or second decade of the twentieth century, what little Black resident population there was in these various places began to contract, sometimes down to one or two individuals or families and often to none at all. A few towns did see a slight increase in the number of African Americans into the 1930s and 1940s, but these were primarily individuals confined to one or another state institution—patients, inmates, and wards in the insane asylums, prisons, and orphanages dotting the countryside—and hardly likely to be seen by Whites as integrated or respected members of any larger community.[8]

As it transpired, the fears Whites had harbored that emancipation would unleash a massive wave of freed people to Minnesota were not realized. Black migration to the state as a whole after the Civil War was slight and mostly directed toward select sections of Minneapolis, St. Paul, and, to a lesser extent, Duluth. From 1860 to 1870, the African American population grew from 259 to 759, half of which was shared between the Twin Cities. During the next decade, the Black population in Minnesota doubled, to 1,564, but two-thirds of that was in the metropolitan areas of Hennepin and Ramsey Counties. The number more than doubled

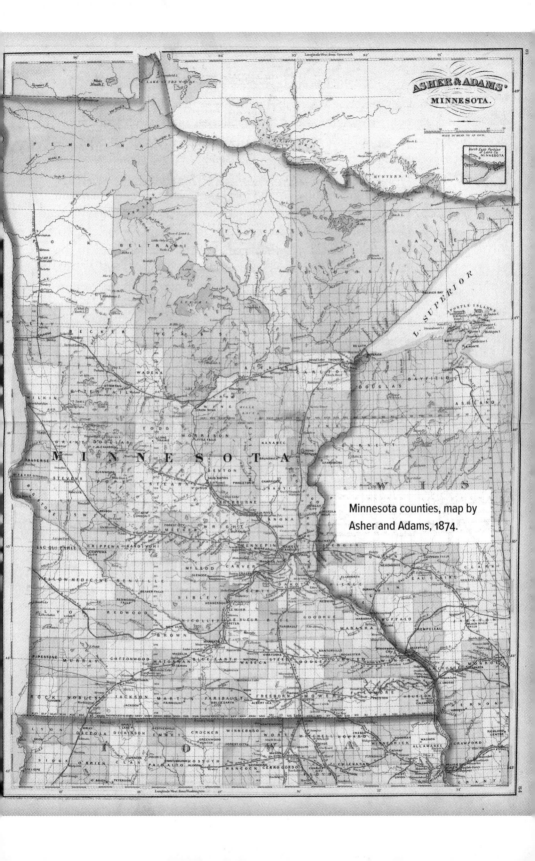

Minnesota counties, map by Asher and Adams, 1874.

again by 1890, reached nearly 5,000 by 1900, and surpassed 7,000 by 1910, though again these African Americans were largely concentrated in major urban areas. At the end of the first decade of the twentieth century there were 2,592 Black residents in Minneapolis, 3,144 in St. Paul, and 510 in Duluth, leaving fewer than a thousand scattered about the rest of Minnesota. During the next decade, total African American population growth slowed dramatically, with an increase of only 1,725 by 1920, and more and more of the newcomers, as well as those who had first made their homes in outlying towns, were moving to the Twin Cities.[9]

Still, the impact of southern slavery's end on communities in the Upper Midwest did not necessarily rest on the actual number of African American migrants to any one place. On the contrary, in greater Minnesota's overwhelmingly White areas, the lone Black individual or family stood out just as much or more than a larger grouping, and their presence provoked a typical response, one that was common from county to county and from decade to decade. Even in communities where the local African American population was minuscule and mostly static, White residents demanded ritualized deference from Blacks, limited them to marginal positions in the economy, barred them from participation in civic governance, and excluded them from influential social roles. Running up against the notion that race relations in the North were significantly different from those in the South, Black and mixed-race residents in Minnesota towns did not possess the same status, rights, and privileges enjoyed by Whites, and there was little that they could do about this. Additionally, much like their southern counterparts, Whites in these towns proved themselves willing to deal with breaches of racial etiquette and assertions of racial equality not only with impudence and hostility but also, in a number of cases, with vicious violence.[10]

"Owing to the Intense Feeling Prevalent Here"

One of the areas of greater Minnesota that did see relatively significant Black migration during the postbellum period was Goodhue County, and at least in part this was the result of efforts made by local Whites. Among them were the brothers Benjamin and Daniel Densmore, who had moved with their parents to Red Wing, the county seat, in 1857. Like Thomas Montgomery, they both participated in the US–Dakota War and then received officers' commissions to command colored infantry units in the Civil War. While they were down South, they engaged in regular correspondence with people back home about sending "contrabands" north to work as household servants and farm laborers. At times, their letters made the pair sound not unlike slave traders, promising to look for a suitable "pair of Africans" and "to make the best selection possible" of their "colored soldiers' wives." In the brothers' own household, their mother, Elizabeth, initially viewed the idea of employing a Black servant "unfavorably," and the live-in Swedish servant disliked the possibility of being "set aside for the ebony article," while their sister Martha believed an honest "darkey woman" would do nicely. Benjamin wrote to let them know that the freed people were "not the most reliable people in the world" and "apt to be trifling," but figured "a girl of 14 years or so of the right stripe would, I believe, please the best." Subsequently, Daniel found a young woman in St. Louis, Mary Prist, and in August of 1864 he sent her to Red Wing. His father, Orrin, wrote to say that Mary was "coarse" and complained that "so few colored people" lived in town, yet assured his son that she "fully meets our expectations and we hope will meet our wants."[11]

Benjamin Densmore, about 1863.

Another conduit for Black migrants to Goodhue County was Julia Nelson, whose ideas about the newly freed people were strikingly different from those of the Densmore brothers. She too had come to the Red Wing area with her family in 1857, and she met her future husband, Ole Nelson, while studying to be a teacher at local Hamline University (not yet moved to St. Paul). Nelson served with the Sixth Minnesota Volunteer Infantry during the Civil War, and the couple married after his return in 1866. They had a child the following August, but the child and Ole both died within the next couple of years. Newly widowed, Julia applied for a teaching job with the American Missionary Association at one of the schools established for freed people in the South and during the next two decades she taught in several different places there. In Athens, Tennessee, she was joined by a Black student teacher, William H. Richards, whom she later helped financially through college and law school at Howard University (and to whom she eventually left most of her estate when she died). Julia also sent a young Black woman, Martha Miller, to live with her ailing mother in Red Wing, and she hired Jeremiah Patterson, whose parents had escaped slavery in North Carolina, to run a farm she owned in nearby Belvidere. She herself returned to Red Wing in 1888 and a decade later went into business with Patterson, opening the Equal Rights Meat Market on Fifth and Plum Streets. This venture failed within a few months, however, and Patterson moved his family (he had married the daughter of the first White residents in Belvidere) and took up farming in Hay Creek.[12]

Still more African Americans moved to Goodhue County after the war on their own or without much assistance from Whites. In 1857, seventeen-year-old George Dennis was the only Black resident in the county, but by 1870, when the total county population was 4,260, a dozen African Americans lived there. Most of them were single men, hailing from various parts of the South and working as farm laborers in White households in Burnside, Cannon Falls, Florence, Hay Creek, Minneola, Roscoe, and Red Wing. By 1880, when the total county population was 5,876, all these migrants were gone, replaced by an entirely new group, slightly different in composition. There were two single men, Stephen and John Bell, possibly brothers, one in Pine Island and one in Red Wing, both working as farm laborers, but the other Black residents belonged to four different large families. This included one in Red Wing headed by Henry Fogg, originally from Tennessee, who worked as a barber, and one in Zumbrota headed by Thomas Jefferson, originally from Kentucky, who worked as a barber too. Another Black family in Red Wing was headed by Emily Johnson, born in Wisconsin, recorded in the census as a "mulatto," and married with several children, their father born in Massachusetts and still living although not there with them.[13]

By 1900, Goodhue County was home to five Black families and a single Black man. Stephen Bell headed one of the families, having married a woman named Sarah, from Missouri, and he still worked as a farm laborer in Pine Island. The others were new to the area, including Lewis and Jennie Foster, both from New England, and their five children, all born in Minnesota. The largest group of African Americans, however, was made up of about a dozen inmates at the recently opened juvenile detention facility in Red Wing, the Minnesota State Training School (MSTS). All were teenaged boys, born to parents who represented the range of Black migration (and White immigration) to the state, including one whose father was from Tennessee and whose mother was from Norway. By 1930, the total Goodhue population was 31,317 and included thirty-one Black residents. Seven of these were children and mixed-race grandchildren in an interracial family headed by Danish immigrant and widow Jenny Faulkner, and another was Lillian Staehli, a Black woman married to a White farmer, although more than half of the county's other African Americans were incarcerated boys at MSTS. Ten years later the total county population had increased slightly yet the African American population had declined to nineteen, including remaining members of the Faulkner family, Lillian and her young daughter, and more than a dozen detention facility inmates.[14]

Just upstream on the Mississippi River, between Red Wing and St. Paul, an even larger number of Black migrants were initially drawn to Dakota County, almost all to Hastings. In 1857, the county seat had only two Black residents, both single men, but within a little more than a decade it counted forty African Americans, a mix of individuals and families. Among the earliest arrivals were Andrew Jackson (A. J.) Overalls, originally from Marion, Indiana. His father, James, was a conductor on the Underground Railroad there, and his wife, Lucinda, was a local minister's daughter. The couple had married in 1854, and after their first child, Nina, was born, they moved to Hastings and A. J. set up as a barber. Those who followed included the Wallace family, who came to town in 1865 and consisted of John and his wife, Nancy, the one formerly enslaved in Tennessee and the other formerly enslaved in Virginia, as well as their two children, James and Louanna. During the Civil War, John served with the Third Minnesota Regiment, which surrendered to Nathan Bedford Forrest at the battle of Murfreesboro in July 1862, shortly afterward was exchanged for Confederate prisoners, and then returned to their home state to join Colonel Henry Sibley's campaign against the Dakota. Wallace went to Minnesota with the regiment, and intent on never returning to Tennessee, he hired someone to bring his family there too.[15]

From the start, as archivist and historian Heidi Langenfeld has found, Hastings's steadily growing Black community showed little hesitation in establishing itself as a public presence and forcefully advocating for racial equality. "On Tuesday morning last," the *Hastings Gazette* reported in August 1863, "we were considerably surprised to see the colored population of our own city, as well as from other points, parading the streets in their best store clothes." The occasion, the newspaper explained, was a dinner party marking the thirtieth anniversary of Britain's Slave Emancipation Act. A few months later, in January, "the colored men of Hastings" established a committee, headed by A. J. Overalls, to draft a petition to the Minnesota legislature in advance of the effort to strike "white" from suffrage provisions. Four years later, in 1869, the *Gazette* reported that "40 colored citizens" from town attended a celebration of the Emancipation Proclamation in St. Paul, and in January 1870 a large group returned to the city to participate in founding the Sons of Freedom, with Overalls chairing the resolutions committee. At mid-decade, in 1875, local African Americans again celebrated the Emancipation Proclamation, and in May they gathered at Germania Hall to "rejoice and jubilate over the passage of the civil rights act," federal legislation protecting Black rights to access public accommodations and serve on juries. A few Whites attended that event as well, and *Hastings Gazette* editors (for some reason reprinting an account from the *Stillwater Gazette*) were particularly incensed about this. "Colored" speakers were followed by "white trash," the story complained, "the affair closing with a dance, both colors freely intermingling."[16]

During the next decade, the number of African Americans in the river port declined by nearly half, to two dozen, yet even then there were new Black arrivals to Hastings. Among them, in 1885, were John and Ella Curry, along with their daughters Georgiana and Ellen. Ella was Nancy Wallace's niece, and initially the Currys lived with the Wallace family, until John got a job at the post office. Together, in 1890, the two families took the lead in forming an African Methodist Episcopal Church, and the next year, the congregation purchased a small frame building from local German Baptists, which they christened "Brown's Chapel." "Experience has taught us the necessity of having a place of our own," they declared, "where we may become permanently situated, and worship God according to the dictates of our own consciences without shame or fear." Subsequently, White and Black donors from other parts of Minnesota as well as Wisconsin helped the congregation pay off their remaining debt on the building, and it became an important social mooring for Hastings's

African American community, which was growing once again. In the fall of 1907, however, tragedy struck the church. On a late October evening, unknown "incendiaries" broke in through the back window, poured kerosene over the floor and pews, and lit the chapel on fire, ruining much of it before firefighters arrived. There were no reports of investigations afterward and, without insurance on the building, the congregation sold it to a local White resident two years later.[17]

As the arsonists likely intended and other Whites in Hastings probably hoped would happen, in the wake of the Brown's Chapel fire the town's Black population began declining once more. In 1910 there were only three African American families remaining—an elderly Abraham Davenport, his wife, and their niece and second generations of the Wallaces and the Currys—along with one single man, John Goodman. In a portentous sign of what was to come, there were also two African Americans at the State Asylum for the Insane, built ten years before. Likewise discouraging, on the eve of World War I, in the early part of 1916, a local doctor and his wife hosted the first meeting of the recently revived Ku Klux Klan, and by the mid-1920s, that group was notably strong, and white-robed members openly paraded through town. Not surprisingly, in 1930, at which point the total Hastings population was a little over five thousand, the Davenports and Wallaces were gone and the Black residents included just James Curry and his wife, Phoebe; William Douglas and his wife, Elizabeth; and one single elderly man, Henry Thomas. There were now a dozen Black patients at the renamed State Hospital for the Insane, however, ranging in age from sixteen to sixty-four, some single, some married, and one widowed, most originally from southern states. Ten years later, the local African American population was merely one, Henry Thomas, while the same group of Black patients were still institutionalized, with the exception of a young man who was discharged, and no new African American patients were admitted.[18]

From one county to the next, many of the same racial demographic patterns that played out in Goodhue and Dakota Counties were mirrored in other parts of rural Minnesota as well, though not without notable variations. In nearby Rice County, for example, the first African Americans to arrive were the Adams family, including James, aged forty-three, from Alabama, and Marie, aged thirty-three, also from Alabama, along with two teenaged sons, both probably born in Wisconsin, and three young girls, whose last name was Beghan, possibly because they had a

White German father. By 1870, the Adams family had left the county, and yet another Black family was living in Northfield, headed by fifty-five-year-old Eliza White, from North Carolina. Four single African American men were in Northfield too, and a single Black man was counted in Walcott. Thirty years later, in 1900, Northfield was home to an elderly widowed African American man and his grandson, two Black families, and one large interracial family that had recently moved there, the Ashleys. This family included Rolla, aged forty-seven and born in Alabama; Pauline, aged forty-five and born in Wisconsin to German parents; and their seven children. Additionally, Faribault had one Black family headed by a widowed biracial man (the census lists him as "W" for White though with a "B" for Black in the corner), one divorced African American man, and several Black residents at the newly opened School for the Feeble Minded. The biracial widower, Oscar Ball, was forty-five years old, originally from New York, and born to a German mother, and his household included a ten-year-old son as well as two boarders, one French Canadian and another who was German.[19]

Rather than an exception, and despite the disdain by Daniel Buck and among many Whites for "race mixing," interracial couples were apparently not uncommon, most often showing up as local residents around the turn of the century. Almost every one of these conjugal arrangements was between a Black man born somewhere in the South and a White woman who was a first- or second-generation immigrant from Norway, Sweden, Denmark, or Germany, or a migrant from some other midwestern or northern state like Iowa, Wisconsin, Pennsylvania, or New York. Many of the men were barbers and others were land-owning or renting farmers, work that allowed them to support a family. The wives were typically listed as "keeping house" or with no occupation at all, and the census listed children alternately as "Negro," "black," and "mulatto." In only a very few cases was a mixed-race pairing between a White man and a Black woman, yet they too were typically not from area families but rather had moved from elsewhere after they had met. There were also a small number of racially mixed households in which a Black family took in White immigrant boarders or where a White family employed a Black woman or man as a live-in servant or laborer.

Among the several other examples of interracial coupling, in 1900 African American Samuel Wright was living in Clark, a town in Faribault County, with his White wife, Annie, and he worked as a barber.

He was fifty-one years old and originally from Tennessee, while she was forty-nine and originally from New York. Their six children were from previous marriages and ranged in age from eight to twenty, four listed in the census as "black" and two listed as "white," and there was one young grandson, listed as "white." Similarly, Louis Boggs was a barber in Blooming Prairie, in Steele County, married to a White woman named Susie. He had been born in Mississippi, and her family had immigrated from Holland, and Susie's brother John lived with the Boggs and their two children and worked with Louis in his shop. Likewise, African American Daniel Weaver was living in Hayfield, a town in Dodge County, with his White wife, Elizabeth, and also worked as a barber. Daniel had been born about 1856 in Michigan to a father from North Carolina and a mother from Pennsylvania, and Elizabeth was a second-generation German immigrant on her father's side. They counted one son, George, whom the census listed as "adopted" and "white" and born in Illinois, probably Elizabeth's by another father.[20]

Slightly different from his Black barbering counterparts, forty-year-old Robert Sterling was a farmer but in 1904 also had married a White wife, Molly, after which they moved to Excelsior. His father was from Virginia and his mother from Iowa while her parents were both from Norway, and in 1910 Robert and Molly had one daughter, Edna, whom the census listed as a "mulatto." African American John Green had moved to Le Sueur from Alabama, where he was a farmer, in 1875, and when he appeared in the 1910 census he was listed as a sixty-five-year-old widower with five sons and one daughter, the oldest thirty years old and the youngest only eleven, all of whom had a German mother. In 1920, he was still living in Le Sueur, with a lesser number of his children, and the oldest boy, Otto, was overseeing the farm. Farther south along the Minnesota River, in the town of Kasota, a Black tailor named T. J. Clay was married to a White woman named Ethel. He had been born in Iowa in about 1870, while she was less than half his age and came from an undesignated part of Minnesota. Moreover, the same town included a Black family composed of African American John Miles, aged eighty-nine, and his son, Ellery, aged fifty, and they took in a White lodger, Edward Graves, who was from Germany and worked as a railroad switchman.

Like most interracial families in Minnesota's rural areas, Samuel Wright, Louis Boggs, Daniel Weaver, and Robert Sterling and their wives and children moved away from their particular towns within a decade or two after arriving, and all of the men were deceased or otherwise missing from the census by 1920. But a few others, including the families headed by John Green and T. J. Clay, lingered a bit longer, and interracial households did not entirely disappear from the state's rural parts until the 1940s. The Ashley family had left Northfield by 1910, for instance, yet twenty years later the town counted six Black residents who were part of two different mixed-race families. African American Robert Boone, aged forty-five, was born in Minnesota to parents from North Carolina, worked as a compositor foreman at a printing office, and was married to Ruth, aged thirty-nine, also born in Minnesota but to a mother and father from Norway. They had one daughter, Ruth Jr., who is listed as a "Negro" in the census. Additionally, there was Gertie Mimms, a widowed White woman, originally from Kansas, with four children ranging in age from seven to thirteen, all described in the census as "Negro," their Black father born in Illinois. By the next census, however, they too were gone, leaving only two Black couples without children, a single African American man, and more than two dozen institutionalized Black men and women, all in Faribault.[21]

Part of what explains the eventual retreat that Black as well as mixed-race families made from rural counties in the first half of the twentieth century was the limited occupational opportunity they faced in a rigidly segregated labor market. With the exception of barbering, Whites in rural towns locked African American men out of almost all professions, and in only very rare cases did they permit Black men to work in packing plants or other industry. More typically, they worked as porters for a local shop, hotel, or railroad, as janitors at a public school, church, or private business, or as hostlers and wagon drivers for delivery companies and stockyards. Married Black women with children were sometimes able to avoid wage labor and attend to mothering and "keeping house," but when they did work for pay, they were allowed only a few choices, most of them taking in washing. Single African American men and women, and those who were married but had no children, were also employed as servants in private homes and as live-in cooks at hotels, including both small, local establishments and larger, resort-type enterprises.[22]

Until the early part of the twentieth century, the resorts ringing Lake Minnetonka, just west of Minneapolis, were an especially popular tourist destination during the summer months, and a good portion of the staff was Black. In 1880, for example, the main hotel in Excelsior employed nearly thirty African Americans as cooks, waiters, and chambermaids, in a community with 417 year-round residents. At the time, it advertised "Old Fashioned Southern Fried Chicken and Fresh Fish Dinner" on a sign posted out front, and after the original building was destroyed by fire and rebuilt in 1886, a new owner constructed several cottages for the mainly White southern clientele's servants too. As business declined, though, the resort's Black staff was reduced to three: Sydney, James, and Mary Woodford. In 1900, they were still in Excelsior, living among more than seven hundred White residents, yet they no longer worked at the hotel, and their household included a Swedish immigrant and a German immigrant. Ten years later, the Woodfords had moved to Deephaven, on another part of the lake, and two new interracial couples had moved to Excelsior. One was Robert Sterling and his wife, Molly, and the other was George W. Johnson, a poultry and truck garden farmer from Missouri, who lived with his White consort Nellie Minis. By the end of the 1920s, however, the Sterling family had moved to Salt Lake City and the Johnson family had moved to Minneapolis, and there were no African Americans among the still steadily growing all-White population.[23]

While some Black migrants did become farmers, very few acquired their own land, and those who did tended to own fewer acres than Whites and had relatively shorter ownership. In 1910, African Americans operated just twenty-nine of the 156,137 farms in Minnesota, and only about half of those were owners, possessing a total of 2,362 acres. Ten years later, the number of Black farm owners had increased to twenty-four, but that was among a significantly larger number of farms in the state overall, and the combined acreage owned by African American farmers had dropped to just 1,657 acres. After another decade, in 1930, there were twenty-seven Black farm operators, yet just nineteen of them were owners and the rest were tenants, and the amount of land they owned shrank even more, to 1,469 acres. At that point, the total African American population in rural Minnesota had decreased by 40 percent since 1910, from 566 to 335, and while seventy-one of eighty-seven counties reported "Negro" inhabitants, only a slight eighteen of those seventy-one reported "Negro" farmers. In fact, five of the farms operated by African Americans in 1930 were part of one interrelated group in Edina, on the outskirts of Minneapolis, and together they claimed a disproportionate share of the land, building, and farm implement value owned by all Black farmers in the state.[24]

The otherwise meager number of African Americans who owned their own farms in the early twentieth century was due in part to the complete failure of various colony plans in the century proceeding, either because of local White hostility or land agents' misrepresentation of the tillable claims. In Todd County, the mere rumor of organized Black homesteading enraged White residents and sank the political fortunes of Timothy Ward, a White doctor associated with the settlement idea. Like Jane Gray Swisshelm, Ward was a Covenanter, a member of a religious group known for its opposition to slavery, as well as a Radical Republican. Also, like Thomas Montgomery, Ward had been an officer in a colored infantry regiment during the Civil War, and during his military stint he adopted a young African American girl from Mississippi, Matilda Rogers. After his discharge in 1866, he moved to Minnesota with his family and, in 1869, the first year African Americans were allowed to vote there, Ward challenged local farmer and Republican Party functionary Jacob Brower for the position of auditor. Brower's supporters circulated a handbill claiming that the doctor was a secretary of the Negro Emigration Society and that he was preparing to bring seven hundred Black men and their families to occupy land in several area townships, with "Officers claims in the centre, Niggers on the outside." Agents for the society had supposedly visited the area, but owing to the intense opposition, they changed their minds about beginning their work. With that, state party officials made sure to block Ward's nomination, and a few years later he and his family returned to his home state of Ohio, leaving Todd County all White.[25]

Another colonization effort in the next county over got further along, although in the end it failed too. When the Grand Army of the Republic held an encampment at the St. Paul fairgrounds in 1896, real estate agents there enticed a few African American veterans from Greenwood, Kentucky, to gather a group of homesteaders to farm in Fergus Falls. In April of the next year, they returned with twenty families but were unable to find either good land or steady employment, and by the summer's end some had already moved away to nearby townships to work as farm laborers or in various menial occupations. Despite this, two years later a real estate agent encouraged yet another large group of Black Greenwood families to go to Wealthwood, in Mille Lacs County, but they also found the soil poor and their venture went bust as well, again sending most of the prospective settlers elsewhere. One family that came with this second group, for example, was headed by Alexander and Josephine

Peneok (or Penick), who were then in their sixties and had four children, ranging in age from fifteen to twenty-three. By 1910 the elderly couple was living in Aitkin, north of Mille Lacs County, their daughters Bettie and Mattie had married and were living nearby (with Bettie working as a "washer woman"), a son Elick lived with Mattie, and a son Frank had moved to Fergus Falls, married, and found work as a janitor. Ten years later, none of the family remained in Aitkin, and at least Mattie had moved to Minneapolis, while Frank still lived in Fergus Falls and worked in a shoeshine parlor.[26]

Besides the evident lack of opportunity to find gainful employment or to own land, Black individuals and families also left rural Minnesota towns and counties in fear of threatened and actual violence. Sometimes this happened over the course of years, like the African American population's decline in Hastings after arsonists burned Brown's Chapel in 1907, and other times it took place in the rush of a few days, as was the case in Montevideo in 1903. In mid-July of that year, historian Christopher P. Lehman recounts, an itinerant Black man, Joseph Henry Scott, attacked and robbed Helen Olson, a Norwegian woman, in nearby Watson. The county sheriff formed a posse, which found and arrested Scott, and several times over the next few days, with newspapers mistakenly reporting that he was a "murderer," White mobs attempted to lynch him. As that was taking place, a group of Whites in Montevideo confronted the town's six African Americans, widower Thomas Jefferson and his children, and gave them until Tuesday to leave, which they did. "If the negroes could be driven out of the United States as easily," the *Montevideo Leader* opined, "the race problem would soon be solved." Having failed to capture and kill Scott themselves, other Whites in Olivia, which had no Black residents to expel, made a life-sized effigy and hung it on a telegraph pole, after which they burned it. "It's rather hard on us Northerners, who have held up our hands in horror at the brutal acts of the southern negro," the *Olivia Times* mused, "to awake to the fact that a terrible crime has been committed in the north, in our fair Minnesota, by a negro, presumably a northern product."[27]

In fact, as the interwar period dawned, many towns and counties throughout the state became all White, and the ones that did not often counted just a single Black individual or family, or increasingly, the African Americans recorded by a census were institutionalized, in places like Red Wing's Minnesota State Training School. The MSTS was just one among a growing assortment of prisons, mental hospitals, and orphanages, all of them located in areas beyond the Twin Cities. These institutions mixed Blacks among Whites, but by definition they restricted the liberties of inmates, patients, and orphans and denied them the chance to be full-fledged members of the surrounding community. Consequently, as African American barbers, cooks, farm laborers, hack drivers, servants, washerwomen, and others migrated away, the only Black people whom Whites in rural towns and counties might personally encounter or know were those they perceived to be lawless, insane (including "criminally insane"), and/or neglected. This was hardly the kind of interaction that would lead them to question their deeply rooted racist assumptions and beliefs, and it certainly did not move them to confront a historical racist legacy and make their towns more welcoming. At the same time, as chronic overcrowding, staff negligence, and building disrepair worsened from decade to decade, life for those institutionalized African Americans (as well as equally unfortunate Whites) became an inescapable nightmare.[28]

Established in 1866, the St. Peter mental hospital originally operated out of the Ewing House, which had been the town's first hotel but was sinking into dilapidation since it had been used as an emergency hospital during the US–Dakota War and afterward abandoned. The town eventually secured state funds to construct new buildings on the site, and in short order the north wing was completed in 1870, the south wing finished in 1873, and an addition made to the north wing in 1876, the latter overseen by the company Thomas Montgomery and T. G. Carter had established. From the start, however, the facility was overcrowded, and within a couple of decades all of the buildings were in poor condition and needed a complete overhaul. Remodeling was finished in 1908, and a facility for the dangerously insane was constructed on-site three years later, although even with expansions in 1917 and 1936 that asylum was perennially overcrowded as well (within the first year of operation there were sixty-four patients in a space meant for fifty). Moreover, the new facility was criticized for being both too secure and not secure enough, "a prison that wasn't a prison and a hospital that wasn't a hospital," particularly following several dramatic escapes, including one that required the governor to mobilize the St. Peter National Guard.[29]

Among the nearly one hundred patients at the newly established St. Peter asylum was an African American man named Marshall (or "Marshal") Rayford, initially admitted to the temporary facility in October

1869 and transferred to the permanent one in 1870. Born about 1848 in Kentucky, he was an unmarried laborer with a "common school" education. He had previously lived in St. Paul, probably with his parents, although hospital and census records say nothing about who they were, listing their origins as unknown. On his admission to the asylum, the White superintendent described Rayford's appearance as "untidy," later adding a diagnosis of "mania." More revealing, however, is the brief explanation of how the young man understood his own personal distress and involuntary commitment. "He says he loves a white girl," the superintendent noted, "but that his parents want to hide him." Subsequently, over the course of the next decade, Rayford exhibited various symptoms of actual mental illness, flatly described by the hospital staff as "alternately excited and depressed," while otherwise he ate and slept well, was in good health, and got along with other patients. Unfortunately, lacking any effective treatment, and without any family coming to retrieve him, he remained institutionalized for the rest of his life, and in the fall of

St. Peter Asylum, about 1936.

1930, when he was more than eighty years old, he died and was unceremoniously buried in the hospital cemetery.[30]

During the sixty-year stretch of time that Rayford was confined, the African American population in Nicollet County grew dramatically, numbering more than forty by 1930, but all of that growth came from institutionalization in one of the asylum's two different wards. Like Rayford, most of the patients were at least fifty years old, slightly more than half were born in a southern state, many had lived previously in St. Paul or Minneapolis, and the large majority were men, although there were some women. Fairly representative of the female patients was Elizabeth Bell, born in Missouri in 1871 to parents who were originally from Virginia. When she was committed to St. Peter in 1924, she was married but living with friends in St. Paul, and her symptoms included auditory hallucinations and various delusions. Six years later, in 1930, she was transferred to the state hospital in Anoka, part of an attempt to ease overcrowding by moving "well-behaved chronic cases," and she died soon after. As patients like Bell were moved away or died, however, others replaced them, and in 1940 the Black population in Nicollet County had not notably changed, with at least forty African Americans institutionalized at the St. Peter hospital, while none were living at liberty in town.[31]

Following World War II, it was becoming clear to many that the state asylums were not only dangerously overcrowded but also very badly run. Disturbed by what was happening, the Minnesota Unitarian Conference Committee on Institutions for the Mentally Ill hired Justin Reese, the former director of Field Work for the National Committee for Mental Hygiene, to make a comprehensive tour of the facilities. In a report to Governor Luther Youngdahl based on the tour, the Unitarian Conference Committee insisted that the seven existing mental hospitals suffered various "bad features" as a result of "inadequate operating funds" and "decades of neglect." The average operating cost allowed for each institution by the state legislature was one-fifth of what the American Psychiatric Association required, and none was even close to meeting minimum standards for the number of doctors, nurses, attendants, and social workers. Consequently, physical restraints were often substituted for treatment, patient hygiene received little attention, clothing was insufficient, and food and food service were poor. Although the majority of the ten thousand patients who suffered these conditions were White, a disproportionate number of them were Black and, considering that this was the only life Whites allowed to African Americans in many counties and towns by midcentury, such neglect was yet another legacy of the aspirations for White supremacy that date back to Minnesota's territorial era.[32]

"This New Land of Ours"

Just as Whites in the South struggled with a racial "Reconstruction" in the aftermath of the Civil War, historian Leslie Schwalm explains, White northerners confronted the fact that slavery's end meant a new geographic mobility for African Americans and, concurrently, a new claim on social mobility. As Black migration out of the South forced the question of Black equality in the North, White resistance to the one became entangled with resistance to the other. Inevitably, White hostility profoundly affected historical memory as well. "The transition to black citizenship," Schwalm notes, involved "an extensive and persistent series of collisions over segregation, civil rights, and the more informal politics of race—including how slavery and emancipation would be remembered and commemorated." Around the turn of the century, a "culture of reunion" emerged, one that allowed for reconciliation among Whites by dismissing the sharp differences over slavery that had led them to war and alternatively portraying slavery as a benign or even civilizing institution. At the same time, the newly forming collective myths "allowed northern whites to ignore or overwrite their region's own history of slavery and its unresolved struggle against black citizenship, portraying African Americans as simple, naïve, grateful non-citizens."[33]

In Minnesota, like other parts of the Upper Midwest, postbellum efforts by Whites to intimidate, subordinate, control, and exclude Black migrants were increasingly part and parcel of Civil War commemorations there. Sometimes this took the form of condescending acknowledgment of an era and a people gone by. In mid-April 1915, for example, the *New Ulm Review* published a heavily rewritten version of a story from the *Spokane (Washington) Chronicle* about African American Mark Cane, formerly one of New Ulm's "well-known characters." Cane had recently appeared at a celebration of President Abraham Lincoln's birthday and related parts of his life story, including growing up on a South Carolina plantation, being sold at age sixteen to a slave trader, and laboring on a large Alabama plantation until the Civil War. Supposedly, he also told the audience that he met Lincoln when he was touring the South with

Stephen Douglas (which he did not), and Cane's enslaver confronted the future president, saying, "I understand you claim that niggers have as much brains as white people," at which point Lincoln felt Cane's head and proclaimed that the slave would be a great man if given a chance. Later, when the Ninth Minnesota regiment passed through Alabama, Cane joined up as an orderly, went back north with the soldiers after the war, learned the barbering trade in Rochester, and in the early 1870s moved to New Ulm with his wife, Lizzie, and opened his own barber shop. The couple were "well-remembered by those who were children forty years ago," the story noted, but like so many other African American migrants in rural Minnesota, at the turn of the century they left, moving all the way to the Pacific Northwest.[34]

In other cases, Civil War commemoration in Minnesota featured unvarnished racist caricature, even by Whites with seemingly open-minded political sympathies for African Americans. In the 1890s, for instance, the *Red Wing Republican* ran a story that mocked one of the area's few remaining Black residents in Goodhue County, Civil War veteran Nicholas Taylor. Somewhat similar to Cane, Taylor had fled a Mississippi plantation to the Fifth Minnesota Infantry camp, soon after joined a colored regiment, and following the war made his way north. The man was "dark in color but white in purpose," the newspaper asserted, and he was known for his "watermelon smile," his attempts to use "half the long words in the English dictionary," and his endless stories about hunting in the South. Purportedly, he did not care whether he was called "Nick Taylor" or "Nigger Nick." In fact, when Taylor died in 1907, Red Wing minister Charles Carter Rollit conducted funeral ceremonies at Christ Episcopal Church and delivered a eulogy titled "Nigger Nick," which the *Republican* reprinted. Taking the opportunity to ponder "the man who had once been a slave," Rollit waxed on about "this new land of ours" and "how it gave / This man a place—tho' the world's underling, / While the church did his requiem sing, / As the equal of chieftan [*sic*] or king."[35]

Among Nicholas Taylor's local contemporaries was the *Republican*'s founding editor and Civil War hero, Lucius F. Hubbard, whose Whiteness allowed him a markedly different life as well as a notably different death. Originally from New England, Hubbard came to Minnesota in 1857, after which he settled in Red Wing and took over what was then the *Daily Republican Eagle*. Like Thomas Montgomery, he enlisted in the army in 1861 and was briefly detached to guard the frontier against the Dakota, although unlike Montgomery he remained with his all-White regiment when it moved south. There, Hubbard regularly posted letters to his mother and aunt, detailing his frequent (unmerited) promotions in rank. "I have done reasonably well for the time I have been in the service," he wrote after only four months, "I was placed in command of the entire regiment without having previously acquired the least knowledge of even the first principles of the [military] profession." Hubbard reported back about the "contrabands" he encountered as well. "I am doing quite a business in the confiscation of slave property," he related in one letter, "I have already sent about eight human chattels away by railroad headed north, and have about fifty more in camp. . . . I have also attached quite a number to my regiment in the capacity of teamsters, cooks and servants." Yet, as Hubbard made clear, the delight he took in watching slavery crumble was less about moral disgust of bondage or concern for freed people than smoldering hatred for treasonous White southerners. "It certainly makes the rebels wince to see their 'niggers' taken off," he explained, "which is a source of some private satisfaction to me even if it does not contribute greatly to the general good."[36]

For the next three years, Hubbard led his troops in numerous critical engagements with Confederate forces and was brevetted a brigadier general before finally mustering out in September 1865. He returned to Red Wing, became extremely wealthy through investments in various businesses, and began a successful political career, as a Republican of course, serving first as a state senator, from 1872 to 1875, and two terms as governor, from 1882 to 1887. By the time the Spanish–American War broke out in 1898, Lucius Hubbard was sixty-two years old and yet President William McKinley personally requested that he return to the military to command a full army division, which he did at a military post in Florida. When that war was done, he came back to St. Paul and shortly after moved to Minneapolis. Then, in 1913, at the age of seventy-seven, with his historical legacy assured, Hubbard died. Both houses of the legislature passed a resolution to adjourn on the day of his funeral, Governor A. O. Eberhart issued a special message about his importance to Minnesota, and the Twin Cities newspapers paid him singular tribute. "General Hubbard was one of the most prominent figures in the development of the state," the *Minneapolis Journal* declared, and "as editor, miller, railroad builder, legislator and governor he has been a leading citizen," while his "gallant conduct" in the Civil War was "an important chapter in the state's military history."[37]

Chicago, Milwaukee & St. Paul rail yards, hotel, and depot, Austin, Minnesota, about 1900. *Courtesy Mower County Historical Society*

CHAPTER 3

Not "a Negro Town": Packinghouse Workers and Whiteness in Austin

BY THE TIME a teenage John Winkels left his family's farm in Adams, Minnesota, for nearby Austin in the fall of 1922, the Mower County seat counted more than twelve thousand residents. Austin, an agricultural town near the Iowa border in southeastern Minnesota, had seen marked growth following the Civil War with the arrival of a branch line for the Chicago, Milwaukee & St. Paul (C.M. & St. P.) railroad, and within a few decades it was a major division point for more than half a dozen other branch lines, where outgoing trains were made up and repairs were done. The links the railways provided to cities north, south, east, and west also drew industry, most notably George A. Hormel's meat-packing plant, established in an old creamery on the Cedar River in 1891. Although starting with just six employees, Hormel incorporated his business after the turn of the century and expanded the plant facili-ties, adding an engine room and machine shop and separate multistory buildings for casings production, beef-kill, and hog-kill, greatly increas-ing the need for workers and enticing migrants to town. World War I prompted yet another expansion in production as well, and still more individuals and families poured in from the countryside seeking packinghouse jobs.

Winkels was among those who came to take a position on the Hormel hog-kill line, and his cousin and one of his younger brothers soon joined him. John and his cousin had also been to Austin earlier in the summer, when they came up for a dance and, while there, the two of them were involved in a violent scene. At the beginning of July, four hundred thousand railroad shopmen across the country decided to strike against a reduction in wages, and by the end of the month the railroad companies were attempting to replace them with strikebreakers, including those employed locally by the C.M. & St. P. Around noon on the twentieth, the day of the dance, thirteen African American strikebreakers arrived in a boxcar, adding to the few White strikebreakers already holed up in the railroad yard roundhouse. That evening, a crowd of a hundred local railroad workers, packinghouse workers, truckers, and others—including the Winkels pair—paraded through the streets, rhetorically asking the many bystanders if they wanted Austin "to be a negro [*sic*] town." Then, once they were in a full frenzy, the crowd stormed the facility. "I had a piece of shovel handle," John recalled, and "we hit them over the head" and "run the niggers out." Back on the farm in Adams, his brother Casper watched the fleeing Black workers go by. "We lived close to the tracks, and they wanted to know if they could have a drink of water and stuff," he remembered, and "they said they'll never come back to this part of the country again."[1]

Like almost all the men and women who flocked to Austin and found work at Hormel, John Winkels, his cousin, and his brother were White. In 1900 only three African Americans lived in town, and over the next decade that number increased to no more than a dozen. Most were single men or married men unaccompanied by their wives, and they boarded with Whites while working in some menial occupation. In 1920, there were only nine Black residents, still mostly men, two of whom worked at the packinghouse. Lloyd Newcomb, aged thirty-five and originally from Kentucky, had a job as a "singer" on the hog-kill line, and he boarded with Albert J. Dallenbach, an immigrant from Switzerland, who was a butcher. Noah Riggs, also aged thirty-five, boarded as well and was employed as a trucker at the packing plant. In the years following the attack on the railroad shop strikebreakers, however, when Austin's total population more than doubled to twenty-eight thousand, Newcomb and Riggs both left, and few other Black residents remained.[2]

As a result of the Black flight from Austin, when workers began organizing a union at Hormel in the early 1930s, there was not a single African American in the packinghouse, although John Winkels later claimed that the company briefly employed a group of Black men from out of town during the campaign, and once more, he was involved in chasing them away. "They hired forty of them and they put them in the plant all at one time," he remembered, and the whole lot lived in "the jungles," a wooded area just east of the packinghouse. "We told them after work, 'You better get the hell out of town because you're not going to come in here tomorrow.'" To make good on the threat, that night Winkels and other White workers armed themselves with clubs, went to the woods, broke up the cooking fires, and ran the African American workers out. "After that," he said, "they didn't come in no more because they knew [Hormel] couldn't hire them." Likewise, the remaining local Black residents also knew not to bother. "We had Frank," Winkels recalled, "he was shining shoes in the barbershop and then afterwards he would bell hop for the bus, and everybody liked him." But, he noted, Frank would "never go in the packinghouse because he knew we didn't want him there."[3]

By 1940, after several hard-fought battles, Winkels and the set of militants he was a part of had managed to establish the Independent Union of All Workers (IUAW) at Hormel as well as to extend its reach to include almost all the "uptown" retail and municipal workers, greatly improving wages, hours, and conditions for thousands. Because of Austin's history of racial violence and exclusion, however, these benefits were reserved for Whites. While the city's population had increased to more than thirty-six thousand, there were only about half a dozen Black residents on the eve of World War II. Working-class Whites had established a color line using violence and intimidation, and that line was maintained over time by Austin's reputation as an inhospitable place for African Americans to live. "They knew it all over," Winkels explained. Once, when he was on union business at a packinghouse in Waterloo, Iowa, he encountered a Black woman employed as a custodian there who testified to Austin's racist reputation. "There's a woman, she was washing the walls going up the steps," he recalled, "and this guy says 'We got some people here from Austin' . . . and he looked up at her and she was colored and she says, 'Hormel packinghouse, they don't like us black people.'"[4]

By midcentury, though, after the IUAW had joined the Congress of Industrial Organizations as Local P-9 of the United Packinghouse Workers of America (UPWA), union leaders as well as some rank-and-file members counted themselves among the most outspoken advocates of Black civil rights in Minnesota. They did this without confronting or disturbing Austin's overwhelming Whiteness primarily by framing White supremacy as a southern phenomenon and disregarding their own active history of racial exclusion. *The Unionist,* the Local P-9 weekly newspaper that was delivered free to every household in the city, regularly featured reports about desegregation battles in places like Alabama, Mississippi, and Kentucky, for example, and it frequently pointed out the interest working-class Whites had in challenging southern Democrats who were defending segregation, since they also were among the leading voices against organized labor. Yet when John Winkels retired from the Local P-9 executive board in December 1955, the paper lauded him for his long and selfless service to the meatpacking union and, of course, made no mention of his violent racist past or the troublesome legacy it left behind. "He developed his philosophy of unionism back in the days when an injury to one was an injury to all," the editor insisted, "when a fellow worker looked upon his union members with a feeling of unity and sympathy."[5]

Three decades later, in the 1980s, there were still fewer than fifty Black residents in Austin, and when Hormel workers started a long but ultimately futile strike against major contract concessions, the workforce there remained all White, with the exception of two young men from Ghana who had come to the United States to attend the University of Minnesota but had run out of money and were apparently overstaying their visas. By both intent and deed, Whites had made sure that for most of the twentieth century Austin was far from "a negro town." Although they never adopted the full array of segregation laws and Jim Crow customs more common in the South, they were similarly concerned with exercising and defending their power and privilege, even in a place where there were very few African Americans, where there was little chance of many more arriving, and where Blacks posed little competition for housing or jobs. Instead of establishing White supremacy by elaborately ordering relations between the two races, however, codifying the terms for occupying the same space or using the same amenity, Whites in Austin and elsewhere throughout the North did it by keeping African Americans away from them altogether.[6]

"We Had No Objection to the Fact That the People Were Colored"

Like millions of other workers in the United States, those laboring on the country's railroads made significant wage gains during World War I, buoyed by a booming economy and enabled by government protection for organized labor. With the war's end and the economy's weakening, however, a newly established US Railroad Labor Board announced wage cuts to various positions across the industry. In response, a majority of the rank-and-file workers voted to strike, setting a deadline for July 1, 1922. Before that could happen, the board organized a meeting of industry executives and union leaders, and with the promise that there would be a reconsideration of the wage reduction, the president of the maintenance-of-way union agreed not to sanction a walkout by his members. But leaders for the six unions representing railroad shopmen refused to even attend the meeting and held to the deadline, calling more than four hundred thousand members off their jobs. The labor board then issued a statement declaring that the striking workers were no longer "employees of the railways." Railroad executives interpreted this to mean that they had government support for replacing the striking workers with strikebreakers, which they eagerly sought to do. This stoked workers' outrage, and eventually they resorted to violent means, including bombing railroad property, burning bridges, and sabotaging trains as well as assaulting strikebreakers and vandalizing their homes.[7]

In Austin, nearly all of the 225 Chicago, Milwaukee & St. Paul employees faced wage cuts, and 184 shop mechanics and freight car men walked out, leaving a few maintenance-of-way men and others still on the job. At the start of the strike, division superintendent E. A. Meyers pointedly let the striking workers know that their positions would be easily filled, canceling their seniority and making them "mighty sorry" that they "ever participated in this Bolshevik movement." At another point he warned that if the men did not end the walkout soon, the company might simply dismantle the roundhouse and arrange for contracts with larger locomotive works elsewhere. Meanwhile, the national maintenance-of-way union finally joined the strike, along with eighteen others, and the potential for picket-line confrontations grew, prompting railroad corporations to seek the aid of federal troops and city police forces. Locally, officers with National Guard Companies G and H left town to join an encampment in Lake City, Minnesota, while the C.M. & St. P. designated several special agents, joined by newly deputized sheriffs.[8]

By mid-July, about a dozen White strikebreakers had collected at the depot in Austin, but this caused no serious disturbance until the group of thirteen African American strikebreakers joined them on the twentieth and, it seems, their race as much as their reason for being there was the provocation for the violence that followed. Within an hour after the Black men arrived, local union members met to discuss what to do. By late afternoon, a mob began to form, toward evening the group paraded through the streets, and finally they surged across the overhead bridge leading to the roundhouse, disarmed a special agent, and rushed the back of the building. The terrified strikebreakers put up little resistance and quickly fled. "That there was no desire on the part of the negroes to return to Austin," the *Daily Herald* reported the next day, "was evident from assertions made to many of their pursuers as they sped rapidly along the railroad ties and through the verdant pastures of the countryside." Although they were supposedly occupied planting trees with Boy Scouts during the time of the raid, union leaders Jacob Herzog and Richard Taylor also issued a revealing statement. "The action last night, we feel, represents the sentiment of the citizens of Austin as to a corporation establishing a 'black belt' in our city," they insisted. "There is no slum district in our city nor is there room for one." Blame for the violence was not on the attackers, Herzog and Taylor claimed, but rather "the ones that were responsible for bringing the negroes here."[9]

During the raid, hundreds of women had gathered on the overhead bridge to cheer on the men, calling to them to clear out "white strikebreakers as well as black," and in fact, four Whites were among those who ran away into the countryside. Yet like the men in the mob, the women directed most of their fury toward any African Americans they saw. In one case, the *Daily Herald* reported, they spotted "a well known colored young man employed at one of the barber shops," most likely twenty-two-year-old Butler Cook, and mistaking him for a strikebreaker, they yelled for the mob to "get him." Fearing for his life, "the courteous and well-liked local boy hastily responded with explanations respecting his identity and emphasized that he was not a member of the workers employed in the shops," and the crowd let him be. The other White strikebreakers who did not flee were local residents, and perhaps because of that, they faced only petty harassment from the mob. One of them, W. J.

Beckel, reported that someone threw rotten eggs at his house following the raid and, later in August, they smeared pink and yellow paint on the front brick wall. But Austin mayor George Hirsh appeared before the aldermen to defend Beckel and make it clear that vandalism directed at men who crossed the picket lines would not be allowed. The man had "the right to work or not to work," he said, and "if it takes two dozen police he shall have protection."[10]

In the immediate aftermath of the roundhouse attack, Chicago, Milwaukee & St. Paul superintendent Meyer bemoaned the "disrespect for law and order," mentioning nothing about the racial terror it included. Ten days later, the company brought in fifty more strikebreakers, presumably all White since no mention was made of their race. "It is true we got a bunch of men," Meyer said, "and the trains are running at 100 per cent." Yet they were not being employed for the "back shop," he explained, because "the kind of repairs done there will be done elsewhere in the future." At the same time, the railroad company reinforced the company guard, sought arrest warrants for the mob ringleaders, and petitioned for a restraining order limiting the number of pickets. The restraining order specifically mentioned eighteen men by name, citing them for "interference with railroad operations, destruction of property, violence against its employes [*sic*] and persons desiring to become their employes," although it included language making it applicable to every individual as well. "We do not anticipate anything but the observance of the law," the marshal serving the notice oddly insisted. "The trouble comes more from outsiders than from the men themselves."[11]

Several weeks following the roundhouse attack, with racist anger still boiling, White residents in Austin's West End ran a Black family out of town—likely the septuagenarians Isaac and Jennie Bailey—claiming that they were "maintaining a nuisance." Their names and the particular violation were unspecified, although what they did was ostensibly serious enough that residents had complained to police and even appeared before the city council. When those efforts came to nothing, they "took matters into their own hands," gathering as a group to confront the family at their home and order them to leave. But the *Austin Daily Herald* insisted that "race feeling was not the motive for their warning" and quoted an unnamed resident saying as much. "We had no objection to the fact that the people were colored," he claimed, "and we would not have taken any action if they had behaved themselves. . . . We want to keep our section of the city clean and similar action will be taken if any further disturbance occurs." If the family had failed to comply with the group's demands, he added, "they would have been escorted out of the city last night, household goods and all." The next morning, however, the only thing left at the home was a sign the couple had tacked to their door: "Gone but not forgotten. Good will to men and women."[12]

While none of the West End residents suffered any consequences for menacing the Baileys, throughout the summer city leaders and railway officials continued to hound the men involved in the earlier attack on strikebreakers, and various union representatives went along with this behavior. The strike was the main theme of that year's Labor Day celebration in Sutton Park, where Mayor Hirsh called on the sizable audience of workers to "purge your organization of radicals," conflating racial violence with class-conscious militancy. Railway union president Jacob Herzog, who had his own political aspirations, followed suit, invoking both patriotism and Christianity as fundamental values for organized labor. "There is not a question, but we have the best government on the face of the earth," he declared, "but it is not wholly perfect—no-one is perfect. There was only one such and he was crucified." Together, it seems, the two men were laying the groundwork to punish the rowdies whose violence had violated the conventional economic order. In fact, in mid-September, when the railroad strike was finally done, nearly two dozen shop employees were forced to resign, as superintendent Meyer explained, on account of their earlier participation "in the trouble that night the colored men were driven from the shop."[13]

Clearly, particularities like class and context both conditioned and circumscribed White residents' expression of racial hatred in Austin, including what they could do and how they could do it as well as how other Whites responded to them. In the years just before and after the railroad shopmen's strike, when the Ku Klux Klan made its first inroads there and in other industrial and agricultural communities around Minnesota, the group's promotion of White supremacy and its reception by local people was similarly nuanced. In predominantly German and agricultural New Ulm, for example, which had been the target of Klan accusations of disloyalty during World War I, a local newspaper reported that an organizing effort by the group saw "but few present and it is intimated that there is little hope of securing a membership here." Nearly seven hundred Whites attended the founding meeting of a Klan chapter in heavily Scandinavian and industrial Duluth, however, not long after a mob of Whites lynched three Black circus workers in the city, and membership more than doubled by 1925. In the end, the Klan lasted for only a few years in Minnesota and elsewhere, undermined by overreaching attacks on increasingly formidable immigrant groups as well as hypocritical pretensions to a middle-class Protestant moral agenda, yet even if briefly it further clarified and affirmed the racism of many Whites throughout the state.[14]

The first iteration of the Ku Klux Klan had been established in the South just after the Civil War, in response to Reconstruction efforts at bringing racial equality to the defeated region, but federal troops and courts had dismantled the terror group by the end of the 1870s. The second Klan, the one that eventually came to the Upper Midwest, was established at Stone Mountain, Georgia, on Thanksgiving Day of 1915. Like the first incarnation, this new Klan was dedicated to preserving White supremacy, but additionally they were concerned with reducing the number of foreigners coming to the United States, and tellingly the founders moved the national headquarters to Indianapolis, Indiana. From that central location it orchestrated the formation of local "klaverns" in every part of the country, in urban areas as well as rural, and by the early 1920s the Twin Cities had several. For the most part these klaverns operated in the open, drawing heavily from fraternal orders like the Masons and Shriners, and membership included many prominent public figures, such as Earle Brown, the Hennepin County sheriff and a Republican candidate for governor. He and others were initiated into the Minneapolis Klan at the Dyckman Hotel, and they continued to use that as a meeting space in the years to follow. They also made annual organized marches down Broadway, dressed in full regalia, and several times burned crosses on a hill in Robbinsdale, a nearby suburb. In 1923 they put up their own candidate for mayor as well, Exalted Cyclops Roy Miner, who at one time worked at the Hormel plant in Austin.[15]

While the Minnesota Klan's rank-and-file membership grew, the state organization's leadership set up a newspaper operation in St. Paul, first publishing *Call of the North*, which ran from July 1923 to February 1924, and then putting out *The Minnesota Fiery Cross*. As tools for building a new Ku Klux Klan, these papers frequently detailed the organization's fundamental principles and beliefs, revealing the ways it went beyond its predecessor. One sidepiece, the "Klansmen's Creed," made this very clear. "I believe in a closer relationship of capital and labor," it read, as well as "the prevention of unwarranted strikes by foreign labor agitators" and "the limitation of foreign immigration." With Catholics (but not only Catholics) particularly in mind, the creed decried "allegiance to any foreign government, emperor, king, pope or any other foreign, political or religious power." Likewise, it insisted that the rights of a "native-born American citizen" were "superior to those of foreigners," at least in the United States. At the same time, however, the statement obliquely articulated a long-held and familiar White obsession with race and sex. "I believe in the protection of pure womanhood," it also declared, and although that did not justify "mob violence," it required "that laws be enacted to prevent the cause of mob violence."[16]

In numerous other cases, the Klan papers were not so reserved about the need to stop Black migration and prevent interracial comingling. By the 1920s, a combination of mechanization and reorganization of southern agriculture, as well as new employment opportunities in northern industry due to World War I and (ironically) restrictive immigration laws, had spurred the start of a huge population shift, later known as the "Great Migration." African Americans were attracted to the North, one *Call of the North* article acknowledged, "because of the larger wages and the assumed greater social opportunity afforded to the Negroes," and most of them gravitated to areas where other Black migrants had already settled. "This natural gravitation enlarges the Negro population, causing it to overflow the space which the white people are willing that Negroes should have, and race antagonism is engendered." The race war the ongoing migration stoked, another article proclaimed, was "quite as murderous and hateful as any similar war in the South," suggesting that the fault was on the migrants themselves, who boldly "assert equality with white people" and seemed to make "an arrogant claim of superiority." Inevitably, the newspapers mused, the very presence of Blacks among Whites led to miscegenation. "The great purpose of the Ku Klux Klan is to preserve in America, as far as possible, the purity and power of the White Race," one article insisted, "to keep our country from becoming a vast Mongrelia." Unlike the southern states, it lamented, many northern and eastern states did little to hinder the "dangerous intermingling of white and colored people," and some even permitted interracial marriage, which "began with the abolition of slavery" and continued as "a curse of ever-growing horror."[17]

★ THE CALL of the NORTH ★

"Eternal Vigilance is the Price of Liberty"

VOLUME I. NUMBER 9.   ST. PAUL, MINNESOTA, FRIDAY, SEPTEMBER 21, 1923 $2.00 A YEAR. 5c A COPY

AUSTIN IN KLANLIGHT

Okla. Governor Running Wild

"Jack" Walton is as Reckless as Bull in China Shop.

Oil State Executive Faces Impeachment and Prosecution.

Klan Stirs Owasso

RESIDENTS COMPLAIN TO SHERIFF OF NOISE MADE BY ROCKETS.

Klansmen Stage Big Ceremonial In View of Thousands Assembled to Witness Naturalization Rites

Mower County Fair Board Would Not Grant Use of Fair Grounds but an Ideal Place Near Austin was Secured.

KLAN LECTURE IN STILLWATER

MARTIN COUNTY KLAN GROWS

THE KLAN'S ATTITUDE TOWARD WHIPPINGS

FIERY CROSS AT GRANITE

By the summer of 1923, some of the Minnesota Klan's most fruitful recruiting was happening in rural counties and towns, where the number of African Americans also happened to be in steady decline. In July, Goodhue County organizers held public lectures in Zumbrota, Kenyon, and Cannon Falls, after which applications for membership were supposedly "coming in rapidly." Toward the end of the month, sixty-seven Red Wing members met on Barn Bluff to erect a cross and initiate thirty-two new candidates, and in September, they hosted a large gathering on Trenton Island for contingents from the Twin Cities, Mankato, Austin, and Albert Lea. Earlier in July, the Albert Lea chapter had hosted *Call of the North* editor Peter J. Orn at the local fairgrounds, where they lit three thirty-five-foot crosses and conducted a "naturalization" ceremony, a ritual that allowed those whose parents were both foreign-born to join. The lecture and ceremony attracted several hundred people, and afterward the crowd made a noisy parade through town, the men in their white robes and women in the lead singing "Onward Christian Soldiers." Additionally, organizers in Fairmont claimed that an August meeting at the Legion Hall brought in one hundred new members, while others in Canby, just west of New Ulm, reported that nearly one thousand people attended their free lecture.[18]

In more than a few areas, however, staunch opposition by local leaders and influential residents seriously hindered Klan recruiting efforts. In Stillwater, Spring Valley, Redwood Falls, Winnebago, and elsewhere, mayors publicly disparaged the group, city council members prohibited organizers from holding meetings within city limits, and halls and churches closed their doors to them. If this failed to stop the Klan, the civic leaders simply shut them down. When a local Protestant minister held a klavern gathering at a hall in Barnesville, the mayor and a policeman "bolted through the door" and disrupted the service before it was over. Taking stock of it all, the Klan claimed the interference was an infringement of their constitutional rights and vowed to confront those who used their official positions "as an instrument of prejudice." The group believed in "free speech," *The Call* declared, "and will fight a legal battle with every person who tries to deny anyone the rights safeguarded by the basic laws of the land." However questionable its credibility, the newspaper also insisted that the opposition did not reflect popular sentiment. "Lecturers have been received in practically all communities in Minnesota with enthusiastic welcome," *The Call* explained, and "we have yet to find the rank and file of people unwilling to permit an honest expression of a cause regardless of merits or demerits."[19]

Perhaps more than any other town, Austin showed the clash between popular support for the Klan and official opposition to the group. Mower County chapters were "growing by leaps and bounds," organizers claimed, after a particularly large outdoor naturalization meeting in July 1923. Seeking to build on the momentum, in early September they applied to use the county fairgrounds for "a religious and patriotic program." Every one of the county board members was a Protestant, the Klan pointed out, which they thought would make them inclined to be more sympathetic, but still the men "flatly" turned down the request. "We would like to know," *The Call* announced, if the decision was driven by "fear of an organized religious minority." Klan leaders were further outraged because other groups they deemed much less worthy regularly received permission to secure the space. "Commercialized Amusements That Savor of Viciousness May Use Fair Grounds," *The Call* announced in a front-page headline, "But Not God-Loving Americans." Among the groups they singled out were traveling circuses, with all their "camp followers," notably "lewd women" and "bunco-steerers," as well as variety shows, including a "colored suggestive, animal-dance aggregation."[20]

The Klan was not to be thwarted, however, and when the fairgrounds application fell through, a farmer who lived on Turtle Creek offered up his land, and the group held the planned gathering there. Early in the day, as participants arrived, there was obvious tension. "The foreign-minded gangsters of Austin were conspicuous by their quietness," *The Call* reported, while "Klansmen in regalia who walked down the main part of town were frequently called 'gutter-rats.'" When some of the men met at a café and gave a rousing welcome to Clark Gross, the Grand Dragon of the state organization, others in a large crowd outside also made "smart remarks." Yet later that night at the farm, *Call* editor Orn delivered a forty-five-minute address to a thousand robed Klan members who had come from various parts of the state, including Minneapolis and St. Paul, Red Wing, Rochester, Mankato, Cannon Falls, Faribault, Zumbrota, Owatonna, and Fairmont. The address was followed by a naturalization ceremony, initiating four hundred new members into what was now the not-so-invisible "Invisible Empire," and the entire spectacle was witnessed by thousands of onlookers.[21]

Throughout the fall, the Mower County klavern continued to grow, with Austin leading the way, and during the next year the Minnesota Klan's membership swelled to what probably were its highest numbers. In the early part of 1924, there was a change in leadership and the inauguration of the first statewide organization for women, and the end of summer saw the first statewide konklave (their German spelling for conclave), held at the Rice County fairgrounds in Faribault. The meeting reportedly drew two thousand men and five hundred women, who paraded through the city in full regalia, many if not most of them from the region's numerous meatpacking towns. In the years to follow, however, Klan membership waned and the group's reach for political power stalled, a change that was happening in other parts of the country as well. A Minnesota konklave was held in 1926 in Owatonna, on twenty acres of land that local organizers later purchased and christened Klan Park, but attendance was down from the year before, and the same was true in 1927, at what turned out to be the last state meeting.[22]

Although the Minnesota Klan did not last beyond the end of the 1920s, its bigoted ideas and ostentatious displays were fresh in the minds of many Whites and Blacks for years afterward, and its legacy cast a long shadow over the state's race relations for decades to come. This was certainly true in Austin during the 1930s, when workers at Hormel successfully organized a union, as well as during the 1940s and 1950s, when the union consolidated its position and presence there and linked rank-and-file members to the larger labor movement. Sven Godfredsen, who worked at Hormel and later became the editor of the packinghouse union's newspaper, vividly remembered one evening during the summer of 1924, when a twenty-car motorcade of robed Klansmen came over from Albert Lea, some of the men riding on the cars' fenders. "Suddenly," he said, "I became aware of the Klan's power." Nearly ten years later, at which point he and other union activists (John Winkels among them) were in the thick of battle, the structure of the old hate-ridden organization was gone, "but it was still there in people's thinking, and they lined up in various ways because of it." This included Austin's hardened reputation for racial exclusion. "We had no blacks you know," Godfredsen noted, and African Americans who were involved in building other packinghouse locals "resented Austin as a lily-white, apart community."[23]

The Hormel union was born out of the efforts of a "militant minority" working in the hog-kill and beef-kill departments, a mix of Trotskyists, Communists, and unaffiliated socialists led by former Industrial Workers

Hormel strike, 1933.

of the World organizer and casing department foreman Frank Ellis. They shared his philosophy of union democracy, shop floor organization, direct action, solidarity among all workers, and industrial union structure, as historian Peter Rachleff explains, and they put these principles to work during the summer of 1933, signing up enough workers to win formal recognition and waging a three-day sit-down strike to enforce their first contract. When this was finished, the newly established Independent Union of All Workers (IUAW) organized city employees and local retail and service workers (an approach called "wall-to-wall"), as well as those employed at meatpacking plants in other cities, including Albert Lea, Faribault, Owatonna, Rochester, South St. Paul, and Bemidji. A few years later, at the start of the new decade, the IUAW affiliated with the United

Packinghouse Workers of America (UPWA) as Local P-9. Testament to the critical role local activists played in building the meatpacking union, this affiliation also coincided with the move several made to positions at the national level. Godfredsen left to edit *The Packinghouse Worker*, Ellis left to become a national officer, and labor lawyer Ralph Helstein became the general counsel.[24]

Oddly, considering southern Minnesota's history of racial violence and racial exclusion, the union that Austin workers joined and helped lead became known for its commitment to Black civil rights. This was due, in part, to the large number of African Americans who found work at packinghouses during the 1920s and 1930s after migrating from the South to Chicago, Kansas City, and elsewhere, and who insisted that their concerns about racial discrimination both inside and outside the plants be heard and addressed. Following the end of World War II, the election of Helstein as president of the UPWA in 1946, and the conclusion of a bitter nationwide strike in 1948, the union redoubled its efforts in that regard. Helstein hired Fisk University's John Hope Franklin to survey the membership about race relations, and he found that while Blacks held a large majority of local steward and executive board positions, they were present in only half as many job categories as Whites. In response, the UPWA established an Anti-Discrimination Department in 1950 and instructed local unions to set up committees of their own to confront hiring discrimination, workplace segregation, and community racism. Building on this, in 1957 the union hosted an Anti-Discrimination Conference and invited Martin Luther King Jr. to speak. In addition to voicing the racial concerns of the Black union membership, King illuminated what White workers had at stake in the fight for civil rights too. "It is certainly true that the forces that are anti-Negro are by and large anti-labor," he said, "and with the coming together of the powerful influence of labor and all people of good will in the struggle for freedom and human dignity, I can assure you that we have a powerful instrument."[25]

Perhaps because of the influence of a progressive cohort that initially helped to build the Austin local, and even though unreconstructed racists like John Winkels were elected to the executive board, the first UPWA contract with Hormel in 1940 included language that was very much in line with the perspective King later counseled at the conference. "We recognize that our industry is composed of workers of all nationalities, of many races, of different creeds and political opinions," the preamble to the contract acknowledged, and "in the past these differences have been used to divide us." Completely disregarding the city's long and bitter history (and likely borrowing boilerplate language from other UPWA agreements), it further asserted that Austin's workers had "organized by overcoming these divisive influences and by recognizing that our movement must be big enough to encompass all groups and all opinions." The preamble also pledged the union to further strengthen its capacity for withstanding efforts to play on workers' differences. "We must destroy the possibility of disunity," it said, "through the education of our membership in the spirit of solidarity with a view to eliminating all prejudices."[26]

One of the primary ways Local P-9 attempted to raise the consciousness of rank-and-file members was through *The Unionist*, its free weekly newspaper. The paper took a somewhat roundabout approach, however, highlighting the principled and pragmatic logic of worker solidarity

The Unionist, May 4, 1956.

across race lines while also presenting racism as a problem particular to the South. Reporting on a successful strike at Godchaux Sugars in Louisiana at the end of 1955, for example, *The Unionist* characterized the outcome as "no ordinary victory" since the company's racist appeals to White workers had been met with "undeviating" Black and White unity among the rank and file. "One can even find ample evidence that after a 55-year extension of the Nineteenth century," Helstein assistant Charles Fisher remarked, "there will dawn a new era of social and economic justice in the backward Southland." In other issues, the paper highlighted the civil rights activism happening in Kentucky, Tennessee, Mississippi, Georgia, and Alabama, with considerable attention paid to the Montgomery bus boycott and the harsh tactics used to intimidate and punish the organizers. "Even those who are most familiar with the efforts of the white supremists [*sic*] in the South to deny the Negroes their elementary rights as American citizens," one article explained, "are amazed at this brazen attempt to force the Negroes to ride in buses where they have been discriminated against and abused."[27]

The perspective on Black civil rights featured in *The Unionist* was shared by most of the union's Minnesota leadership, as was evident at the UPWA's District 2 convention in Austin during the spring of 1956. This was a high-profile event attended by Governor Orville Freeman and Austin mayor Baldy Hansen as well as International union president Ralph Helstein and many other prominent labor leaders, every single one of whom was White. The newspaper's headline for the meeting declared "Civil Rights Gets Strong Backing from UPWA Convention," and a subsequent story listed the resolutions delegates passed, one of which supported the NAACP in the fight to reinstate African American Autherine Lucy as a student at the University of Alabama after White mobs attacked her and the board of trustees forced her out. Helstein mentioned this fight specifically in his speech, criticizing Alabama officials "for denying a girl the right to continue her education because of the color of her skin," while IUAW founding member Frank Ellis made a point to highlight inclusive activism generally, drawing a standing ovation. There was class struggle going on, the union veteran said, and by following the belief that "an injury to one is an injury to all" workers could build a powerful "union philosophy."[28]

Later that summer, the UPWA held its international convention in Cincinnati, but unlike the Austin district convention this was not an all-White affair, counting a mix of White and Black workers among the various leaders and eight hundred delegates from all parts of the country. Not surprisingly, the racial rhetoric there was not so typically branded with the idea of northern exceptionalism. On the eve of the opening day, President Helstein released a report declaring civil rights "a major issue of our time" and taking stock of the "brighter and more hopeful developments on the national and international scene since the union met two years ago." The *Brown v. Board* decision, he noted, "had awakened the responsible citizenry of the nation to the shame of segregation and all forms of discrimination both in the north and the south." Positioning the union in a leading role in confronting these wrongs, the president added, was critical to the labor movement's survival "as an instrument for democratic progress." The report itself likewise detailed gains the UPWA had made against discrimination, again "both in the north and the south," and in his keynote address to the convention Helstein declared that he knew of "no other union that has fought as hard against second-class citizenship as the UPWA."[29]

Following the convention, back in Austin, Local P-9 initiated and led some public efforts of its own to address racial discrimination. In mid-September, twenty residents who represented a "cross section of the community" met at the Normandy Café and established the Austin Committee on Human Rights and Fair Employment Practices, with Frank Schulz elected as the chair. The committee was to be one of twenty-two throughout the state, and it was charged with supporting the work of the Governor's Human Rights Commission (established in 1943 as the Governor's Interracial Commission) as well as the state Fair Employment Practices Commission (formed the year before, in 1955). It did not meet again before the year was out, but in mid-December, during Human Rights Week marking the United Nations adoption of the Universal Declaration of Human Rights, Schulz released a statement that echoed Governor Freeman's own. Minnesotans had to make a serious "re-examination of the guiding principles of our Constitution and Bill of Rights and a critical appraisal of how these rights are enjoyed in their own communities by all men," he said, "with rededication to the aim of securing their enjoyment by all members of the human brotherhood under God."[30]

Despite all good intentions, however, a combination of collective nearsightedness and historical denial plagued the human rights committee's work from the outset and eventually undermined its efficacy. When members gathered for a second time at the end of January, in the UPWA union hall, Schulz opened the meeting by noting that "the group agreed that although no specific problems of racial or religious discrimination exist in Austin, the committee could do constructive work to insure that people's attitudes on race, religion, color or national origin are healthy and based on qualities of a person as an individual." Then they viewed a film about steps labor and management could take to eliminate segregation in industry, with no apparent discussion of why Hormel was an all-White workforce or why Austin was practically an all-White community. They also began preparations for Brotherhood Week at Austin Senior High School and Junior College, which would include a student panel on discrimination. Additionally, committee member Wilfred Leland made a point to mention that the federal Fair Employment Practices Commission required a nondiscrimination clause in all government contracts with industry and that a 1953 state law prohibited the register of deeds to record a deed with restrictive covenants barring a property transfer because of race, religion, or national origin, again without any discussion about how these were locally relevant.[31]

Some glimmer of hope appeared in March when the committee announced plans for an "intensive human rights study" of local conditions and divided the members into working groups. One on "Housing and Public Accommodations" was tasked with examining "if there is equal opportunity for adequate housing available to all groups" and "if there are fair and equal practices for all groups in the community's public transportation system, hotels, restaurants, theatres, and cultural activities." Another on "Education and Employment" would investigate "whether people of all races, religions and nationality backgrounds have full opportunity for jobs on basis of merit" and "to see if there is a school-wide policy which implements and supports continual improvements of intergroup relations in the school and community." And two others were charged with looking at similar concerns for local "Health and Hospital Facilities" and "Recreation." None of the working groups reported on any serious problems, though, if in fact they found any problems at all. They were supposed to report back to the full committee within sixty days, yet that apparently did not happen, and their conclusions seemed not to inform the work that followed.[32]

Later that fall, the Austin Committee on Human Rights hosted a region-wide "joint workshop" at the UPWA union hall, featuring several notable speakers. The day began with a tour of the Hormel plant, led by Fayette Sherman, the head of industrial relations and a member of the local committee, who presented the plant and its workforce as progressive models to emulate. After the tour, the group returned to the union hall for a panel on educational projects and community organizations. This panel was chaired by Benjamin E. Darby Jr., owner of the Owatonna *Daily People's Press* as well as chairman of the Citizens Committee there, and it included presentations by the principal of Albert Lea High School, a social studies teacher at Faribault, and a supervisor from the Rochester schools, besides others representing the League of Women Voters in Owatonna, the Lutheran Walther League in Fairmont, and the Coordinating Council in Austin. That discussion was followed by a luncheon panel chaired by Frank Schulz that began with a welcome from Mayor Hansen and an opening address by Governor Freeman on "The State Responsibility for Equality of Opportunity," which focused on intransigence in the South as a foil for action in the North. "We cannot directly influence the governor of Arkansas," he said, but "we must redouble our efforts to advance equality here where we are responsible."[33]

Despite the engagement of a considerable number of influential people, however, in the end the October workshop did little more than stimulate a superficial conversation about racial discrimination in southern Minnesota, and it prompted no serious efforts to address the area's legacy of racial exclusion. If anyone from Austin and other participating communities were going to evolve a broader view of things at some particular historical moment and finally take action, these would have been the people, and this could have been the time. Yet overwhelming Whiteness and the long history of racism it rested on was hidden in plain view, and this continued to be the case in the years to follow, partly because most of the same individuals stayed in place. Ralph Helstein was reelected to another term as UPWA president, and he tapped Frank Schulz to be his vice president, although they worked out an arrangement for Schulz to stay in Austin as Local P-9 president, which allowed him to continue to serve as chair of the human rights committee. Otherwise, the committee's executive board was relatively unchanged but featured increasingly active leadership by Vice President Luella Galstad and Secretary-Treasurer Helen McMillan.[34]

By the early part of 1962, the staff on the newly formed State Commission Against Discrimination (SCAD) was growing frustrated with the lack of initiative by the Austin committee. In January, Viola May Kanatz traveled from St. Paul for a meeting with Galstad and McMillan to check in on their work and prompt them to do more. The latter apparently told Kanatz that she was "well pleased with the members of the citizens committee," and according to the SCAD representative, she "evidenced no particular concern about the necessity of additions to make it function the way they would anticipate it doing so." Galstad further explained that "an organization like this should perhaps not attempt to have more than four meetings a year." In response, Kanatz suggested that the committee concentrate on housing discrimination and recommended that they organize screenings of a film, *Property Values & Race*, as well as plan a fall conference with local church groups, law enforcement officials, and educators. But the two Austin women pointed out that "there were only two Negro families" in town and they had "no difficulty in their housing accommodations," adding that "religious problems" were more significant than "color problems." Frustrated with their reluctance, Kanatz again suggested showing the film, which she noted in her report "might have real value in a community where the informal natural contact with Negroes is by virtue of the population not possible."[35]

While Helen McMillan was obstinate with SCAD staff when it came to discussing Austin's racism, she had a local reputation for principled liberalism, and over the next few decades this was a foundation for her career in public service. Helen had married Kenneth McMillan in 1938 in the Twin Cities, and after he returned from service in World War II, they moved to Austin, where he became a municipal judge and she served as president of the local League of Women Voters for fifteen years as well as president of the state organization from 1953 to 1955. In the fall of 1962, at the suggestion of Democratic-Farmer-Labor Party officials McMillan ran for the district's house of representatives seat and became the first woman to represent Mower County in the Minnesota legislature. She was reelected five times, and during her twelve years in office she was a passionate voice for social welfare, workers' compensation, mental health care, environmental quality, and women's rights. In 1973, the year before she retired, Governor Wendell Anderson appointed her secretary for the Governor's Human Rights Commission as well. By then, perhaps, she might have been somewhat more aware of racial inequality and its complementary Whiteness, but there were few signs of that in her advocacy and policymaking.[36]

During the time McMillan was in office, the district she represented remained mostly White, a result of both intentional exclusion in the past and a failure to acknowledge and correct the cumulative effects of those efforts in the present. Still, after midcentury, Austin was probably not a "sundown town," as Jim Loewen contends, at least not in the strict sense of the term—where posted signs told Blacks to be gone by nightfall, or public sirens sounded in the evening to remind them to leave, or local police escorted lingering African Americans beyond the city or county limits. Racism certainly permeated White thinking and race relations there, and that undoubtedly suppressed the Black population, but explaining the color line this way is overly simple. In fact, as early as 1962, *The Negro Motorist Greenbook,* a semiannually published guide for Black travelers navigating a segregated nation, listed the local Fox Hotel as a place they could find welcome, and bars in Austin regularly brought in female African American dancers, a few of whom stuck around, married White men, and had families. To be sure, Austin still had very few Black residents in the 1960s, and this was true for other nearby meatpacking centers as well, including Albert Lea (with only two Black residents), Fairmont (one), and Owatonna (eleven), but by this point the question was whether Whites even noticed at all.[37]

"All for One and One for All"

One of the practical consequences of racial exclusion in Austin was that for many decades only Whites had access to the good-paying, well-benefited, mostly secure union jobs at Hormel, which in turn allowed them to buy homes and build up equity as well as send children to college and launch them into new socioeconomic levels. Even for local Whites, though, those privileges did not last indefinitely. As job loss from automation and wage cuts continued into the 1980s, during the summer of 1985 Local P-9's 1,700 Hormel members decided to buck orders from the national union and go on strike. Briefly, at least, their struggle attracted support from activists across the country hoping to revive the labor movement with a renewed emphasis on militancy. In the end, however, the strike failed, undermined by the 460 workers who crossed picket lines to join 550 newly hired replacements. "The only way to have gotten anywhere was if nobody had gone back," reflected Pete Winkels, Hormel employee and the (adopted) son of Casper and Blanche Winkels.

Instead, he mused, the company was able to say, "Look, even their own people are coming back." Management played on that, claiming that "they had one-half old scabs and half new scabs," and within a year the company had won. The rebel Local P-9 was put in trusteeship, and the old benevolent contract lay in ruins.[38]

When the strike began, most participants as well as most observers gave little attention to the racial uniformity of the Hormel labor force. At two particular moments, though, race and Whiteness did come up. In the spring of 1986, as mounting demonstrations at plant gates turned into violent clashes with police and county sheriffs, dozens were arrested, and thousands of supporters streamed into Austin to march in solidarity with the strikers. On April 13, civil rights activist and Rainbow Coalition founder Jesse Jackson came to Austin and visited workers in the Mower County jail, praying with them and linking arms to sing "We Shall Overcome." Afterward, he went to Hormel's corporate headquarters with an offer to mediate the strike, which officials rejected. That evening Jackson delivered a rousing speech to more than one thousand strikers and strike supporters in the auditorium at St. Edward's Church. During the speech, as historian Hardy Green noted, he showed discomfort in speaking to an all-White audience as well as uncertainty about whether rank-and-file members accorded him legitimacy as a leader. Nevertheless, he made a point to draw connections between the civil rights movement and the P-9 labor fight. "What Selma, Alabama, was to the voting rights movement in 1965," Jackson declared, "Austin, Minnesota, has become that to collective bargaining in 1986."[39]

Button used to protest at the Hormel plant in Austin, Minnesota, 1985–86.

The next month—after a court injunction limited demonstrations at the plant gates and the first trusteeship hearings had begun—a group of strikers undertook a massive art project on one of the union hall's exterior walls. Over the course of several weeks, more than one hundred union members helped to paint an eighty-by-sixteen-foot mural featuring a female meatpacker holding an axe labeled "P-9" over the head of a green serpent as well as a line of workers marching into and out of an industrial plant and carrying a banner that read "All for one and one for all." The workers dedicated the mural to jailed South African activist Nelson Mandela, and on May 27, one thousand people turned out for the dedication ceremony, with special guest Babs Duma from the African National Congress. In his remarks, strike leader Jim Guyette observed that Mandela could be out of prison if he would give up his fight for freedom and, similarly, "we could have a contract agreement if we would give away our freedom and self-respect." Unfortunately, though, the dedication of holdout union members was not enough, and the strike came to an abrupt end that summer. Then, in October, union trustee officials sandblasted and painted over the mural.[40]

For many of Austin's striking White workers and supporters, the fight against Hormel played an important part in broadening their worldview for the better while changing their economic situation for the worse. Subsequently, the two decades following the strike saw the most significant increase in the city's Black population. There were only 47 African Americans among the more than 21,000 residents in 1990, but this number increased to 749 among nearly 25,000 by 2010—still only three percent of the population but by far a much larger number than Austin had ever known. On the other hand, in the same year the city had 3,796 residents who identified as Hispanic or Latino, a demographic fact that showed the different histories of the two racial minority groups and introduced new racial tensions, at least in some parts of the community. "They're not enforcing any of the legal things they could as far as illegal immigration here," former Hormel worker Jim Doughty complained in 2013, and "that undercuts the labor movement," an opinion that sounded not unlike the narrow-minded notions expressed by John Winkels nearly one hundred years before. Latinos or other immigrants who were willing to be low-wage labor, Doughty contended, made worker unity impossible and thwarted collective bargaining—missing the fact that many unions were doing little to organize the new labor force and build worker unity that way. "If you run out of illegals you can always find an immigrant or a refugee that might do the work, and as long as you head in that direction wages won't come up." Although evolving, White working-class commitment to the philosophy of solidarity and "an injury to one is an injury to all" still had not been entirely stripped of contradictory and deep-rooted racial prejudice.[41]

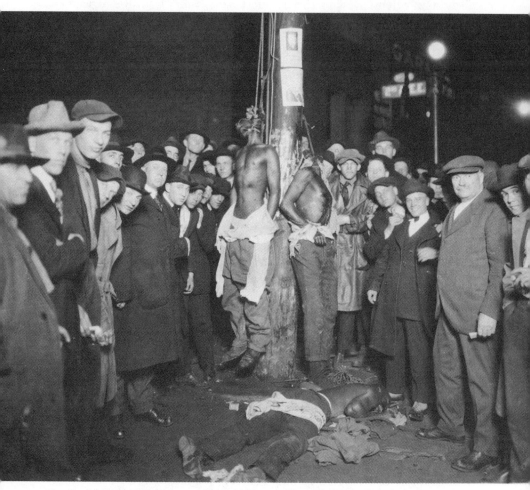

The lynching of Elias Clayton, Elmer Jackson, and Isaac McGhie in Duluth on the night of June 15, 1920.

CHAPTER 4

"In That Very Northern City": Making the Color Line in Duluth

IN THE LATTER PART OF APRIL 1920, John Robinson's Circus left its winter home outside Cincinnati, Ohio, to begin a tour through various parts of the United States and Canada. As was the case with other circuses during the era, numerous reports of burglary, theft, and assault often followed in the wake of the show's arrival and departure from town after town, and those reports frequently made a point to mention the race of those involved. At the end of May, in Alliance, Ohio, for example, while John Robinson performers and animals paraded down Main Street, robbers "looted" several homes, mostly stealing cash, and many of those who visited the circus grounds reported losing money to "short changers" as well as pickpockets working the crowd. In that instance, the local newspaper described the criminals as "colored men," although the few who were actually arrested (and skipped bail) were White. A few weeks later, after the John Robinson passed through South Bend, Indiana, the *News-Times* explained that the show "made" the town "with a vengeance," stealing "everything that wasn't nailed down," including a team of horses and substantial amounts of money, by outright theft as well as rigged gambling operations. The paper also noted that a young White woman and a White male companion were accosted by three Black circus hands behind the tents. They allegedly held a razor at the young man's throat, warning him against making a sound, and then took the woman away and raped her. The couple told the police and there was some investigation, but no arrests were made, and the show train continued on its way north.[1]

Although the alleged sexual assault in South Bend was unusual among the "circus" crimes reported, something like it supposedly happened again when the John Robinson visited Duluth, Minnesota. Early on the morning of June 15, Police Chief John Murphy received a call from Patrick Sullivan, who reported that five or six Black circus workers had raped his son's female companion the previous night. Seventeen-year-old James Sullivan and eighteen-year-old Irene Tusken claimed that they had been watching roustabouts take down tents when another group of Black men surprised them, held a gun on Sullivan, and marched him and Tusken to the woods, where she fainted. According to Sullivan, each of the men forced themselves on her, after which they told the couple to go away from the circus grounds. Sullivan and Tusken then took a street-car to her family's residence and sat on the front porch briefly before Tusken went to bed and Sullivan left to meet his father for the night shift at the ore docks. He told his dad what had (allegedly) taken place, thereby setting in motion a series of other events. By the end of the next day, more than a dozen Black circus workers were arrested and a White mob had forcibly taken three from the jail and gruesomely hanged them from a utility pole before a crowd of thousands. The other Black workers remained in police custody awaiting indictment and trial for rape, and eventually they were joined by several Whites who were arrested for murder and riot following the lynching.[2]

Even before the rape charge was aired in court, however, there was good reason to think that Sullivan and Tusken had not told the truth, or at least not a reliable version of it. "In the first place," the muckraking *Duluth Rip-saw* editor John Morrison declared after several days of gathering evidence, "back of a circus is a peculiar place for a decent boy and a respectable girl." Morrison had asked around about James Sullivan's "character" and heard numerous stories detailing his excessive drinking (despite local and county prohibition ordinances) as well as his "chasing women." On at least three occasions, he and friends had broken into lake cabins, partied through the night, and left the cabins in "a nasty condition," with "signs of drunken revelry evident such as whiskey bottles together with hair pins." More recently, around the time Sullivan started dating Tusken, he was spied in a cabin with a lone young woman, "both of them drunk." All of this suggested, at least to Morrison, that the two were probably up to no good when they were wandering the circus grounds. But beyond this speculation, the editor also learned that the Tusken family physician had visited Irene Tusken on the morning after the alleged assault and concluded that she had not been raped, which he was openly talking about with medical colleagues.[3]

As the *Rip-saw* continued its independent investigation, various members of the Twin Cities National Association for the Advancement of Colored People (NAACP) were trying to figure things out for themselves as well, and they learned that the jailed Black men's insistence that they were all innocent of any wrongdoing was similarly doubtful. Most concerning was a letter from St. Paul branch member Andrew Jackson, who was in Winnipeg when John Robinson's Circus stopped there, following its Duluth show, and he talked to some of the Black workers about the alleged assault. Jackson reported what they told him to his wife back home, and she passed this correspondence on to the NAACP St. Paul president, Dr. Valdo Turner, who then communicated it to national NAACP vice president Mary White Ovington. "They say there was a white man selling whiskey on the grounds," the letter explained, "and the men ganged on him and took his whiskey away from him." The man "had some women hustling at the same time" and, angry about being robbed of the liquor, "he caused the woman to holla *rape.*" The workers offered this information to prove that the men who were lynched had not sexually assaulted Irene Tusken, and Jackson made a point to say they told what they knew in the presence of a group, which included Odd Fellows and Masons, his manner of giving assurance for the story's veracity. Turner and Ovington and other officials must have understood that this account would not be helpful to the defense they were preparing, however, and the NAACP never revealed the letter or mentioned it publicly.[4]

Considering how vengeful lies and concealed evidence muddled the facts, it was difficult to know for certain what actually happened that fateful night "back of the circus," and to piece together the sequence of events that followed the next day. Observing the lynching from afar, though, the national media focused less on the details and more on its larger significance. This included an editorial in the *New York Times* that centered on what the murders in Duluth meant for characterizing racial violence as a southern phenomenon. "In that very northern city," it explained, "there were certain variations in the actions of the mob which may or may not have been due to the moderating effects on temper of a high latitude." Most notably, the editorial pointed out, members of the mob briefly attempted to conduct their own "semblance of judicial proceedings" and spared three of the six men they had taken from their cells. But, it insisted, the White northerners' familiar frenzied reaction to the purported rape of a White woman by Black men showed that "human nature is much the same in both sections of the country." Just as well, "as so often in the South, the resistance to the mob offered by the local authorities must have been half-hearted, or worse, otherwise it would not have been so ineffectual, and the storming of the jail would have been accompanied with fatalities among its assailants." Even city leaders' unusual promise to punish the perpetrators was "dubious," the *Times* concluded, and surely there would be no consequences for the five thousand residents who stood around to witness, "all as guilty, morally, as those who pulled the avenging rope."[5]

In the immediate aftermath of the lynching, city leaders and others feared that Duluth's emboldened Whites would take matters into their own hands once again and violently expel African Americans altogether. A few Black residents fled on their own across the bay to Superior, Wisconsin, but that city's acting police chief, Louis Osborne, publicly declared that Whites there would soon "run all idle Negroes out," and a local carnival fired its Black employees and told them to leave. Uncertain and afraid, most African Americans in Duluth stayed put and prepared to defend themselves. "We'd decided that we'd just barricade ourselves in our house," Edward Nichols recalled, "and I had a .45 Colt automatic that I'd brought back from the war." The steel plant also distributed rifles and ammunition to Blacks in Gary, an adjacent suburb not too far from West Duluth, where many of the most enraged Whites lived. Meanwhile, Governor Joseph A. A. Burnquist mobilized a National Guard unit after guard member and local businessman Major Fred Beecher contacted Adjutant General W. F. Rhinow in St. Paul to explain the situation and the sheriff made a formal request. Once the troops arrived, all equipped for riot duty, they began patrolling Black neighborhoods with orders to shoot to kill if Whites attempted a raid. A few days later, African

American residents organized a community meeting, which the assistant county attorney attended, NAACP representative Charles Sumner Smith explained to executive secretary James Weldon Johnson, "to tell people what was being done for their protection and to offset any misrepresentation of purpose."[6]

By the end of the summer, relative calm had been established, and by fall the promised trials had concluded, though just three White men were convicted only of inciting a riot, while one Black circus worker was convicted of rape. Thwarted in any attempt to remove African Americans from Duluth, yet suffering no real consequences for the lynching, Whites acted to preserve the city's racial order in the months, years, and decades to follow. The next summer, in 1921, a large group of White men met at the Owl's Fraternity Hall and organized a Ku Klux Klan klavern. Membership grew to seven hundred by the end of the year, and it was double that by the summer of 1923, making it one of the largest in the state and including two dozen police officers among its ranks. To mark Christmas and the New Year, they burned crosses on a prominent hilltop above the city, but after mid-decade the klavern had declined in numbers, like others throughout the state. More lastingly, with little in the way of official sanction or legal tools, Whites maintained a rigid color line throughout Duluth, excluding Blacks from living in all but a few sections of the city and limiting their work to a handful of low-paying occupations. Facing these conditions, as well as job losses during the Great Depression, a sizable number of African Americans did eventually leave, and others simply stayed away. As the city's total population increased from 99,000 in 1930 to 104,000 in 1950, the Black population declined from 416 to 330.[7]

It was not until the early 1960s that Duluth began to make any significant advances toward addressing the city's deeply rooted patterns of discrimination, and this started with an attempt by the African American couple Matthew and Helen Carter to integrate an all-White neighborhood along the lakeshore. White Unitarian Universalist Congregation minister Reverend Thomas L. Smith covertly bought a lot for them there, and once that was revealed it provoked considerable resistance from Whites in the community. At the same time, the Carters' years-long battle to move into the neighborhood demonstrated Whites' ability to hide their racism behind a facade of benign motivations and racial myopia. In a scene that was repeated in cities, towns, and suburbs across the state and country, White homeowners organized themselves and pitched their objections to the Black family's request for a building permit as a matter of practical considerations, citing traffic hazards and other concerns. Then, after Whites repeatedly vandalized the Carters' new home with racist graffiti, the mayor, police chief, and *Duluth Herald* editorial board all claimed to be shocked that such sentiment was present in the city and variously suggested that the acts were perpetrated by one or two "deranged" individuals. "I am hopeful that this is just an isolated case of vandalism," Mayor Ben Book declared after one incident, since "it is contrary to the feelings of this community."[8]

"Didn't Think Anything Would Happen in This Part of the Country"

Wedged between the Mesabi Iron Range and Lake Superior, Duluth centered its economy for most of the twentieth century around steel, mining, and shipping. The single-largest employer was Minnesota Steel, owned by the U.S. Steel Corporation, along with two subsidiaries, the Oliver Iron Mining Company and the Pittsburgh Steamship Company. At least a quarter of the city's African American population came to Duluth to work at the steel plant, before and after World War I, encouraged by recruiters who scoured the South promising good jobs to all. Fred Douglas Bell, for example, left Greenville, Texas, among a group of twenty other men, with their transportation paid, and once established in Minnesota, they sent for their families and set about making better lives for themselves. Some Black workers were also enticed by the *Twin City Star*, an African American newspaper published in Minneapolis, which ran an advertisement announcing that "Negro laborers" could earn three dollars per day at the steel plant. Unbeknownst to them, however, part of the company's motivation for their recruitment was to suppress White workers' demands for increased wages and hinder a union campaign, under the assumption that Black workers would accept lower pay and not participate in labor organizing. Very likely, that calculated policy of racial division stoked White anger, and over the years this tension was held to a low but constant simmer only by vigilant observance of racial separation and discrimination in other aspects of life.[9]

Although Minnesota Steel had built model company housing in Morgan Park in 1915, and officials publicly declared that they would allow "no race segregation," that area was reserved for White employees.

U.S. Steel's Minnesota Steel Plant, 1940s.

Instead, African American employees lived in what Black steelworker Edward Nichols referred to as "tumbledown shacks" in a "shantytown" called Gary, where they were expected to stay. His son, Charles, remembered that he always felt "a twinge of fear" riding through Morgan Park on the streetcar to downtown Duluth, after his parents and others made it clear that if something went wrong with the streetcar and they had to get off, they "might be in harm's way." Compounding this residential racial exclusion, among the more than one hundred Black residents in Gary, forty of the men worked as laborers in the coke plant, doing some of the most grueling and dangerous jobs at some of the lowest pay rates, at lower rates than Whites doing the same tasks, while only one Black employee held a foreman's position, presumably supervising the African American cohort. Another ten Black men were employed as factory laborers, construction workers, and restaurant waiters, along with one barber, a janitor, and a farmer. Similarly, while just a handful of the men's wives worked outside the home, those who did had to settle for poorly paid labor, one as a hairdresser, another as a cook, a third as a restaurant helper, and a fourth as a laundress.[10]

Elsewhere in the city, African Americans were limited to housing in the Central Hillside, East Hillside, and downtown areas, barred from

the surrounding exclusively White sections of the city. Typically, in the places where Blacks were allowed, whole buildings were designated by landlords as solely for Black (and Native American) renters, often families with notably meager or irregular incomes. Some of the men worked in segregated galley crews on lake boats and others worked for the railroads, mostly doing dining-car service and cooking, with at least one or two hired to prepare engines at a roundhouse. About sixty men and women worked at Erwin Oreck's exclusive Flame Night Club as servers, cooks, busboys, doormen, and washroom attendants, and a few did similar work in local saloons, restaurants, and hotels. Additionally, some women were employed as housemaids for wealthy White families, while other men were custodians at schools and banks, and a fortunate

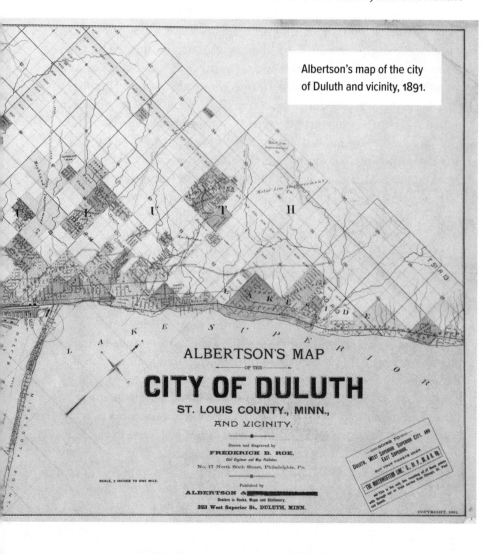

Albertson's map of the city of Duluth and vicinity, 1891.

number—as many as twenty at one point—were employed in the post office, often more reliable because it was a federal job. One of the latter, Henry Williams, was a classical musician who also published his own weekly newspaper, yet for lack of vocational opportunity he had to settle with being an elevator operator to the day he retired. Duluth had only one Black dentist (who eventually left), a couple of Black lawyers (who worked out of their homes), and one Black police officer.[11]

Besides housing and employment, the color line showed up in routine interactions between Blacks and Whites as well. At the steel plant's soup house, for instance, White workers could sit down to eat their lunch whereas Black workers had to take their food away. Similarly, the company-built Morgan Park Good Fellowship Clubhouse was closed to African Americans, even though they paid monthly dues for it. When a "colored club" from Gary tried to press against this policy, their request was denied because of "the large number of dates now booked for Club activities." Among those activities were "burnt cork" performances by a minstrel show group that also performed at venues around Duluth. In fact, this group was just one of several in the city, and local schools even rented their space when classes were not in session for regular "blackface" programs. Given how common such public displays of racism were, it is not surprising that most if not all other social spaces were marked by racial prejudice too. Only certain downtown restaurants would serve African Americans, according to Edward Nichols, and movie theaters limited Blacks to seats in the first rows on the floor or in the balcony, while just two hotels allowed Black guests.[12]

This segregation in public spaces was contrary to the civil rights law Minnesota had enacted in 1885, legislation that met its first legal test in Duluth a decade later. In mid-September 1897, a White man named Tom Shannon met formerly enslaved African American Edward Rhone on West Superior Street and invited him to have a drink at the Merchants Hotel saloon, owned by Robert Loomis. Shannon went inside but Rhone lingered at the door, and the Black porter warned him that he would not be served there, as indeed happened. In court, Loomis claimed it was because Rhone was drunk, though Shannon testified that the saloonkeeper told him it was because "he did not serve colored people," and that Shannon returned days later to apologize and explain that he had not known that was the rule. Surprisingly, the all-White Duluth jury decided in favor of Rhone and awarded him twenty-five dollars, the minimum compensation under law, but Loomis appealed to the state supreme court. After hearing the case, the justices overturned the verdict on the grounds that saloons, and "the sale of intoxicating liquors" generally, were intentionally excluded from the civil rights law, and because saloonkeepers were not "in public business," their right to choose whom they served could not be restricted. This decision prompted African American attorneys Fredrick McGhee of St. Paul, William Morris of Minneapolis, and Charles Scrutchin of Bemidji (who would later play a role in defending the Black circus workers) to push for amended legislation adding "saloons" to the civil rights law. To do this, they turned to J. Frank Wheaton, the first African American elected to the legislature, and during the 1899 session he succeeded in getting it done.[13]

Despite the strengthened civil rights protection, however, Duluth's public accommodations and establishments were either off-limits or restricted for Blacks well into the next century. Yet in a barely hidden underworld, which thrived more than ever after saloons were closed by local and county prohibition ordinances enacted in 1917, the line was muddled. In numerous illicit "blind pigs" and "tiger dens" scattered around the city, Whites and Blacks regularly sampled the pleasures of liquor, gambling, and prostitutes, often in the same place and sometimes intimately together. This violation of racial separation, as much as any concern about illegal activity, prompted White residents' growing demands to curb the pervasive vice, and a prominent contributor to that was *Duluth Rip-saw* editor John L. Morrison. "Dark Girls Woo White Men, Bold Negro Prostitutes Elbow Decent Families" one of his headlines read, "District Near Lake Front Now Swarms With Colored Courtesans, Innocent Little Children Contaminated by Immoral Surroundings." In fact, in Morrison's mind, overlapping moral and racial transgressions at least partly explained what took place "back of the circus." It was no coincidence that the *Rip-saw* was also the most skeptical voice about what Irene Tusken and James Sullivan were really doing that night as well as the lynch mob's claim of chivalry to defend their murderous violence. "The mixture of white and black women for immoral purposes very often leads to race riots and lynchings," Morrison later declared in a story about brothels operated by a Black couple that had both Black and White prostitutes, and "of the latter, Duluth has had enough."[14]

To be sure, some vice venues were purposefully segregated spaces, including clubs and brothels operated by and exclusively for African

Americans. One of the more popular was the Gary Canteen, owned by George B. Kelley, a Black veteran of the Spanish-American War and a former post office clerk. "It is supposed to be a literary and social club for the special benefit of colored people employed in that section of the city," Morrison explained about the Gary Canteen, but as the *Rip-saw*'s undercover "colored inspector" confirmed, the primary draw seemed to be "craps, poker, and intoxicating drinks." This was not much of a secret, however, and Kelley likely operated only by the sanction of the police. Likewise, authorities tolerated "a combined boarding and gambling house" in Gary that "keeps several girls who are reputed to cater to the lustful desires of the male boarders but who pose as chambermaids." But other Black venues were intermittently raided or closed. Toward the end of 1918, police busted Luther Dawson's gambling "resort" and arrested half a dozen "colored gentlemen with sportive inclinations," fining each of them ten dollars and fining Lawson one hundred dollars. The year before, they also shut down illicit "negro clubs" on Michigan Street, and after some of the clubs moved to Superior, patrons there were swept up in a mass arrest of "immoral colored folk" ordered by the mayor.[15]

Still, the most notorious "red light" district in Duluth was in a somewhat racially integrated section on the downtown waterfront, between South First Avenue East (formerly St. Croix Avenue) and St. Croix Alley. This area had long been a notorious haunt for brothels, and as White madams and their White prostitutes left, they were replaced by African American prostitutes, who continued to serve both White and Black clients. The women sat in windows, stood in doorways, or strolled the street, according to Morrison, and he claimed that "many a white man is seduced by the blandishments of black Sirens who smile, beckon and call out." Meanwhile, increasing numbers of working-class Finnish immigrants settled on the other side of the avenue, and outraged by the bustling activity they organized a mass meeting at the Finnish Temperance Hall in the late summer of 1919. At the meeting they established a committee (which Morrison chaired) and drafted a petition. The St. Croix district "is infested by a large number of immoral individuals," it said, "particularly Negro women of dissolute habits," as well as "a large number of moral, reputable, law-abiding families unable to remove to more pretentious localities." Because their previous complaints had been ignored, residents were appealing to the county grand jury to investigate and remedy the problem. At the same time, the *Duluth Herald* reported, an anonymous individual or group circulated letters "in which the writers threaten race riots to clear the St. Croix avenue district of its negro residents." Newly installed public safety commissioner William Murnian and police chief Murphy downplayed the letters, though, and at another mass meeting, Morrison made a point to say, "many speakers urged caution against words or acts that would arouse race feeling."[16]

The grand jury looked into the petition's complaints and, within a few days, issued a report with several recommendations. One was to have the county attorney start abatement proceedings against any property involved in convictions for prostitution, which would put pressure on White landlords, many of whom were prominent public figures, political leaders, and business owners. Additionally, without explicitly stating that police assigned to the St. Croix area were implicated in the vice, the report called for changing the patrolmen who walked that beat, with the exception of Victor Isaacson (one of the police officers later present when the lynch mob stormed the city jail and who afterward joined the local Ku Klux Klan klavern). County attorney Mason Forbes agreed to initiate the abatement proposal, and two officers were moved out of the district while Isaacson and others stepped up arrests. While acknowledging these improvements, Morrison continued to encourage White residents to demand more, and in his pleas the editor often fused race and vice, ignoring his earlier cautions against arousing "race feeling." "As Dennis Kearney stood on the sandlots of San Francisco over forty years ago and declared that 'The Chinese Must Go,'" Morrison wrote, "so now do the decent Finnish fathers and mothers stand in Duluth's former redlight district, surrounded by their children, coming citizens of city, county, state and nation, and stubbornly declare: 'The Immoral Element in this Neighborhood Must Go.'"[17]

Clearly, by the time of the lynching in the summer of 1920, the *Ripsaw* had done its part to put Whites in Duluth on edge with its consistent race-baiting. Yet the newspaper also displayed an awareness of the role of White citizens in the city's underworld, which is why, unlike many others, Morrison was immediately doubtful about Irene Tusken's allegations against the circus workers. It is also why he was unsurprised by the violence the allegations provoked. "The lynching of those unfortunate colored boys was the crowning tragedy of a generation," the editor declared. "The plot was conceived in a lawless resort, carried out by hoodlums and permitted by a weak and incompetent police department." The "resort" he was referring to was a pool hall known for illicit activity in West Duluth, the neighborhood where many of the dozen working-class Whites initially arrested for rioting lived. As it turned out, various things became apparent that indicated the purported rape before the lynching was probably a liquor sale and prostitution transaction gone wildly wrong, and that the criminal enterprise James Sullivan and Irene Tusken were involved in was tied to chief of police John Murphy, deputy US marshal Frank Bradley, and other public authorities.[18]

Although it is certain that the young White couple had some inter-action and confrontation with Black circus workers, during the weeks and months after the incident, the two changed their story in significant ways. Ten days after the lynching, for example, the St. Paul NAACP hired a detective service to dispatch an "operative" to Duluth, and when the man, who was White, asked Tusken about the night before the lynching, she said Sullivan had come to her house and they walked to the circus, where she met some friends whom she had known for years, though she did not know their names. Months later in court, Tusken explained that friends Eudora McVeigh and Dorothy Beaver came to her house, they went by streetcar to the circus grounds, and after she unexpectedly met Sullivan she decided to part with her companions and walk around with him. In addition to factual inconsistencies, major parts of the cou-ple's story did not rest well with the evidence either. When the operative asked her "if she felt any ill effects after the assault," for instance, she told him "my arms were a little sore." He also talked to the Tusken family physician, Dr. David Graham, who had examined Irene Tusken the day after the incident, and he said that she was not raped and might even still be "virtuous." Subsequently, the doctor offered similar testimony in court, explaining that he found no inflammation, tears, or bruises and no evidence of soreness or sensitivity.[19]

The likelihood that Tusken had sex with some of the roustabouts was given a bit of credence by another investigator sent by the St. Paul NAACP almost immediately after the lynching, although for obvious reasons the group never made his full report public, and defense lawyers did not use it in court. The investigator, former Duluth resident and attorney J. Louis Ervin, who was African American, obtained sworn statements from the fourteen circus workers still held at the St. Louis County jail. One of them, Nate Graves, recalled that he was loading a wagon when William

Miller called out to him that he and Frank Spicer had "a jaz [a good-looking woman with unusual sexual talents] out in the woods." Another man, Clarence Green, said he saw "a white boy and girl" heading toward the Big Top with "six colored fellows following them," including Miller, Spicer, Louis Hayes, and three others he did not know. Lonnie Williams remembered that a man named Isaac, possibly Isaac McGhie, who was lynched, was also among the group, and that one of them, "Lewis," likely Louis Hayes, told him they were out with a girl. Yet Hayes insisted he was working that time of the evening and only overheard another circus worker saying that some of the crew "had a girl over in the woods," adding that he "did not say whether they were buying it or what they were doing." Miller also denied involvement but told Ervin that he saw "three colored men coming out of the woods," while Spicer maintained that he knew nothing about any assault.[20]

Because the men had made similar statements at the time of their initial arrest, police probably had a good idea what had happened as well, including chief John Murphy, and this took on added significance as events continued to unfold. Less than a month after the lynching, Murphy and US marshal Frank Bradley were arrested by a treasury department deputy for violating federal prohibition law. They had been indicted along with six others by a federal grand jury, and the indictments were quite specific. On May 20, the *Duluth Herald* reported, the men purportedly received 1,236 quarts of whiskey at a shack three miles from the border and, the next day, loaded it into two separate cars and took it to Tofte, a town in Cook County. Despite the evident facts, though, in November all the indicted men were acquitted and Murphy, who had resigned as police chief the day after his arrest, left Duluth. Although nobody ever openly speculated about this, it is possible that Murphy had known what James Sullivan was doing at the circus because it was his whiskey the young man was selling, and it was no coincidence that the elder Sullivan called him directly, which presumably not everyone in the city could do. Additionally, while the crime Tusken accused the circus workers of committing was a serious one, it is at least unusual that after (supposedly) hearing of the rape accusations the city's police chief immediately met the father and son at the ore docks and was personally involved in stopping the departing circus train and removing the entire crew of 150 Black workers to identify the culprits. Later in court, perhaps revealing that at the time Murphy was worried about the consequences of his knowingly unwarranted actions, he recalled wondering how the White public would react, "that is as to taking those niggers out." One of his detectives had put him at ease, however, saying "he didn't think anything would happen in this part of the country, that if it were down South it might."[21]

With the police chief and other public figures indicted for violating liquor laws, another reckoning of sorts occurred among Whites during the subsequent lynching trials as well. From the end of June to late July, police questioned hundreds of men about their role in the violence, and by early August a special grand jury indicted twenty men on various charges of rioting, instigating a riot, and first-degree murder, the latter charges eventually dropped. Rather than acknowledging that the lynch mob was large and diverse, though, all the young men who were indicted came from the same White working-class part of town in West Duluth, where Tusken and Sullivan also lived. Likewise, two of the eight who were ultimately tried were first-generation Swedish immigrants, two were second-generation Swedish immigrants, and one was a second-generation Norwegian immigrant. This selectivity made the city's racism turn on class and ethnicity, absolving the majority of White residents of responsibility for the lynching and at least notionally distancing them from accountability for the city's long-established color line. As the trials began, it became even clearer that the judicial process was not intended to purge the city of racism but merely to provide a check on how it was manifested, to contain commonly held racial hatred within the rule of law and conventional social custom, which was critical to preserving the idea of northern exceptionalism.[22]

In all these respects, the composition of the grand jury was telling, and the instructions Judge William Cant gave them as well as their statement back to him were even more so. Most of the nearly two dozen White men were from neighborhoods east of downtown and a few were from smaller towns outside of the city. William McCabe, "a leading member of the Duluth Board of Trade and leader in the religious circles of the city," who lived in a stately home in the Hunters Park neighborhood, was elected foreman. Among others he was joined by A. W. Taussig, the owner of the exclusive Kitchi Gammi Club, where Duluth's business elites had long socialized. In setting them all to their task, Judge Cant, who had himself waded into the mob with another judge to dissuade them from lynching the circus workers, explained that the possibility the men who were lynched "may have committed another crime, also heinous, is not the slightest excuse" for what happened to them. "Viewed either locally or nationwide," he said, "human progress is made possible only by safeguarding those rules designed for the control of human conduct, which have been crystallized into law." The jury members agreed and, after weighing evidence and deciding on indictments, they made a similar statement. "If the law is not severe enough," they noted, "the remedy is not mob action" but rather "to go to the legislature and have laws placed upon the Statute books that are adequate for this crime." Instead, the jurors lamented, "with mob authority only, some set themselves up as a kangaroo court to pass on the guilt or innocence of men accused and in custody of the city authorities."[23]

The class and ethnic dimensions of the effort to hold someone accountable for the lynchings, and the emphasis on restoring the rule of law, were also on display in the criminal trials, particularly the trial of Carl John Alfred Hammerberg, who was eventually convicted of instigating a riot. Born in Sweden in 1902, Hammerberg came to the United States with his parents in 1908, not long after which his father was convicted of murder and imprisoned at Stillwater before being deported. His mother raised Carl and his sister on her own, doing "shopwork" and washing, and he left school to work at a West Duluth box factory, though at the time of the lynching he had a job at the shipyard passing rivets. In court, the young man explained that he had just gotten off work when he met friends who "heard about a big crowd coming up to lynch them niggers" and "they asked if the rest of us was going up." He went along, at least part of the way on a truck driven by Louis Dondino, also from West Duluth, full of other rowdy men hollering about a "necktie party." Once at the jail, Hammerberg claimed, he went inside and observed the scene, then walked down to the street and witnessed two of the three lynchings. Without much evidence presented that he had done any more than that, Judge Cant instructed jurors that it was "not necessary that he have thrown rocks or that he have struck an officer or battered down the door, but did he do anything of a substantial character which aided in the defiance of the officers." After deliberating, the jury asked for further clarification about the definition of "riot," and following that, they returned a guilty verdict and Cant sentenced him to two years in prison.[24]

Testimony in the Hammerberg trial as well as others left no doubt that the lynchings had attracted a diverse array of cheering spectators, and that the raid on the city jail and the violence that followed involved a mass of people who went unpunished. After getting a ride on Louis Dondino's truck, steel plant machinist Herbert O'Brien recalled that he had "a good opportunity" to see the gathering crowd, which he said numbered in the thousands. "They were men and women both . . . lots of women with babies in their arms, lots of baby carriages . . . there were laboring men and businessmen," he recalled, and "lots of women hollering and clapping their hands and saying, 'Good for you, boys. You have got the backbone in you. Stick up for women's rights.'" Police sergeant Oscar Olson, who was in charge of the officers at the jail, confirmed O'Brien's description. He put the crowd at around four or five thousand, including young and old, and also noted the presence of "laboring men and business men" and women. Additionally, dozens took part in breaking into the cells, bringing the three circus workers out, and hanging them from a utility pole. "Men much worse than he and leaders far beyond what he was in this unfortunate matter," Judge Cant admitted to the jurors in the Hammerberg trial, "will go entirely free." This was despite the fact that witnesses named names and offered vivid firsthand accounts of what they did. Several described Ed Goneau carrying a sledgehammer, Lawrence Brotherton leading one of the Black men to the utility pole, and Edward Jackson on the utility pole helping with the rope, for example, but none of the three was indicted or questioned in court. Even with overwhelming evidence of his central role, Denfeld High School student and Hammerberg acquaintance Leonard Hedman was acquitted too.[25]

Still, while Duluth's Whites settled accounts among themselves by pitting blame for the lynchings on a handful of working-class young men and ignoring the culpability of many more individuals, class tensions surfaced among Blacks as well. In late June, nearly seventy African American residents met at St. Mark's A.M.E. church and formed a branch of the NAACP, but when members of the already existing Civic League were unsuccessful in electing some of their own as executive committee officers, they demanded a reorganization. This did not happen, and instead George B. Kelley, who had spearheaded the NAACP effort, continued as the first branch president. Although he was a captain in the Minnesota Home Guard and a founding member of the Minneapolis NAACP, he was also, as some frustrated members wrote to the national NAACP office, "a keeper of a 'dive' of low repute." Because of this, the letter writers pointed out, the "better class" of "colored people" were staying away. Minneapolis branch president (and fellow Home Guard member) Charles Sumner Smith defended Kelley in his own letter to NAACP executive secretary James Weldon Johnson, however, calling him a "leading representative of our people for several years," one "recognized by the best white citizens." Smith also noted that the two of them had already been talking about establishing a branch since the start of the summer and, so far, the initiative had been "a success in every way." Among other accomplishments, by mid-December they could report that significant fundraising had allowed them to hire some of the best lawyers for the circus workers' rape trials, and as a result eleven of the men were discharged from prosecution, one, William Miller, was acquitted, and only one, Max Mason, was convicted.[26]

Unfortunately, over the next couple of decades, the Duluth NAACP was unable to affect racial prejudice and discrimination in any meaningful way. Workers at the steel plant had finally organized in the mid-1930s, and one of the main organizers was African American Lee Wiley, but Blacks continued to fill lower positions there, and none were members of the clerical workers union because they were barred from office jobs. Moreover, other major unionized manufacturing companies in the city, including American Steel & Wire, Universal Atlas Cement, and the Diamond Tool & Horseshoe Company, did not hire African Americans at all. Likewise, Seafarers International Union leaders claimed that "the union has never had a Negro applicant for membership from the Duluth area or a Negro union member applying for assignment to a ship through the Duluth hiring hall," although there were dozens of Blacks living in the city and working on boats out of Two Harbors. "There are certain types of jobs that Negroes will never apply for," a 1950 local study explained, "because they know it would not be useful to do so." In fact, only a little more than 10 percent of Duluth's African American residents were employed in "skilled" work, and none were recorded in "the professions." This was reflected in household incomes, with more than half of Black households earning less than the national average wage of fifty-one dollars per week, 12 percent of those earning under twenty-five dollars per week, and 36 percent making fifty-one dollars or more, most of those being unskilled workers at the steel plant. This was despite comparatively high levels of education, including 16 percent of heads of households with one or more years of college and 35 percent who had attended or finished high school.[27]

In terms of housing, by midcentury two-thirds of Duluth's Black residents owned their own homes, yet almost all of those homes had been built before 1917 and nearly half of the families were doubling up with parents or someone else. Housing discrimination was routine, though not necessarily measured in formal complaints since, the 1950 study said, it was not so much "obvious" as "subtle" discrimination that maintained "segregation of Negroes into certain areas." Similar to the unwritten rules about what jobs were closed to them, Duluth's Black residents also knew not to bother trying to buy homes or rent apartments in most parts of the city. Nevertheless, at least a third of African American residents reported difficulty finding housing in Duluth because of their race, suggesting that when they did try to go beyond allowable areas, Whites made sure to block them. One respondent in the 1950 study recalled that when he attempted to obtain housing in a locality that he left unnamed, "the neighbors got up a petition to keep me out." Another noted that "real estate companies just won't show places east of Eighth Avenue," citing a boundary between the Central Hillside and East Hillside neighborhoods, while some put the line at Ninth or even Tenth Avenue East. Otherwise, by far the largest group of African Americans remained in the Gary and New Duluth suburbs, well west of the city center and adjacent to the steel plant, although no Black employees of the plant lived in Morgan Park, the company-built neighborhood that had long been all White.[28]

Along with the solid color line in employment and housing, Whites' deeply ingrained racist attitudes continued to define Duluth's social spaces too. A fifth of all Blacks said they had experienced discrimination at restaurants, and there was little that they could do about it. In one case, an African American woman went to "one of the better-known eating establishments in company of 22 outstanding White persons" following a meeting, but the wait staff let them linger and the manager told them they would not be served "with that nigger." In addition, most Blacks attended all-Black churches, and White ministers made a point to keep it that way. When an African American man attended what he described as "one of the largest and most prominent [White] Protestant churches in the city," he was tolerated for two consecutive Sunday services, yet when he brought several friends, the minister told him that members of the congregation had complained and asked that he not return. The tradition of Whites performing minstrel shows also went on unabated, even by those who would seemingly be predisposed to recognize the offensive nature of the racist caricatures they paraded. Local Jews had established the Covenant Club because they had been excluded from "gentile" clubs, for example, and yet the B'nai B'rith women's group was performing semiregular minstrel shows there during the 1940s, with actors wearing oversized suits and huge polka-dot bow ties as well as the requisite "blackface." Less surprising, the White male members of Mason's Trinity Lodge 282 put on an annual minstrel performance at the Shrine Auditorium on East First Street, not far from where the lynching happened, well into the 1950s.[29]

In the face of this unrelenting racism, the Duluth NAACP struggled. As Black residents fled the city, branch membership declined, the proportion of African American members dropped, and the national office began to threaten to revoke its charter. Intent on reviving the local group, William (Bill) Maupins replaced steelworker and union organizer Lee Wiley as president in 1958. Born in Duluth in 1922, Maupins was raised by adoptive parents, William F. Maupins and Cornelia Maupins (Williams), both of whom were originally from the South. As a young man, he grew up hearing stories about local Whites' racial hatred from his father, including one about the Ku Klux Klan burning a cross in Central Hillside, and he had a vivid notion of the local color line's injustice from witnessing the disappointments of his maternal grandfather, Henry Williams. Later, as a teenager, Maupins became personally aware of the fact that Duluth was "very segregated" when he and his friends were barred from "the most desirable places." Also, after graduating from Duluth Central High School and then serving in the navy, he earned a political science degree from the University of Minnesota Duluth (UMD), yet he had difficulty finding work suitable to his qualifications. When Maupins attempted to get an office job at the steel plant, he was told they would only hire him for work in the yards, and other companies like Minnesota Power and Light would not even take his application. Eventually, after encountering a few more dead ends, he found employment as a lab supervisor at the university, married and had several children, and moved to a house on Ninth Avenue East, although by the time he became NAACP president he was a widower.[30]

Soon after assuming his new leadership position, Maupins directed much of his attention to housing discrimination, particularly a statewide effort to pass a fair housing law. That campaign had gained traction in the late 1950s when two urban renewal projects and a highway expansion

Bill Maupins, upper left, with W. J. Musa Foster (upper right) and Seitu Jones (lower right), about 1975.

project in St. Paul displaced thousands of African Americans, who then struggled to find new homes or apartments other than in the city's non-White neighborhoods. Since an earlier 1953 law only prohibited discrimination in public housing accommodations and forbid new racial covenants, residents had little legal recourse when they encountered other forms of exclusion, and the Twin Cities NAACP chapters mobilized their membership to pressure the legislature for greater protections. But Maupins knew that discrimination was not limited to St. Paul and Minneapolis. "There is no realtor in Duluth who will even show a house in an improved area to a negro," he wrote to St. Louis County representative Arne C. Wanvick. "Their refusal is uniform." Acknowledging the extent of the problem, Wanvick and a narrow majority of state lawmakers passed a measure in the 1961 legislative session that prohibited racial discrimination in rentals and property sales more broadly, although it excluded apartment buildings where one of the units was owner-occupied, rooms in an owner-occupied house, and single-family dwellings without government financing (Federal Housing Administration or Veterans Administration mortgages). The latter exception meant that most real estate, which used conventional financing, fell outside the law. Nevertheless, after the governor signed the bill, to take effect in 1962, Maupins and other local advocates began to press the Duluth City Council to enact a complementary municipal fair housing ordinance, which they believed would facilitate enforcement of the state legislation.[31]

One of the first chances for Minnesota NAACP leaders to test the new law, as well as for Maupins to demonstrate the need for a city ordinance, arose later the following year, when the African American couple Matt and Helen Carter attempted to buy property and build a house in an all-White neighborhood on the city's lakefront. Originally from Mississippi, the Carters had first migrated north to Chicago, where Matt worked in a galley crew on a lake boat out of Milwaukee while Helen worked as a teacher in city schools. They lived in one of the South Side Lake Meadows buildings, a development that appealed to them in part because it was the first (intentionally) racially integrated housing constructed in Chicago. NAACP members also held their meetings in the Carters' building, and Matt and Helen joined them. The Democratic Party precinct captain lived in the building as well, and he encouraged them to be politically active. The couple happily stayed there for six years, until the summer of 1960, but then moved with their two children to Duluth, where it would be easier for Matt to work on the lakes and be with his family more often. He found a new apartment for them through a White boat engineer, whose wife managed several buildings in the Central Hillside area that she rented only to African Americans and Native Americans. Unfortunately, like the seafarers union, the Lake Carriers Association refused to allow Blacks to join ship crews in Duluth, and Matt had to work out of Two Harbors, thirty miles away. Likewise, when Helen went to apply for a teaching position, she was told that the school system had no "colored" teachers. Fortunately, while sitting dejected in the board of education office, she was befriended by Richard Weatherman, a sympathetic White administrator who hired her to replace a woman who had recently died, teaching "exceptional children" at the Jefferson School, making her the first Black teacher in the city.[32]

Within a year after coming to Duluth the Carters moved to a second apartment, just two blocks away, and as the children grew, the family realized they needed even more space and started looking for another home. Matt encountered a range of responses in his search, though all of them were rejections. He would find a "for rent" sign and could see people in a front room watching television, but when he knocked on the door they would look out and refuse to answer. Or, if they did come to the door, they would claim that the place was already rented and, in a few cases, they would say explicitly that they would not rent to him and slam the door in his face. Matt also tried working with a realtor to buy a house, yet the realtor made it clear that everything for sale of any quality was off-limits to African Americans. "I could show you the place," he would say, "but you can't live there." Instead, the realtor directed him to Gary and New Duluth, where other Blacks already owned homes. After enough of this, the Carters decided to buy a lot and build their own house. They planned to do that somewhere on the city's eastern end, which would be closer to the port where Matt worked and not too far from the school where Helen taught. The one particular lot they liked there was at Forty-Fifth Avenue East and London Road, property owned by Edmond (Ed) H. Hebert, who lived at 4623 London Road, but when the couple made an offer, and Ed realized that the family was Black, he refused to sell as well.[33]

Truly fed up with the ordeal, Matt went to the office of county attorney Keith Brownell, who said he sympathized with him but claimed there was little he could do. Instead, he recommended that the Carters work with Reverend Thomas L. Smith, a White minister at the Unitarian

The Carter family, about 1969. Left to right: Tony, Bill, Kai, Helen, and Matt. *Courtesy Matt Carter*

Universalist Congregation, and the best way to do that, Brownell said, was through a local White attorney, Andrew Larson. Smith, who first came to the city in 1957, was a fiery advocate for racial equality, so when Matt tracked down Larson and Larson talked to Smith, he readily agreed to be a straw purchaser. Without being fully transparent about what he was doing, the minister bought the lot in March 1962 for $1,300, $450 less than what Hebert originally paid for it. Smith then let several months pass before transferring the property to the Carters, and Matt waited to begin the process of getting a building permit. In mid-February of the following year, however, during National Brotherhood Week, a member of Matt's Sacred Heart Church Bible study group was on the radio discussing discrimination in Duluth, and he revealed that he knew of a Black couple who had a minister purchase a lot for them in an all-White neighborhood. Some London Road residents put two and two together and confronted Smith, telling him they "didn't want the neighborhood ruined." At that point, Matt decided to file for a permit, including a request to modify the standard setback from twenty-five to fifteen feet so he could build a two-car garage. In March, neighbors responded with a petition to the city planning commission, signed by more than fifty residents, opposing the request. They claimed that a shorter setback on the

corner lot would create a traffic hazard and "alteration of existing building lines" would "detract from the property values of existing homes in
the area."[34]

Meanwhile, Bill Maupins also got involved in the fight, and he became
a frequent dinner guest at the Carters' apartment, providing a steady
measure of encouragement and advice. In early January, he wrote to Viola
May Kanatz at the State Commission Against Discrimination (SCAD) to
ask about how to employ the new fair housing law. She replied at length,
and shortly after residents declared their opposition publicly to the planning commission, Minnesota-Dakota NAACP State Conference president
Donald Lewis wrote to encourage Maupins to have the Carters file a
complaint with SCAD to be the law's first test case. Emboldened by this,
Maupins showed the London Road petition at the next NAACP branch
meeting, which was packed, and several days later he joined others at the
planning commission meeting, which was also full and unusually heated.
At one point, Smith boldly called out the White residents. "The issue is
not the setback of the house," he said, "it is the man's race," and besides,
he noted, the city regularly made exceptions to setbacks in similar situ-
ations. In a subsequent meeting and letter to the commission, Newton
S. Friedman, the lawyer for the NAACP, was less blunt but made the
same basic argument. The Carters faced discrimination when they tried
to buy the lot for their home, Friedman explained, and "bias" was evident among opponents at the public hearings, suggesting that the decision to vacate the setback was not about traffic safety or property values,
and thus the issue should not be decided by those criteria. Ultimately,
however, the commission decided against the exemption and required a
redesigned building plan for a permit, one allowing for only a single-car
garage, while the NAACP decided not to file a formal complaint.[35]

Discouraged but determined, the Carters began construction of their
home at the end of April—slowed initially by someone stealing all the
plywood for the flooring—and in early June civil rights activists resumed
the campaign to pass a local fair housing ordinance. They met in the
mayor's reception room and began the meeting with "extensive discussion" of the situation Matt and Helen had faced. Maupins then reported
that he had reason to think the mayor and city council would like to
enact legislation, while Duluth Fair Employment Practices Commission
chairman William Van Evera said he had been in communication with
council member Donn Larson about introducing a bill similar to the

one they had drafted a year before. Another commission member, Anna Paine, announced that nearly two dozen people had formed a Duluth Citizens Human Rights Committee (DCHRC) to support the fair housing ordinance, to set up a task force to investigate discrimination complaints, and to make contacts in neighborhoods where "minority group members" were attempting to move. More outreach and lobbying followed over the next couple of months, and in early September, the city council passed the bill. Oddly, only afterward did the DCHRC ask Maupins to send NAACP members as representatives to serve on their board. The committee was dedicated to educating "the public in the truths of equality by quiet work or public testimony," secretary Robert Cameron explained, and they wished to invite the group to a meeting "where we may share ideas and offer services in cooperation to each other."[36]

Later the next month, Reverend Smith participated in a debate with real estate broker O. E. Thompson at a meeting of the Saturday Lunch Club, and his remarks again carried a confrontational tone. "We can no longer afford to continue the housing policy of the past," Smith declared, and he bemoaned the "appalling apathy" in Duluth about racial discrimination, which he explained was rooted in the notion that there was no problem because few Blacks lived in the city. "We are under obligation," the minister concluded, "to bring integrated housing into our community." Thompson replied with a standard objection, claiming that "when Negroes move into white neighborhoods, real estate values decrease by as much as 50 per cent," and that apartment rentals were also adversely affected when Black tenants moved in. "This is not the fault of the Negro or the white race," he said, and the best way to solve the problem was "negotiation." "Time is a great healer," he concluded, "and will help us find a solution." But Smith challenged Thompson's claim about declining real estate values, insisting that it was simply not true. Maupins, who was present as well, explained that any drop in values was only temporary, and property values eventually returned to their former levels.[37]

Growing more at ease as homeowners, the Carters adopted another son, Bill, in the fall of 1963, and the family settled into the London Road neighborhood. Three years later, on a mid-October night, when Matt was away on a boat, vandals defaced their home and sidewalk with graffiti, including "Koons Get Out," "Burn Baby Burn," and "Get Out Nigger." Police Chief Edward Bird was reportedly shocked by what happened to what he called the "law-abiding family," and while pledging that everything would be done to prevent another incident, he bemoaned the need for change "in the hearts of men." "We in Duluth have believed we are free of racial problems," he said, "but apparently some deep-rooted feelings can be found here." The editorial board at the *Duluth Herald Tribune* wrung its hands too, speculating about what might motivate a person to do such a thing. "Now we know that we have at least one ugly mind or two in our community," they wrote, people who want to "condemn every member of a group because of a belief that somewhere, at some time, some members of the group were not desirable neighbors." More practically, the newly established Duluth Jewish Federation Community Relations Council offered a five-hundred-dollar reward for information that led to the arrest and conviction of those involved, although the money was never claimed.[38]

Less than a year later, on the night of August 9, 1967, vandals struck again, defacing the Carters' house with more graffiti, including "Kill Niggers," "Get Out Niggers," a swastika, and the initials "KKK," as well as coating one of their cars with varnish remover. This time none of the family was at home. Matt was on a boat and Helen had taken the children to Washington, DC, to visit her brother, who worked for Senator Walter Mondale. In the months since the last incident, though, the Carters had decided to host a student from Uganda, Al Lwami, a freshman at UMD, and he was there. Lwami reported hearing a noise like "rushing wind" around 10 PM but did not discover the damage until the next morning. After viewing the scene, Maupins declared that Blacks in Duluth were "outraged" and demanded "an all-out effort to put a cessation to this type of intimidation." Yet the official White response was once again understated and nearsighted. The *Duluth Herald Tribune* editorialized about the incident, calling it a "blot" on the city that demanded residents search their "collective conscience." The paper further suggested that it was "contrived by one or no more than a few deranged persons" and compared it to "the recent violence of a very small percentage of Negroes in several cities," apparently referring to the urban riots of the past few years.[39]

Fortunately, harassment of the Carters ceased, in part because a few of their neighbors banded together to form a volunteer watch detail. Local philanthropist Julia Marshall also bought the four open lots adjacent to the Carters and offered to sell however much of the land they wanted, bringing flowers to the couple when they signed the papers to buy another twenty feet. More surprisingly, several neighbors who had initially opposed the family's presence befriended them, including Ed Hebert and his wife, Adeline. They became close enough that Matt and Helen would invite them over on holidays, and when Adeline was later diagnosed with Alzheimer's and moved into a nursing home in Superior, the Carters did various things to help. Then, when Ed got sick, the Carters found a nursing home for him too. Ed was so thankful that he offered to sell his house to the Carters, underpriced, although they passed on that because they were concerned that Ed needed money for his own health care. Instead, the dying man—"the person," Carter noted, "that wouldn't sell me the lot when he found out I was black"—willed Matt Carter all of his furniture.[40]

"Look Its Nightmare Squarely in the Eye"

By the time the Carters built their house on London Road, the Black population in Duluth had begun to recover from its decline in the 1930s and 1940s, rising from 334 in 1950 to 565 in 1960 and then doubling over the course of the decade to 1,100 (among a total population of more than 108,000). Much of this increase was due to the expansion of an air force base, not because Whites' racism had dissipated. As Bill Maupins explained to his colleagues on the local Fair Employment Practices Committee, the African American servicemen often had difficulty finding adequate housing, especially if they brought their families with them. At least half a dozen property owners renting to base personnel refused to sign a nondiscrimination certificate, and in a 1964 study nearly two-thirds of Black servicemen said they experienced discrimination when they tried to rent an apartment. Duluth was more or less still geographically segregated, with African American residents concentrated in East Hillside and parts of Central Hillside as well as in what was called the Heights, to the northwest, either in the Capehart Airbase Development or the low-income Harborview Homes Project. Generally, the cost of buying homes or renting was lower in these areas, and the quality of housing was typically lesser too. This reflected the city's long history of racial exclusion in housing, of course, as well as ongoing job discrimination, limiting Black workers to lower-paying occupations. More than a third of African American families in Duluth lived at or below the poverty level and nearly half had a household income less than the city median.[41]

Forty years later, at the turn of the twenty-first century, very little had changed. Only a small fraction of African American residents in Duluth were homeowners, and the number of Blacks living below the poverty level had actually increased. Matt and Helen Carter still lived in their London Road home, and yet they were mostly an anomaly, a rare break in the city's color line that was less a preview of its imminent dissolution than a confirmation of its deep historical roots. Despite the slow progress toward racial equality, however, some of the city's residents, both Black and White, did at least begin to reckon with the gratuitous violence of nearly a century earlier that had helped to make and preserve Duluth's racist social order. On October 10, 2003, thousands gathered downtown, this time not with murderous intent, as they had eighty-three years before, but rather to unveil what was one of the only memorials in the country dedicated to lynching victims. And, once more, the *New York Times* took the opportunity to question the notion of southern exceptionalism and its corollary northern exceptionalism. "Americans who know of the violence of this period at all tend to believe it was confined to the segregationist South," the editorial board explained, "but the fact that lynchings took place in many parts of the country was underscored recently in the northern Minnesota city of Duluth." Although there had been a long stretch of time when many people tried to forget the racist violence that plagued both the South and the North, they mused, "the country now seems more ready to look its nightmare squarely in the eye."[42]

CHAPTER 5

"A Bigoted, Prejudiced, Hateful Little Area": Racial Exclusion in Edina

WHEN THE CORNERSTONE WAS LAID for St. Stephen's Episcopal Church at the Wooddale Avenue and Fiftieth Street intersection in Edina, Minnesota, in the fall of 1938, two other relatively new buildings already stood nearby. A clubhouse for the recently developed Country Club District had been constructed below the bend on Minnehaha Creek in 1924, and a school opened across from that on Wooddale two years later. In fact, because the St. Stephen's parish was formally organized in the spring of 1937, before the church was built, its congregants initially met for Sunday services at the Edina School. When their guild hosted its first "All Black Face Minstrel Show" the next April they did so at the school auditorium as well. Directed by Albert and Florence Allen, who lived on Casco Avenue, the event was billed as an "after-lent show" with proceeds going to St. Stephen's, and a whole host of their Country Club District neighbors contributed their time to make it a success. "Rehearsals are producing new talent every week," the local *Crier* reported, "and entertainment is promised for the entire community." Among a cast of nearly three dozen actors, Florence and her sisters, Minnie Livingston and

Blackface minstrel show, probably 1950s, Edina High School.
Courtesy Edina Historical Society

Charlotte Young, performed as the "Yes Sah! All Sister Mammy Act," and a group of men took the stage as the "Black Face Boys," while additional volunteers worked to assemble costumes and construct the set. And all this effort was well worth it, the newsletter noted afterward, making for a "Big Smash Hit!" When the amateurs "blacked their faces, donned bandanas, and padded their figures with pillows," it declared, "they ran the laugh-temperature of their large and appreciative audience almost beyond the breaking point!"[1]

Besides the "entertainment" it provided, though, this first "burnt cork" event, and the annual minstrel shows that continued in Edina at least into the mid-1950s, also served another purpose. Even if some among the all-White participants and audiences did not fully grasp or consciously acknowledge it, the performances allowed them to affirm and sustain a deep racial prejudice as well as to justify and maintain the exclusion of African Americans from their community, without, in their minds, violating pretensions of gentility. The fixation on an imagined, "traditional," rural South that the shows perpetuated associated Blacks—or rather, Blackness and assumed Black inferiority—with a time, place, and culture profoundly not the "modern" urban North. This racist alchemy enabled the Country Club District residents, and the many other White northerners who regularly hosted and attended minstrel shows, to simultaneously reveal and deny their bigotry, to both display and hide their own racist beliefs and practices. The various standard roles and storylines established a particular caricature of African Americans and yet put responsibility for the supposed living reality behind it on stunted southern Blacks and static southern Whites. Moreover, by casting racial prejudice and inequality as distant and remote, the performances gave Whites an excuse to avoid confronting and eradicating those prejudices. The attitudes and wrongs were not their own, and northern Whites were too far away to measurably influence or alter them in any case, willfully ignoring the obvious manifestation of those attitudes and wrongs in the very intentional and unchanging Whiteness of their neighborhoods.[2]

Yet, only a few decades prior, this sort of insidious racism was not a part of the common culture in the area, principally because the different set of people who lived there would not have permitted it. Situated immediately southwest of Bde Maka Ska and Lake Harriet, Edina was a racially integrated village of small farms, and the spirit of tolerance and coexistence that prevailed was strongest among the Whites and Blacks who settled on the land where St. Stephen's, the Country Club clubhouse, and the Edina School were later built. One of the original residents was Jonathan Grimes, who had become an ardent abolitionist growing up among Quakers in Virginia. During the Civil War, he owned and operated the Minnehaha mill to supply flour to Union troops at Fort Snelling, after which he and his wife, Elizabeth, moved to a small plot north of Minnehaha Creek to establish the Lake Calhoun Nursery. The Grimeses' neighbors included James Bull, a migrant from New York who settled on a quarter section just downstream from the mill and, after his first wife died in 1865, married Amie Leah Cooper, the daughter of local Quakers. Both of those plots were originally owned by George and Sarah Baird,

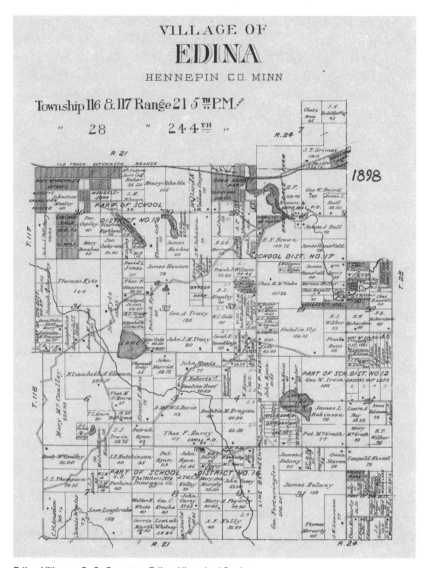

Edina Village, 1898. *Courtesy Edina Historical Society*

who had come from Pennsylvania and raised purebred Hackney horses, Holstein cattle, and Merino sheep on land abutting the Grimeses and Bulls and diagonally adjacent to the mill. Additionally, Henry and Susan Brown came from Minneapolis in the latter part of the 1860s and purchased the acreage that surrounded the mill, on both sides of Minnehaha Creek, to establish a farm they named "Browndale." Perhaps encouraged by the presence of these and other welcoming Whites, a few African American families began to arrive too. This started at the end of the 1870s with Beverly and Ellen Yancey, who settled on the upstream side of Browndale and quickly became full members of the community. There were regular social visits with the Grimeses, Bulls, Bairds, and Browns, as well as berry-picking parties on the Yancey land. The Black couple were also founding members and officers of the local grange chapter, while Ellen helped found the school district's parent-teacher association and served as its first president.[3]

In the 1920s, however, with the extension of a streetcar line linking Edina more directly to Minneapolis, developers began turning the various tree nurseries, pastures, dairies, and fruit farms into housing tracts, transforming the village through what might be called "suburban renewal." This happened first when the Yancey children and another Black family sold much of their land to the developers of the Emma Abbott Park and Cleveland subdivisions, after which the Grimeses' and Browns' heirs sold some of their land to become part of the Morningside subdivision. Then, following World War I, Thorpe Brothers purchased the rest of Browndale and what was left of the Bulls' property to make the Country Club District. "Twenty minutes by automobile and less than thirty minutes by streetcar from the heart of downtown," a 1924 promotional booklet read, the "new restricted residential addition" offered "discriminating seekers of homesites advantages that have heretofore been unheard of in Minneapolis real estate." Subsequently, within another decade, most of the original residents were gone, many of them to Minneapolis or St. Paul. After that, the only African Americans living in new Country Club District homes were those employed by White families, and exclusion as well as that exception were explicitly delineated by racially restrictive housing covenants. "No lot shall ever be sold, conveyed, leased or rented to any person other than that of the Caucasian race," one deed restriction for a Casco Avenue home read, "nor shall any lot ever been [*sic*] used or occupied by any other person than one of the white or Caucasian race, except such as may be serving as domestics for the owner or tenant."[4]

The Twin Cities metropolitan area was not completely immune to the gathering midcentury battle against segregation in America, however, and the first integration effort in Edina began in 1959. This was a reintegration effort, of sorts, bringing what fair-housing advocates called "black pioneers" to a place where other Blacks had lived several decades before. Forced out of their home by a highway project in Minneapolis, African Americans Marion and Mary Taylor bought a lot in the Morningside neighborhood that was formerly orchard land belonging to Jonathan Grimes and his wife, the close social acquaintances of the Yanceys and other Black families who had lived nearby. Yet the Taylors faced significant opposition from White residents, including former mayor Otto Wolin, and it was an ordeal for them to win the right to build, secure necessary loans, and finally settle in the neighborhood. As was the case with the Carters in Duluth, opponents initially pitched their resistance as a matter of practical considerations, citing concerns about stormwater drainage, but when the village council dismissed this objection, they more openly expressed worries about property values and "race mixing." In the end, the Taylors only succeeded because of their own exceptional fortitude, aid from the newly established Greater Minneapolis Interfaith Fair Housing Program, and a supportive petition campaign initiated by two White families as well as intervention by the sitting mayor, Ken Joyce. Even after they succeeded, it was a decade and a half, into the mid-1970s, before another Black family, one that was interracial, followed them. For all intents and purposes, the area remained predominantly all-White, demonstrating the obstinate legacy of racial exclusion.

"No Better Than a Portion of the South"

Located west of the confluence of the Mississippi and Minnesota Rivers, the area that eventually became the St. Louis Park, Edina, Richfield, and Bloomington suburbs of Minneapolis had long been occupied by Dakota Indians. Three decades after the US government established Fort Snelling and began to assert military control, however, the government dispossessed Dakota inhabitants of the land by the treaties of Traverse des Sioux and Mendota. Within two years, by 1853, surveyors had mapped this countryside into sections and lots, and within two years of that, Whites had claimed or preempted most of them, including all of the Richfield Township. These new titleholders included speculator Richard Strout, who platted a town he called "Waterville" in the heavily forested western section of the township and, in 1857, erected a flour mill there on Minnehaha Creek. Jonathan Grimes purchased the mill from Strout and, after operating the mill nonstop during the Civil War, sold it to Daniel Buckwalter and moved with his wife, Sarah, and their children to sixteen acres they bought from George and Sarah Baird to establish their tree nursery. There they tended apple orchards and experimented with various other trees, many of which eventually lined streets in Minneapolis and earned them enough renown that Jonathan was elected the first president of the Minnesota Horticultural Society. Meanwhile, in 1869, Buckwalter sold the mill to Scottish immigrant Andrew Craik, who christened it the "Edina Mill," from a line in the Robert Burns poem "Address to Edinburgh."[5]

Among the other Whites who first came to the area around Minnehaha Creek was James Alvah Bull, whose family went on to have an outsized influence not only on agricultural endeavors of the community but also on farming in Minnesota more widely. Born in 1834, Bull came to the territory in 1853 with his father and his first wife, Mary E. Comstock, and the young couple remained after the father purchased land from the Bairds and deeded it to them before returning to New York. Mary died several years later, however, and James married Amie Leah Cooper, who had come to Minnesota with her parents from Lancaster, Pennsylvania, in 1857. The Coopers had settled with fellow Quaker farm families in nearby Interlachen, where Amie grew up, but for several years before her marriage she was an itinerant teacher in Hennepin County schools, and later served on a committee appointed by the state grange to open the University of Minnesota's School of Agriculture to female students. For his part, James was a founding member and the first master (president) of the local Minnehaha Grange, a founder of the School of Agriculture, and a master of the Minnesota State Grange, followed (not coincidentally) by the first female state master, Sarah Baird, who served from 1893 to 1912.[6]

Not long after the Bulls established their place in the village, Henry and Susan Brown joined the community too. Henry was born on a farm in Baldwin, Maine, in 1843 and came to Minneapolis by 1859. Initially, he found work driving a team hauling lumber out of the woods, and following that he took up farming, supplementing his income by teaching school in the winters. Through this work, Brown earned enough to accumulate substantial savings and make various investments, and within a short period of time he owned an immense amount of timber land and many large sawmills and yards, extensive iron ore property in the Mesabi Range, a large share in the North American Telegraph Company of Minnesota, as well as a majority interest in two flour mills. In 1865 he married Susan Fairfield, who was from Saco, Maine, and together they resided at a "pleasant" home in south Minneapolis (the first in the city with indoor plumbing) and became generous philanthropists. They built a second home in Edina and turned the land into the celebrated "Browndale" stock farm, adding the nearby grain mill to their holdings when Andrew Craik died in 1892. The couple held annual public auctions of shorthorn cattle and won prizes for their stock at the Minnesota State Fair and the Chicago World's Fair, and Henry served as president and board member of the Shorthorn Breeders Association.[7]

Drawn by this mix of prosperous, liberal-minded Whites, the African American Yancey family settled in the area as well. Beverly Yancey had been born in 1828, in Ross County, Ohio, to parents who had been born in Virginia, likely enslaved. In 1850, he married Ellen Nancy Bass, whose parents had been born in North Carolina, also likely enslaved, and they moved one county over to Oxford, Ohio, where Beverly worked as a farm laborer. Over the next decade and a half, the couple had five children, but in 1864, Ellen died giving birth to their last, a daughter named Maggie. Meanwhile, Beverly had joined a colored infantry regiment, serving to the end of the Civil War, and after mustering out he moved his family to Minnesota. There he managed a farm belonging to prominent Minneapolis doctor Calvin Goodrich, in St. Louis Park, a position he attained because he had been good friends with the doctor's son in Oxford before the Goodrich family moved to Minnesota too. Shortly after, Yancey purchased land of his own in Edina, fifty acres within sight of Minnehaha Creek, not far from the grain mill, and in 1870 he married Ellen Maria Bruce, who was originally from Washington, DC. They had two children of their own, Charles and Ellen, and while Beverly's other sons and daughters left to be on their own, Maggie continued to live at home for a few years longer. The family also housed three boarders who worked as farm laborers: African Americans Calvin Ayley and Morto Mitchell, both in their twenties, and Swedish immigrant Peter Johnson, who was in his thirties.[8]

In 1873, three years after they settled in Edina, the Yanceys joined with neighboring White families to establish Minnehaha Grange #398, a local branch of the national progressive farmers' organization founded by Minnesota farmer Oliver Hudson Kelley in 1867. James Bull served as the first master, and initially Beverly served as treasurer while Ellen served as flora, a position designated to care for members during illness

Browndale Bridge on Minnehaha Creek, about 1893. *Courtesy Edina Historical Society*

or death, and the Black couple held various other elected positions over the years. Grange meeting minutes also recorded a genuine amiability among the mixed membership. After one gathering that Beverly did not attend, the secretary wrote that it was noted "Brother Yancey be on hand with ice cream and raisins at our next regular meeting . . . and he will be required to explain in a satisfactorily manner why we were subjected to the disappointment of not seeing him." At another meeting, following Maggie's induction as a new member, she and her brother Charles put on a musical performance with the Bulls' daughter, Annie, and it was "much applauded." Likewise, near the end of the decade, when the growing organization decided to build a hall, the first meeting of the "Hall Association" was held at the Yanceys' house, and Beverly was appointed the association's vice president. Constructed on land leased by James Bull, at the intersection of Wooddale Avenue and Fiftieth Street, where the Edina School and St. Stephen's Church were later located, the Grange Hall functioned as the town hall too, hosting regular meetings of voting residents. This included one in 1888, at which Beverly acted as the official recorder, when residents formally incorporated as Edina.[9]

As the Yancey children became adults and married, they decided to stay in the village, and like their parents, they were fully integrated and well-regarded members of the community. In 1883, Maggie Yancey married Thomas Fite (or Fyte), a member of one of the other Black families in the area, and three years later they had a son, whom they named Thomas. Shortly after, however, Maggie's husband died, and she remarried to Swedish immigrant Claus Johnson (possibly related to the Yancey boarder). The new couple purchased land to start a berry farm adjacent to Beverly and Ellen, and five years later they had a son of their own, named Alfred. At the same time, the younger Ellen had returned to serve as a church organist after studying music at the University of Minnesota, and she married William Gillespie, who was from another newly arrived Black family. Following this, the two of them took over operation of the Yancey farm, and both were highly involved in the grange, alternately serving in various leadership roles. When they were formally inducted in 1908, they were appointed assistant steward and lady assistant steward, and a few years after that "Brother Gillespie" was named "worthy master" and "Sister Gillespie" was made the secretary. Similarly, Beverly and Ellen's son Charles went away to school in Canada, where he met Helen Watkin, whose grandparents had fled from slavery years before, and the couple returned to Edina and married. They were active in the grange too, and Charles organized a local orchestra, served as school board treasurer, and made his living as the village clerk.[10]

As further testament to the important role the Yancey family played in Edina, local residents took special notice when Beverly and Ellen died. Although James Bull used his daybooks primarily to record purchases, payments, and wages, for example, his brief entry for October 31, 1905, unusually mentioned that "B. C. Yancey" had passed away. More effusive was a memorial resolution by the grange, a common practice for deceased members but, in this case, quite atypical for its length and

Helen Watkins Yancey, wife of Charles, with their children, Beryl, Edgar, and baby Helen, 1917. The woman at right is probably her mother, Amelia Abbott Watkins. *Courtesy Edina Historical Society*

demonstrative sentiment. "It is fitting that we who loved our brother in life should express our high appreciation of his services," it began. "In the death of Bro. Yancey the Order loses a firm friend and constant supporter . . . his family a tender loving husband and father, and all a genial comrade and faithful friend." A decade later, in March 1915, when Ellen Yancey died, the full grange membership attended her funeral services. At their next regular meeting, her longtime friend Sarah Baird temporarily took over as secretary to write an adoring tribute. "Our hearts are saddened by the loss of one of our most beloved and esteemed Charter members," the first part read. "Always remaining loyal and faithful to our cause, though unable in recent years to attend all meetings, she exhibited spirit of helpfulness, tolerance and love recognized by all of her coworkers." Ellen had been known for "her wise counsel, her gentle presence and nobleness of character which drew all hearts to her," Baird recalled, and grange members mourned "for one to whom all looked with love and respect."[11]

Despite several decades of interracial harmony, however, that aspect of the Edina community was already starting to be undone by the turn of the twentieth century, as real estate developers began buying land and platting subdivisions in the northern section. This started when Charles Yancey and William Gillespie sold much of the family's acreage to Seth Abbott (who named his development "Emma Abbott Park" after his opera-star daughter) and to other investors who created the adjacent Cleveland subdivision. Then, in 1905, the Grimes heirs sold their family land and the Browns heirs sold part of their family plot for what became the Morningside subdivision. These initial developments were made possible by the extension of the Twin City Rapid Transit's newly electrified Lake Harriet line out to Lake Minnetonka, which made it easier for middle-class professionals who worked in the city to live outside Minneapolis. As lots began to sell along the railway line, though, a split formed on the village council between the remaining farming interests resistant to paying assessments for "necessary improvements" and those hoping to draw homebuyers to the area, sparking calls by the latter to make a formal separation from Edina. Oddly, the final push for this came after Charles Yancey was arrested for embezzling over $5,000 from the roadwork payroll, which created an unsettling controversy. Indicative of the trust the clerk still had among some residents, attorney George Grimes (son of Jonathan and Eliza) posted his bond and served as his lawyer, while the council minutes only discreetly mentioned that he had resigned. Yancey repaid the money and left for Minneapolis with his family, but the incident prompted a new call for separation and, soon after, those urging for development voted to split from the village of Edina and incorporate as Morningside.[12]

By the mid-1920s, the entire area that once was Edina Village was experiencing a general shift from farms to suburb, and with that the village turned toward racial exclusion. The tipping point came when the Brown heirs sold the rest of Browndale to Thorpe Brothers developers to build what they called the Country Club District. This development was modeled on exclusive suburbs in Kansas City, Cleveland, and Baltimore, and like those it included various features meant to attract "the better class." It was not their intention to make the neighborhood "a community of 'snobs,'" the Thorpe Brothers declared in a 1924 brochure, but the lot sizes, home prices, bucolic layout, "sparkling" lake, and an eighteen-hole golf course were very much about pitching it as "select." Additionally, all the property deeds carried racially restrictive covenants, language that prohibited owners from selling their homes to anyone who was not "of the white or Caucasian race." Promotional literature never explicitly mentioned these covenants, however, suggesting that prospective buyers understood the developers' various euphemisms and, perhaps, appreciated the need for concealing vulgar racism. The district would be "a community where you can be proud to live, proud of your home, your grounds, and your neighbor's home as well," one flyer explained, "a place where you can rear your children with the freedom of mind that comes with knowing they are more protected than would be possible in any 'hit or miss' city neighborhood."[13]

While the Country Club District was being built out and occupied, a few African American residents from the original farm families were still around, but this was a dwindling group. Maggie Johnson lived in Edina with her White husband, Claus, on their berry farm, and in the 1930s he was working as a laborer at the golf club. By the 1940s, she was widowed and lived some distance away, on Eden Prairie Road, with her son Thomas, his wife, Florence, and Florence's two young children from another marriage. Thomas worked for a Minneapolis building contractor, and after his mother died in 1963, he moved the family out of Edina and into the city. African Americans George and Ora Payne had come to the area sometime before 1910 and also had a berry farm, next to the Gillespies', though by the 1930s George was employed at a "hog works," and by 1940 they too had moved to Minneapolis. John and Viola Leggette arrived a bit later, with their two children, and by 1920 they had purchased a modest home on Van der Voort Avenue, west of the Country Club District. In the 1930s he worked as a "slusher" at a seed mill, and by 1940 the family was in Minneapolis as well. Lastly, one house over from the Leggettes, Noah Siggers lived with his wife, Addie, their daughter Ernestine, and Addie's brother John McIntosh. Noah worked as a carver at a furniture factory starting in the 1920s, and he stayed on after Addie died in the 1930s. Ernestine continued to live in Edina following Noah's death in the 1950s, although she too disappeared from the city directory by the early 1960s.[14]

To be sure, for at least two decades after Edina's Country Club District was developed, a significant number of other African Americans were living in the neighborhood, yet they were all live-in "domestic" workers, allowed under an exception to the racial covenants. By 1930, the community counted nearly one thousand White residents and almost one

Edina school, 1920s. *Courtesy Edina Historical Society*

hundred Black servants. Among the latter were George and Elizabeth Walters, employed as a butler and maid, respectively, for title insurance company vice president Ellis Southworth and his family. George was originally from Arkansas and nearly fifty years old, while Elizabeth was from Tennessee and in her mid-thirties. The stately house where they lived and worked was at 4607 Edina Boulevard, just a couple of blocks north of the Wooddale and Fiftieth Street intersection. Similarly, Gertrude Alexander was employed as a maid by regional auto sales director Grover Smith and his family, and their spacious home was at 4507 Wooddale. The Smiths had previously lived in Rockford, Illinois, where Gertrude first started working for them after her husband died in an Alabama coal mine accident, and the family brought her to Minnesota when they moved. By the 1950s, however, she as well as George and Elizabeth Walters and all the other live-in domestics had moved on, most to Minneapolis or St. Paul. Some African Americans likely continued to travel by train or bus to clean houses, care for children, or tend yards for the day, but otherwise the resident population had become entirely White.[15]

Of course, Edina was not the only place in metropolitan Minneapolis that practiced racial exclusion, and the methods to accomplish it

were not always so discreet. In one 1909 case, in the heart of "an aristo-
cratic district" near Bde Maka Ska, White residents harassed two Black
families who rented apartments from a local doctor, repeatedly ringing
their doorbells, breaking windows with rocks, and circulating a petition to have one of the men fired from his job. In several different incidents during the 1920s, Whites attempted to intimidate African American families who moved into other south Minneapolis neighborhoods
by breaking windows, pouring gasoline on porches, and shooting into
their homes. And in what was probably the most extended display of
local White harassment against African American residents, beginning in
the summer of 1931 World War I veteran and postal worker Arthur Lee
and his family faced several demonstrations by White neighbors outside
their home at 4600 Columbus Avenue, midway between Lake Harriet
and Lake Hiawatha. Previously, homeowners in the area had signed an
agreement among themselves not to sell real estate "to colored persons,"
but the Lees moved in before neighboring homeowners could stop them.
Frustrated in their efforts to keep the area all White, crowds ranging
from a few hundred to several thousand in number began gathering in
front of the house nightly, taunting the Lees and throwing rocks, occasionally prompting police to respond and make arrests. A year later, when
a group of White youths gathered outside "hurling epithets," an exasper-
ated Arthur Lee struck one of the boys. A sympathetic judge fined him a
nominal sum and ordered police to take measures to end the harassment,
but the family soon had enough and, in 1934, they moved away.[16]

White mobs were not always successful at removing African Americans, however, and there always seemed to be a few among resistant
Whites who counseled other approaches. When Black restaurant owner
Evan Bridges bought two lots not far from where the Lees lived, only
a year after the dispute started there, Thirteenth Ward alderman and
alleged charter member of the local Ku Klux Klan Walter C. Robb rallied
his neighbors in another protest. One evening, he led about 150 residents
at the Linden Hills Branch Library in a discussion about what could be
done. Robb "made a masterful subtle appeal to the racial prejudices of
his hearers," and other speakers cited cases "where Negroes were fright-
ened from a neighborhood by stone throwing," but, according to the
Twin City Herald, "many of the people were obviously unfavorable to any
suggestion of violence or coercion." A local attorney also "reminded the
audience that there was no legal way to keep a citizen of any color from

purchasing property," presumably because there were no racially restrictive covenants in that neighborhood. And at least some of the residents of what the *Twin City Herald* called "the Lake Harriet District" did not even agree that Bridges would make "an undesirable neighbor." In the end, a handful of meeting participants formed a committee to call on him and see if he would sell his property, and then report their findings at a following meeting.[17]

Increasingly during the 1930s and 1940s, the federal government responded to White threats and violence against their African American neighbors by formalizing and even codifying a range of other options to help them create and preserve racially exclusive enclaves. Modeled on the approach of its New Deal–era predecessor, the Home Owners' Loan Corporation (HOLC), the Federal Housing Administration (FHA) spelled out a protocol for racist mortgage lending in its regularly updated *Underwriting Manual.* "Recorded restrictive covenants should strengthen and supplement zoning ordinances," the 1938 manual explained, and they "should be recorded with the plat, or imposed as blanket encumbrance against all lots in the subdivision." Among these "recommended restrictions" was "prohibition of the occupancy of properties except by the race for which they were intended." Likewise, borrowing from earlier HOLC maps, the agency demarcated metropolitan areas and rated lending risk in individual neighborhoods according to a color-coded gradient, from green and blue to yellow and red, largely determined by housing-stock quality and racial composition. By this system, "red-lined" African Americans were typically prevented from securing loans to purchase homes even in Black areas (because they were supposedly risky borrowers), and they faced difficulty getting a mortgage for homes in White areas (because the FHA discouraged mixing of "inharmonious races and classes"). At the same time, White homebuyers could not get loans to buy in "risky" Black or mixed neighborhoods, restricting them to all-White sections of town. Just as importantly, Whites in racially exclusive communities had an incentive to block integration in order to maintain their FHA-defined mapped ratings and select home values, which were critical for attracting other White homebuyers as well as for existing homeowners to get second mortgages.[18]

When Congress crafted the 1944 Servicemen's Readjustment Act, or GI Bill, southern segregationists and their northern allies arranged for it to have decentralized administration and oversight, knowing this would also aid in perpetuating racial segregation. Veterans Administration (VA) district office staff were under the direction of state headquarters, and the various benefits were implemented by local governments, schools, and banks, making the law's generous home loans (as well as business loans and education benefits) vulnerable to common White prejudice. In 1947, only two of the 3,200 VA-guaranteed loans in thirteen Mississippi cities went to Black borrowers, and fewer than one hundred of the 67,000 mortgages insured by the GI Bill in New York and northern New Jersey suburbs went to non-White recipients. Likewise, the law was written in such a way that Black veterans had few places to turn if they wanted to appeal a decision. "The stipulation that approval lay in the hands of the bank or lending institution, simple enough on its face," historian Kathleen Frydl notes, "disqualified large numbers of African Americans from receiving Title III benefits, so much so that it is more accurate simply to say that blacks could not use this particular title." This kept African Americans confined to particular neighborhoods, which in turn reinforced the assessment of those areas as high financial risks and unattractive to most if not all White homebuyers.[19]

Local and state governments assisted Whites by stalling on fair housing ordinances and laws or by passing only weak measures and underfunding enforcement too. In Minneapolis, during the summer of 1957, a city council standing committee decided against recommending an "open-occupancy" ordinance after City Attorney Charles A. Sawyer declared that it would violate the Fourteenth Amendment. "It very obviously interferes very substantially," he explained, "with the right of individuals to acquire, use, and dispose of property as they see fit." The next year, after fourteen meetings and testimony from more than two dozen individuals, organizations, and government agencies, the Minnesota legislature's Interim Commission on Housing Discrimination voted not to recommend a fair housing bill for similar reasons. In considering a justification for use of the state's regulatory power, their report declared, "no vital necessity is apparent for depriving private property owners of their rights for the benefit of a few." Instead of legislation, the commission suggested "a campaign of education of the entire population towards a complete tolerance of Negroes and other minorities." This would necessarily be a slow and difficult process, they acknowledged, though "much of the present friction can be avoided if . . . the Negro people can recognize the need for, and actually practice, great patience." Representative

F. Gordon Wright, from a Hennepin County district, even went so far as to brand "open housing" a "communist doctrine" and claimed that his constituents were overwhelmingly against such a law for that reason. "I sent out 3,000 letters," he said, "and received 540 replies, [and] only two favored open housing."[20]

When Minnesota legislators did finally pass an open housing law, to go into effect in 1962, opponents not only added enfeebling exceptions for numerous rental and real estate purchases but also made a concerted effort to deny adequate funding to the oversight agency the bill established, the State Commission Against Discrimination (SCAD). In 1963, agency officials requested a small increase in their operating budget, beyond the biennium funding of $192,000, and Twin Cities realtor groups and organized homeowners joined forces to lobby against it. "The anti-discrimination housing law has one main objective," the coalition declared in an open appeal, "to mix the races in housing." In a bid to halt or at least slow that from happening, they asserted (again) that the only way to accomplish desegregation was by "educational means, such as persuasion, conferences, and conciliation," and they cast the fines and other penalties allowed under the "unjust" legislation as "coercion." SCAD's funding should be limited to the former, their appeal argued, "because none of the races are ready for so great a social change" and "forced integration" simply would not work. Besides, the coalition explained, the state's House Un-American Activities Committee, established to investigate subversion, had received only $360,000 for its 1963 operating budget, and SCAD's was an "infinitesimal task by comparison." The agency had dealt with just a small number of cases in its first year (opponents claimed five, although it was closer to five dozen), and those were "resolved without difficulty."[21]

Operating together, Minnesota's weak open-housing laws and racist rental and real estate practices effectively empowered suburban Whites as well as those in urban neighborhoods to create and maintain racially exclusive communities with few constraints. The corollary to this was an increasing concentration of Blacks in slowly expanding central city "pocket areas." Even as the total population declined in Minneapolis, from 492,000 in 1940 to 482,000 in 1960, the number of Black residents grew more than twofold, from 4,700 to nearly 11,800, and they continued to be confined to the same six pockets where they had long been stuck. On the near north side, for example, where more than a third of the city's

African Americans lived, the total number of residents decreased from 9,800 to 8,600, but the number of Blacks more than doubled, from 1,300 to 3,500. Moreover, most of that growth took place in one particular census tract, which saw the number of African American residents increase from only two dozen to 1,200. Making the situation even worse, all of the 1,700 newly built, privately owned rental units and all but 100 of the 10,000 single and two-family homes that had been constructed in Minneapolis after World War II were off-limits to Blacks, while housing in neighborhoods where African Americans lived tended to be older and deteriorated. Consequently, as Urban League executive director Robert L. Williams pointed out in testimony to state legislators, those neighborhoods were more likely to be designated as "blighted" by the housing and redevelopment authority and transformed by urban renewal and highway projects. Those projects, in turn, displaced residents, he observed, who were then absorbed back into other Black sections of the city and thereby further accelerated residential segregation.[22]

Among the African Americans who were displaced by highway construction in Minneapolis were Marion and Mary Taylor, who lived just east of Bde Maka Ska at 3833 Stevens Avenue, which put them directly in the path of Interstate 35W. Not wanting to move to any of the other neighborhoods where Blacks were segregated, they were challenged to find an alternative. "In every Public Hearing the Highway Dept. had," Marion Taylor wrote to state attorney general Walter Mondale, "I asked if the Dept. had for our use a Relocation Office." They did not, he recalled, because the "feeling is if the Negro population stay[s] in the channeled area [there] should not be any problems." Nevertheless, the intrepid couple decided to look for a place to live in the city's White suburbs. Like many African Americans of his generation, Marion had served in the army during World War II, which gave him at least nominal access to GI Bill benefits. In addition, his well-paying job as a Veterans Administration biochemist, along with Mary's position as a schoolteacher, would easily qualify them for a construction loan and home mortgage. As they began their own personal battle for fair housing, they also filed formal cases for employment discrimination, demonstrating a determination to fight the color line in its various forms. In the early part of 1959, before she went into teaching, Mary had been refused a job at the Heldwood Nursing Home, and three years later, according to the State Commission Against Discrimination, her case was finally "satisfactorily adjusted," though what specifically that meant is unclear. Similarly, in 1962, Marion filed a discrimination case when he was denied a promotion at the VA, but two years later SCAD dismissed it for lack of "probable cause."[23]

The lot the Taylors found to build their new home was in Morningside, at the end of Scott Terrace, one of several parcels that were once part of the Grimes estate but which were left open because they were situated on a hill slope. Unlike the more ostentatious Country Club District nearby, the Morningside subdivision had been developed as blocks of modest bungalows, including about six hundred homesteads, all without restrictive housing covenants attached to their titles. Still, realtor schemes and social pressure had insured that every one of the families who moved there was White. When Morningsiders learned about the likely integration of their community, they quickly organized house meetings and developed a strategy to prevent it. Led by former mayor Otto Wolin, a sales agent who lived on Scott Terrace, as well as attorney Keith Bradley, who lived one block over, on France Avenue, the Whites claimed that the lot the "Negro couple" had bought had to be left open for drainage purposes, and they demanded in a petition that the village government take possession of it for the public good. The council delayed a vote on this, however, and opponents became more vocal about the impact the Taylor move would have on property values,

Miss Baker's first-grade class at Morningside Elementary, 1961. Greg Taylor is in the middle row, sixth from the right. *Courtesy Jim Joyce*

as well as the possibility of "race mixing" and "intermarriage." As the exclusion campaign became public news, Whites who did not even live in Morningside also joined in making racist appeals to keep the neighborhood free of Black residents. St. Paul resident Al White wrote a letter to the council, for example, warning that letting "one Negro" into their "'select community'" would lead others to follow. "The white man must be on the alert if for nothing else, but for the protection of their children and grandchildren," he declared, "so we hope you take heed before it's too late."[24]

The Taylors were not entirely alone in facing this resistance, however, and they were particularly fortunate to get help from the Greater Minneapolis Interfaith Fair Housing Program (GMIFHP). Initial efforts toward organizing that group had begun in 1957, when the Minneapolis city attorney ruled the proposed open-occupancy law unconstitutional and various religious, civic, and business leaders met to decide how to respond. The next year, after coming together under the direction of the mayor's commission on human relations, they held several meetings to discuss how to respond to individual cases of discrimination as well as to consider the possibility of a "long range education program." In December 1958, they established the Citizen's Committee on Discrimination and Housing and elected Allen Anderson, from the Minneapolis Council of Churches, as chair. The following spring, he contacted Galen Weaver and Chester Marcus of the United Church of Christ (UCC), who told him that the UCC's Christian Council for Social Action was seeking partners in northern cities to fund pilot fair housing campaigns, and they wanted Minneapolis to be one of them. The council pledged to fund the pilot for three years, contingent on matching funding from local Protestant, Catholic, and Jewish groups. Once agreed, in April 1959 the Citizen's Committee established the GMIFHP, and members elected Louise Walker McCannel to chair the group. During the summer they conducted a search for an executive director, eventually hiring James A. Tillman Jr., who had been working as a foreign service officer at the US State Department.[25]

In early January of the next year, Tillman began visiting the Taylors to work with them on a plan for going forward. At the same time, he got in touch with Reverend Richard Sykes at the First Unitarian Society in Morningside, and the minister recommended that the GMIFHP reach out to society member Sherman Hasbrouck, who lived on Scott Terrace just a few doors down from the disputed lot. After meeting with Tillman, Hasbrouck agreed to take the lead in organizing a grassroots community campaign, as the executive director put it, "to build and communicate to the council a substantial body of positive opinion in favor of Taylor's building in the village." Hasbrouck then put together a core group of neighbors who crafted a petition against housing discrimination and collected more than two hundred signatures (some representing whole households) by taking it door to door. Meanwhile, Edina Morningside Congregational Church minister Merrill Beale preached a sermon on the subject and posted copies of the petition for his parishioners to sign, which nearly two dozen did. A week later, Mayor Ken Joyce hand-delivered to every household an open letter that he titled "A Matter of No Prejudice." The letter called on Morningsiders to dedicate the community to "fair play," to live by a commitment to "the Brotherhood of Man," and to follow the Golden Rule. Since the regional and national media had picked up the story, as an emblematic example of the civil rights battles happening throughout the Upper Midwest and Northeast, Joyce used the South as a foil as well. "We are now in a position to demonstrate the real spirit of an honest, God-fearing community," he declared, "or to act impulsively, unthinkingly, and become known as a bigoted, prejudiced, hateful little area that is no better than a portion of the South that we have probably in the past presumed to judge."[26]

With a large number of Morningside residents on record in support of the Taylors, and with an official endorsement by the popular mayor, at their next meeting the village council declined to take possession of the Scott Terrace lot for drainage. That evening a group gathered to celebrate at a party hosted by the Hoags, who lived at 4215 Morningside Road and who had played a key role in the grassroots effort. The dozen guests included others involved in the petition campaign as well as Marion Taylor, the *Edina Courier* reported, "whom they expect to have as a neighbor soon." Yet, despite the initial council victory and the welcome by some Whites, the Black family's ordeal did not end there, and they faced still more obstacles. During the summer, the village tax assessor's office delayed getting necessary tax information to their bank, and bank officers blocked their construction loan. "We feel very, very unjustly treated, in the light of two (2) months stalling off by injudicious bank personnel, resulting into two (2) months set back in getting our home built," Marion complained in a letter to the Farmers & Mechanics Savings Bank president. "As bonafide loan seekers with qualified income, character references, and credit references we would like to know if this is the Banks Policy with all of its loan applicants?" Responding to this pressure, the bank did eventually put the loan through, and the Taylors hired a Black contractor, but the village engineer subsequently delayed permitting at various stages, and the council refused to extend the public water line until the Taylors agreed to pay for it. Additionally, because the move was taking so long, the state highway department began to insist that the Taylors pay a monthly lease to stay in their old house, which, Marion insisted, made his family responsible for Whites' "Racial Prejudice."[27]

In the fall of 1960, Marion and Mary's son Greg started first grade at Morningside Elementary, although, because the Taylors' house was still under construction, he joined the Hoag children when students went home for lunch. Later, after the family was finally able to move in, many Morningside residents befriended them and would visit and invite them to dinners and picnics. Mary was also asked to join the PTA and League of Women Voters, and Marion got involved with the local Boy Scouts troop. These displays of tolerance and acceptance were far from universal though. The next-door neighbors immediately moved out, more than once groups of teenagers called Marion and Mary "niggers" to their faces, and one night someone shot a BB through their front window. Moreover, while Greg reportedly attended school without serious trouble, he was always the only African American in his school, and the halls and classrooms were festering with White prejudice. The year he graduated from Edina East High School, in 1972, for instance, some teachers and students organized a two-day Human Affairs Conference, focused on "racial problems" and "the interrelations of blacks and whites," but the response was mixed and many students simply walked out.[28]

"A Better Chance"

Not surprisingly, the gauntlet the Taylors had to pass through to live in Morningside, and that other Black families had to navigate to move into all-White suburbs elsewhere in the Twin Cities metropolitan region, effectively dissuaded all but a handful of African Americans from making a similar move. Likewise, the early "black pioneers" who did venture into the White suburbs often struggled to be accepted. "Although Minnesota residents are working to bring about a total change in the 'traditional' community attitude," the State Commission Against Discrimination reported in 1968, "there are at present, few communities which would welcome minority families into the mainstream of activity and encourage them to participate in the total spectrum of community life." In fact, after Edina's transformation from a racially integrated village of small farms to a racially exclusive "streetcar suburb," there was no larger demographic or cultural shift there for quite a while, even after it reabsorbed Morningside in 1966. Except for the Taylors, the area remained all White until 1977, when Sandy Berman, a White librarian, moved in with his wife, Lorraine, an African American schoolteacher, and her two kids from a previous marriage to a Black man. They bought a house at 4400

Edina High School's yearbook the *Whigrean* included a spread featuring A Better Chance participants, 1973. *Courtesy Edina Historical Society*

Morningside Road, several doors down from the Hoags and a few blocks over from the Taylors, and nobody tried to stop them or harass them away. But while overt displays of racial prejudice may have been less tolerated, and some White residents continued to openly express their belief in racial equality, incremental change like this did little to fundamentally transform the suburb.[29]

Even the small efforts to address Edina's half century of exclusion betrayed how far the village had regressed from the earlier interracial era. Perhaps most notably, the year after Greg Taylor left Edina to attend college at the Tuskegee Institute, his former high school began hosting participants in "A Better Chance" (ABC), a national program that took "highly motivated students" and located them in "more challenging schools" than they had in their own hometowns. The first group numbered eight Black students and one White student, and a decade later a dozen students were typically enrolled at one time. In 1982, the group included African Americans Kelly Jones, who was from Cleveland, Linda McClora, who was from Memphis, and Johnette Arroyo and Yomi Ajaiyeoba, who were from the Bronx, the four of them living with three other (unnamed) female students at a house on France Avenue. There were also four boys who lived with host families, among them Teo Martinez, who was from Oakland. "What is really interesting about A.B.C.," local director Timothy Young insisted, was "that both the students and Edina High School benefit." The students got a "first rate education," he noted, and "they bring to Edina the diversity which is important in an outstanding school." Yet, in practice, the program separated Black teenagers from their families and communities, housed them as if they were exchange students encountering a foreign culture, and marked them out as oddities at school, which only further highlighted Edina's racial homogeneity. There were certainly "problems involving racial differences," the school newspaper dispassionately reported, "since most A.B.C. students have non-white backgrounds." As Yomi Ajaiyeoba explained, "it's like they [Edinans] are scared to talk to you because of your color."[30]

CHAPTER 6

"This Vicious Vice":
Black Removal in St. Paul

NOT LONG AFTER COMING with his family to St. Paul in 1852—which was a decade after Father Lucien Galtier established the city's namesake chapel, three years after St. Paul was designated the territorial capital, and two years after the city was made a diocese—Irish immigrant John Ireland entered a Catholic seminary. A decade later, on the eve of the Civil War, he was ordained a priest and appointed chaplain to a Minnesota infantry regiment. Within a few years of his discharge, in 1863, he became pastor at the city cathedral, and in the next two decades Ireland became a bishop and then archbishop. As he steadily advanced through the local institutional hierarchy, the unusual White prelate exhibited a pronounced sense of duty to bringing African Americans to the church as well as to advocating for Black civil rights. One of the St. Paul residents he convinced to convert was Afro-American League cofounder Fredrick McGhee, and when the latter organized the league's Emancipation Day celebration in January 1891, he gave the archbishop a prominent place on the program. In Ireland's speech to the crowd, he unequivocally condemned local incidents of discrimination and called for African Americans' full political and social equality, even specifically

146

mentioning interracial marriage. The next month he issued a letter to be read from all archdiocese pulpits expressing similar sentiments, and in April he delivered a sermon declaring that Catholics were "compelled to forget color in all walks of life." Likewise, in May, Ireland traveled to Washington, DC, and voiced his resolutely liberal beliefs there too. "As to substance the colored man is equal to the white man," the archbishop said to one audience. "He has a like intellect, the same blood courses in their veins, [and] they are both equally the children of a common Father." Framing the question in secular terms, he appealed to the nation's founding principles as well. "Every prejudice entertained, every breach of justice and charity against a fellow citizen because of his color," he insisted, "is a stain flung upon the banner of our liberty."[1]

As part of Archbishop Ireland's larger effort to bring African Americans to the Catholic Church, a couple of years before the Emancipation Day event he had directed a curate at the St. Paul cathedral to rent a Swedenborgian church near the racially mixed Rice Park neighborhood for a weeks-long mission. Subsequently, in 1892, McGhee, local black newspaper editor Samuel Hardy, and White priest Edward Casey signed incorporation documents to establish the St. Peter Claver parish, and the assortment of Black and White congregants moved to their own church building a few blocks west from the Swedenborgian church, at Farrington Street and Aurora Avenue. Within three years, the congregation numbered more than three hundred members and had a vibrant parish life, including the Toussaint L'Ouverture Society, a literary study group, the St. Monica's Guild, a women's altar society, as well as an organized choir. Meanwhile, a young journalist named Stephen Theobald, who was born in British Guiana and educated at Cambridge University, made his way to Montreal, Canada. There he befriended some Jesuits and expressed his desire to become a priest, and they referred him to Ireland, who brought him to St. Paul to enter the seminary. Five years later, in the summer of 1910, Theobald was ordained, making him one of only five Black priests in the country. He then became pastor of St. Peter Claver, by which point the congregation counted nearly four hundred "coloreds and whites." Under his capable leadership over the next two decades, the parish continued to grow and serve as a model of integration, not only locally but also nationally, as Father Theobald wrote numerous articles and gave lectures across the country emphasizing the Catholic Church's essential role in ending racial discrimination.[2]

During the time that Fredrick McGhee was helping to establish St. Peter Claver, he and his wife, Mattie, adopted a toddler, whom they named Ruth Lamar McGhee, and in the early part of 1893, the family moved into a large house at 665 University Avenue. Located just a few blocks from the church, the McGhees' new home put them closer to the center of the neighborhood that eventually became known as Rondo. A decade later, in 1902, McGhee and other Black leaders in the Twin Cities hosted the National Afro-American Council's annual convention, which was attended by many prominent Black figures of the era, including Booker T. Washington, Ida B. Wells, William Monroe Trotter, and W. E. B. Du Bois. Disillusioned with Washington's efforts to dominate the council, however, McGhee broke with the group and joined the Niagara Movement launched by Du Bois, whom he had entertained as a guest at his University Avenue home on several occasions. The Niagara Movement evolved into the National Association for the Advancement of Colored People (NAACP), and in 1912 McGhee and St. Paul doctor Valdo Turner established the Twin Cities Protective League in the hopes of affiliating with the national group. Unfortunately, by then McGhee was ill, and he soon died of pleurisy, leaving Turner and others to organize a St. Paul NAACP chapter without him. Additionally, Mattie and Ruth faced worsening financial circumstances, and in 1919 they sold the family home to another Black couple, and Ruth left for a job with the federal government in Washington, DC, with her mother in tow.[3]

Father Theobald remained the pastor of St. Peter Claver Church until shortly before his own death in 1932, and he was replaced by Father Charles Keefe (1933–42), who was succeeded by Father Jerome Luger (1942–54). Following World War II, though, the city of St. Paul began an urban renewal project that would clear the areas adjacent to the state capitol, and Father Luger prepared to move the church once again. Since it was the policy of the archdiocese to build a school before a church, in 1947 he brought three nuns from the Oblate Sisters of Providence in Baltimore to oversee that endeavor, Mother Barbara, Sister Anthony, and Sister Celine, like others in the order each of them African American. The site they chose was on the far western edge of the Rondo neighborhood, at Oxford Street and St. Anthony Avenue, and the new school building was finished in 1950. Open to all regardless of race, income, or faith, the school continued the church's commitment to serving and sustaining an integrated community, and its mix of students, half of whom

The family of Fredrick and Ruth McGhee at their home, 665 University Avenue, St. Paul.

were Black and half of whom were White, reflected that institutional culture. When the church building was completed in the spring of 1957, and Father Arnold Luger (Jerome Luger's brother and replacement as pastor) celebrated the first mass there, the growing congregation and the surrounding neighborhood did too. Gloria Jeanne Lindstrom Lewis met her husband, Robert "Sonny" Lewis, at a Catholic Youth Center dance, for example, and despite the fact that she was White and he was Black, they married and moved in with his parents. They lived at 222 Rondo Avenue, four blocks from St. Peter Claver, where the family regularly attended mass and where all the children eventually went to school. On one side of the Lewis household was a Native American woman named

Susie and on the other was the Jackson family, also racially mixed, while down the block lived several White families. "Everybody practically knew everybody," Lewis remembered, "everybody spoke to everybody, and we weren't really uncomfortable there."[4]

Within a few years of St. Peter Claver's move, however, the neighborhood began to disintegrate. The city's housing and redevelopment authority initiated additional urban renewal projects in the area, and the state highway department started a highway project along St. Anthony, directly in front of the church. Together, the projects displaced thousands of people from their homes, shuttered numerous businesses and social clubs, and gobbled up several of the scarce playgrounds and ballparks. "Rondo," as former resident Nieeta Laurene Neal Presley put it, "was just no more." Additionally, although displaced White residents were

Aerial view of the Western, Eastern, and Mount Airy Projects, preserved in the Union Gospel Mission Records at the Minnesota Historical Society.

able to find new housing in various parts of the Twin Cities and outlying suburbs with little trouble, African American and mixed families faced pervasive discrimination and were limited to housing in the immediate vicinity. In effect, state and local government agencies, with predominantly if not exclusively all-White staffs and largely unaccountable to residents, dismantled the city's most integrated community, forced its largest concentration of African American residents into an ever-smaller area, and thereby intensified the racial segregation of St. Paul. Similar to what Whites did in Edina Village, but on a much larger scale, by the end of the 1960s Whites had fundamentally transformed Rondo, and racial exclusion was a significant feature of the process. Moreover, they did this using federal, state, and city tax money, in collaboration with White private capital, and the greatest benefits went to White suburban dwellers (who utilized the new highway), commercial developers (who profited off property acquisition and rebuilding), and large national corporations (which replaced small local businesses), along with middle-class Whites who gentrified the district in the aftermath.[5]

"I Live Only Where You Let Me Live"

African Americans first began moving to the area west of the state capitol at the end of the nineteenth century, extending along St. Anthony, Rondo, and University Avenues as their numbers increased. By 1930, nearly half of the population there was Black, representing a large majority of St. Paul's Black population overall, although they were noticeably divided by social class. Closer to the capitol, from Rice Street to Dale Street, in what locals called "Cornmeal Valley," the families were lower-middle class and tended to be more recent arrivals, often from the South but many from parts of rural Minnesota counties as well. West of Dale to Lexington Parkway, in what residents called "Oatmeal Hill," the families tended to be more affluent and longer established. Yet both sections had a high proportion of single-family dwellings, often with spacious yards, making for low population densities, and at least until the 1940s they were relatively free of blight. Likewise, numerous public spaces allowed opportunities for African Americans from various backgrounds to meet and interact. For the many residents who were not Catholic, for example, there were several Black Protestant churches. Among them was Pilgrim Baptist Church, at Central Avenue and Grotto Street, and when half of the Pilgrim congregation split off in 1914, they formed another church, what became Mount Olivet, at Central and Mackubin Street. In between was St. James AME, at one time attended by a young Roy Wilkins, who later became editor of the NAACP's *Crisis* magazine and then executive secretary of the organization. Besides these churches, Rondo was also home to a number of Black social clubs, including the Sterling Club, started by members of Pilgrim Baptist Church who were postal workers and railroad porters, with a clubhouse on Dale, and the Wheels Club, for retired railroad workers, with a building on St. Albans Street. There was the lodge for Local 516 of the Brotherhood of Sleeping Car Porters too, the African American union organized by A. Phillip Randolph, which included a women's auxiliary.[6]

Still, greater Rondo was never entirely Black, and racial integration was a daily fact of life among adults as well as children, in peoples' homes, on the streets, at local businesses, in schools, and at various other community spaces. African American Kathryn Corman Gagnon lived at 495 St. Anthony and remembered that, along with the "smattering of Black families" on her block, there were the Adelhelms, who were German, and the Tolendouskys, who were Polish, and the Gottesmans, who were Jewish and owned a grocery at Rondo Avenue and Mackubin Street. Gagnon's class photo from second grade at the McKinley School, in 1941, is further testament to the area's racial mix, counting nine Black girls and four Black boys and twelve White girls and twelve White boys, with one of the Black boys sitting in the front row holding the class sign. Similarly, Anisah Hanifah Dawan, who grew up in a house about a block away from Gagnon, at 403 Carroll Avenue, lived between a Black family and a White family, with numerous other White families nearby, whom Dawan described as Italians, Irish, Swedes, and Poles. "All the kids played together, . . . and parents would be mingling and talking," she recalled. "They weren't prejudiced . . . so we all got along good." Like many of the neighborhood youth, Black as well as White, Dawan frequented the Hallie Q. Brown Community Center, opened in 1929 under the direction of the St. Paul Urban League and, for its first few decades, located in the Masonic Hall at Aurora and Mackubin. Additionally, boys and girls "of both white and colored races" participated in clubs sponsored by the Union Gospel Mission at their Welcome Hall near Rondo and Farrington, while in the summer racially mixed groups attended the Gospel Hill Camp.[7]

Residents were aware of how unusual it was to live in such an integrated neighborhood, and they understood that Rondo's physical boundaries were the boundaries of racial tolerance, beyond which was more typical White hatred. "In the smaller community where we lived, we really didn't see racism or discrimination," Black former resident William Collins Jr. explained, "but then you'd wander too much outside of your neighborhood, if you went north of University, if you went west of Lexington." When he was on a local youth baseball team, for instance, the team typically played at the Oxford Pool and Playground, on the east side of Lexington Parkway. One year, after a game, the White coach, twenty-one-year-old Marine Bill Peterson, who had recently returned home to St. Paul after getting out of the service, decided to treat the mix of Black and White players at a restaurant on University and Snelling, several blocks west. The owner refused to serve them, though, and Peterson was enraged. He filed a complaint with the NAACP, after which there was a boycott and only then did the restaurant finally welcome all. Another year, on Halloween, Collins and a dozen Black friends decided to trick-or-treat on the north side of University Avenue. As it got warm, they removed their masks, revealing that they were not White despite being in an all-White neighborhood. At one house, an older White man came to the door and told them to go back "where you belong," but they continued on and eventually, after residents on the block called the police, officers came and made Collins and his friends leave.[8]

Given the type of neighborhood that Rondo had become by the 1950s, when city officials entertained plans for urban renewal and highway construction they recognized that those projects would displace both Black and White residents. It took several years, however, before they acknowledged the disparities in opportunities for members of the different racial groups to find new housing. The first redevelopment effort by the St. Paul Housing and Redevelopment Authority (SPHRA) focused on the immediate vicinity around the state capitol, on both its western and eastern ends, between Rice and Jackson Streets. With boosterish confidence, and prior to any direct community involvement, SPHRA members presented their plans to a group of realtors and businessmen at the Athletic Club in the latter part of 1951, to give them "a chance to understand and make suggestions for changing the plan before it is submitted to the City Council for approval." Chairman William Randall explained that the housing and redevelopment authority would clear the "slum areas" to make way for private capital to build modern residential units, office buildings, and light industry, which would revitalize commerce in the downtown district as well. He further emphasized that because buying the different parcels and clearing them would take several years, it was "not felt that relocating the families now living in the two areas will be a major problem."[9]

Early the next year, in February 1952, the St. Paul planning board and redevelopment authority convened a joint meeting to officially approve the eastern and western projects, one encompassing fifty-five acres and the other covering sixty-six acres, with the expectation that these would also entail building a "superhighway" along Mississippi and Twelfth Streets and a "double highway" along Rondo Avenue. Together, the two redevelopment projects were expected to cost more than $9 million, of which $6.5 million would come from federal Housing and Home Finance Agency grants-in-aid, $2 million would come from city-owned land sales, and the rest would be covered by local tax funds. Additionally, with 370 parcels to clear in the eastern area and 450 parcels to clear in the western area, the SPHRA put the number of total housing units to be removed at 1,300, which they would purchase "through eminent domain if necessary." With those details worked out, and weeks before taking the plan to a city council meeting, the (White) authority members once again solicited the opinion of (White) business leaders. At a gathering at the exclusive Minnesota Club, William Randall outlined the updated projects to several members of the St. Paul Association of Commerce, including executive director Fred Fisher, and they decided to authorize a special committee to make a report to their board of directors. Meanwhile, the *St. Paul Pioneer Press* published an editorial that ominously warned residents against "doing nothing," leaving "blighted sections" to grow and property values to decline, in turn lowering tax revenues and putting a greater burden on taxpayers outside the district. The only choice, the editorial claimed, was to enact the program proposed by the housing authority and "take advantage of federal aid, clear away the slums, and let private enterprise put in new apartments, homes and businesses."[10]

The SPHRA brought their capitol area plan to the city council during the first week of March, packing the long afternoon meeting with their own members and other public officials. This time, however, local White and Black residents were present too, and they made their opposition clear. A few individuals sarcastically castigated Mayor Edward Delaney, while attorney Joseph J. Ermatinger, representing a group of more than three dozen residents, said he was filing a lawsuit in the district court to halt the projects to protect his clients from "personal injuries." Most of the people who spoke, though, focused on the racial prejudice inherent in the removal process. One resident who spoke up was Sallie Mae Weddington, who, along with her husband, were leading figures in the community, members of Pilgrim Baptist Church, the St. Paul NAACP, and several neighborhood social clubs, and regular volunteers at the Hallie Q. Brown center. The couple was also active in the Aurora–St. Anthony block club since they lived at 260 St. Anthony, on the edge of the western redevelopment boundary (as well as the future path of the double highway through Rondo). "Where are you going to put me?" Weddington rhetorically asked. "I live only where you let me live." Unmoved by her plea and despite the overwhelming public sentiment against the housing authority's plan, the city council voted unanimous approval. Moreover, the next year, in February 1953, District Judge Arthur Stewart dismissed the residents' lawsuit against the SPHRA. They had claimed that the matter was legislative rather than administrative, and therefore the city charter allowed them to put the issue before the voters, but Stewart ruled that the "facts do not constitute a cause of action or grounds for relief" and "do not represent any real controversy."[11]

Although the projects may not have been a matter of legitimate legal dispute or compelling public controversy in the judge's mind, as the housing and redevelopment authority began moving residents, it stoked even more neighborhood opposition. This culminated in a final act of resistance by Reverend George Davis during the summer of 1956. The son of a former White slaveowner and formerly enslaved Black woman, Davis was more than eighty years old and lived with his blind wife, two daughters, and several grandchildren at 304 Rondo, on the far side of the western redevelopment area. He had owned his home for twenty-five years and was the last remaining resident on the block. Davis was, as a *St. Paul Dispatch* reporter put it, "the one holdout against the path of inevitable progress," but the well-known street-corner preacher was not going to go easily. "I don't care about this old shack," he told the reporter, "but this ground is the Creator's and mine." He refused to accept the eviction order a judge had granted as well as the $3,000 that was deposited in an account for him by the SPHRA. "He expressed a bitterness towards White people that I had never heard him express before," his grandson

Nathanial Abdul Khaliq (Nathanial Raymond Davis) later recalled, and "he kept saying over and over again how he wasn't giving up his house." The standoff continued until late fall, when White sheriff's deputies, St. Paul police officers, housing authority officials, and hired movers showed up at the Davis home. "If you force your way in here," Davis told them, "it will be the last time you force anything." Eventually, he relented, and over the objections of his screaming wife, the authorities escorted the family to the curb and the movers took their household items to an apartment building on east University Avenue, leaving it all at the bottom of multiple flights of stairs. Nathanial returned to the Rondo Avenue house after school that day and found White men tearing it up with sledgehammers and axes, not to demolish it but rather to make it unlivable, preventing the family from surreptitiously moving back in. After the confrontation, though, his grandfather was "a shell of a man," beaten down and with no fight left in him, and almost exactly a year later he died.[12]

In the wake of their battle with Reverend Davis and the completion of the removal process, SPRHA members belatedly acknowledged that they had overlooked the obstacles displaced African American residents faced in finding new housing. At the start of the redevelopment projects, the agency had determined that more than a thousand families and more than 250 individuals had to be moved, including 43 Black families and 24 Black individual residents on the eastern side of the capitol and 136 Black families and 52 Black individuals on the western side. To accommodate their needs, the SPHRA had established two offices where staff would help residents with rental listings, housing inspections, and loans to cover a first month's rent, but the racial divergence of relocation was stark. While White families and individuals scattered widely, including 77 families that left the city entirely, most to homes in the Minneapolis suburbs, nearly every single Black family and individual simply moved west of Rice Street, deeper into Rondo, bounded by University Avenue on the north and Dayton Avenue on the south. Describing what had happened in the western area in particular, at a meeting of the St. Paul Council of Human Relations in the latter part of 1957, executive director Warren Shippee admitted that the efforts to move African Americans had been "a complete and total failure." Anticipating the same problem as future urban renewal and highway projects went forward, he insisted that the city pass an open-occupancy ordinance, making it a misdemeanor to refuse to rent or sell property to a person because of their race. "The people will have to decide which they prefer," the director concluded, "the evils that develop from compact ghettoes, or dispersion."[13]

Further tarnishing the SPHRA's record, many local business leaders began to sour on the redevelopment projects as well. The main point of their opposition was the agency's decision to sell nearly half of the thirty-six acres available in the western area to Sears, Roebuck & Co. to build a massive $4 million store. After the authority received the company's bid in early August 1957, Downtown St. Paul Inc., a trade group of small merchants, passed a resolution noting that the original redevelopment plan had called for making the majority of parcels available for residential use, but that portion would be significantly reduced if the Sears deal were allowed to go through, while the portion allotted for commercial use would dramatically increase. This shift to more commercial use would draw shoppers away from downtown businesses, rather than add to the number of residents who might bring their business there. In response to the merchants, the SPHRA agreed to study the group's concerns, yet in November the authority accepted the Sears bid, and later the following year, in March, Downtown St. Paul Inc. sued to stop the land sale. Before the lawsuit was presented in court, chairman Nick J. Smith defended the western area project's land use by noting that the SPHRA, planning board, and city council had approved it multiple times since 1951. Testifying before Judge Stewart, though, Shippee allowed that changes had been made to enlarge the commercial portion, from fifteen to twenty-four acres, and to reduce the residential portion, from twenty-four to seventeen acres. Likewise, he conceded that the number of housing units had been cut in half, from 700 to 350, arguing that surveys had concluded that there was no market for more. Nevertheless, the judge dismissed the suit (as he had with the previous one), and construction for the Sears store began shortly thereafter. The residential portion of the project was then reduced further when another large parcel was developed as a sculpture park.[14]

Even though the SPHRA had inequitably upended the lives of Black residents and thwarted the interests of some of its strongest White supporters in executing its capitol area plan, city and state officials were able to forge ahead with another equally contentious project, construction of an interstate highway segment through Rondo. Running east to west just below the western redevelopment area, between Western

Avenue and Rice Street, the highway would displace another 433 families, almost three-fourths of them African American. This constituted nearly 15 percent of the city's entire Black population, and some of the affected residents had only recently resettled in the wake of previous urban renewal clearances. Additionally, by breaking up the northern section of the neighborhood along St. Anthony Avenue, the highway would shrink the one part of the city where African Americans could find housing without encountering discrimination, thus concentrating their population into an even smaller area. As the reorganized Greater St. Paul Development Inc. contended, drawing on a report that the group hired a private engineering firm to do, the proposed route would make a "Twin Cities of St. Paul," rendering a "permanent split-city which can never be physically or psychologically united." Even city engineer George Herrold opposed the plan and alternatively advised building the highway adjacent to the railroad tracks north of St. Anthony Avenue. Funding from the federal bureau of roads in 1952 and 1954 anticipated the southern route, however, while the capitol redevelopment plan had assumed the same, and in May 1956 the city council approved an order to initiate St. Paul's participation.[15]

Fortunately, because Pilgrim Baptist Church pastor Reverend Floyd Massey was a member of the city planning board, Rondo's Black leaders were aware of the highway project from the start. A year before the city council's vote, Massey joined local businessman Timothy Howard to establish the Rondo–St. Anthony Improvement Association to advocate on behalf of the neighborhood's interests. Although the two men were under no illusions that the highway plan could be stopped, they sought to lobby for a "depressed" rather than "elevated" design (below rather than above grade), assist residents in getting fair appraisals for their homes, and pressure the city to pass a fair housing ordinance that would enable residential integration outside of Rondo. They also sought assurances that the project would stimulate development and bring economic opportunity for those who remained in the neighborhood. Pushed by growing awareness that Black residents displaced by redevelopment found it especially difficult "to procure adequate housing," Governor Orville Freeman also announced the formation of a sixteen-member housing and relocation committee, Massey and Howard among them. Chaired by University of Minnesota professor and Governor's Human Rights Commission member Matthew Stark, the committee included St.

Paul NAACP president Frank Smith, St. Paul Urban League executive director Ernest Cooper, St. Paul Council of Human Relations president Reverend Daniel Corrigan, and SPHRA executive director Warren Shippee as well, along with representatives from the state highway department, municipal public works department, local chamber of commerce, and St. Paul realtors. Together, the organization of the neighborhood association along with the creation of an official committee seemed to promise a more responsive and fair process and outcome, one that did not simply treat Black residents as necessary casualties of what the *St. Paul Dispatch* had called "inevitable progress."[16]

By the end of 1956, Massey and Howard had convinced the St. Paul planning board to recommend a below-grade highway, which was seconded by the city engineer and referred to a city council committee for study, and the highway department eventually approved that design. Yet even after galvanizing and marshaling Black community concern, and with the support of some White political and business leaders, the Rondo–St. Anthony Improvement Association struggled to achieve its other objectives. In the summer of 1957, anticipating the first parcel condemnations, the group organized a meeting with state highway commissioner L. P. Zimmerman at the Pilgrim Baptist Church, which three hundred neighborhood residents attended. The commissioner opened by explaining the reasoning for the Rondo–St. Anthony route to the audience and attempted to prepare them for their removal. "Let me assure you that the department will do everything it legally can do to lighten the impact on your lives," he said. "We know that you are reasonable people and understand that someone has to pay the price of progress." The next year, state officials began systematically disputing the property appraisals made by court-appointed appraisers and countered with offers that were 25 to 30 percent lower. In May, the highway department's deputy attorney general filed appeals in Ramsey County District Court against thirty-seven property owners. Howard urged the residents to not compromise until "competent counsel" studied their cases, pledging that the Rondo–St. Anthony Association would "give whatever assistance . . . to see that justice is done." The St. Paul NAACP came to residents' aid too, threatening to file an injunction against the highway department to stop further condemnations. "The differences between the court and state appraisals in many instances are fantastic," new branch president Leonard Carter wrote in a letter to Governor Freeman, and this was made worse by "a vicious vice" that confined residents to relocation only "in the fringe areas of the so-called ghetto," where prices had gone up "in anticipation of frantic buying."[17]

Earlier that year, realtors had begun approaching White neighborhood residents who lived away from the Rondo–St. Anthony route, asking them to sell their homes to the firms so that they could be resold to people who were being forced out by the highway. The local NAACP and Urban League flagged this as "an effort to obtain property within the area so that Negroes will continue to be contained." Additionally, the two groups reported, when realtors showed those and other Rondo homes to prospective buyers, the sale prices were thousands of dollars higher than the market value. "These practices are typical of a pattern," they insisted, "that has been observed many times in the past whenever there have been mass movements of Negro families either in the expansion of a residential area or as a result of relocation due to urban development or highway programs." In response, St. Paul Board of Realtors executive director David Birt made a public assurance that his organization did not condone such practices, and that they were working with the Urban League to craft a report about relocation, but he did not deny that these things were happening. At the very least, as Birt was certainly aware, with few exceptions displaced Black families were not given the chance to leave Rondo. "We had to honor the color barriers," former resident Teresina Carter Frelix later recalled, "we couldn't move past Lexington." Her parents had a house at 717 Rondo Avenue, and when they looked at a house for sale one block beyond that western boundary, they were rightfully doubtful that they would even be considered. "We went in and the people were nice," Frelix explained, and "they showed us the house and we liked it." Afterward, however, the White owners refused to sell it to them. Instead, the family moved to a house at Aurora and Oxford, one block east of Lexington and just two blocks north of the highway route.[18]

As accounts of bigotry accumulated, the local NAACP held its April monthly meeting at Pilgrim Baptist Church and dedicated it entirely to a discussion of the "housing crisis," which drew another audience of more than three hundred residents. "Housing has become the number one problem facing non-White citizens in St. Paul today," branch president Leonard Carter declared. This was a consequence of several factors, he pointed out, though at the moment it was due in large part to the highway project. "The families to be displaced must be offered an opportunity to purchase decent and attractive housing at current market prices," Carter insisted, "in neighborhoods where they choose to live." And what was really needed to accomplish that, he and St. Paul's other Black community leaders believed, was the kind of open-occupancy legislation that Warren Shippee had recommended, prohibiting racial discrimination in selling or leasing property. The NAACP had first brought the issue to the city council in March 1956, and later that summer the council directed the city's corporation counsel, Marshall Hurley, to draft a proposal, which he did, but the effort quickly stalled. In an attempt to revive the issue, Carter joined Reverend Massey, Timothy Howard, local NAACP housing committee chairman Richard Fox, as well as St. Paul Urban League executive director Ernest Cooper in presenting a petition they had circulated as the Citizens Committee for Open Occupancy, calling for enactment of the open-occupancy bill. Subsequently, by June a city council committee was considering a revised proposal drafted by new city corporation counsel Thomas Ryan, yet their deliberations were slowed by Mayor Joseph Dillon's insistence that the councilmen make a "full report" that provided "more factual data and evidence of citizen support." Then, in July, Citizens Committee chair James Levy and a large delegation of the group's members descended on city hall, and the city council agreed to schedule a public hearing on the "advisability" of adopting an ordinance at the end of August.[19]

On the day of the hearing, the council's chambers were "bursting at the seams," with hundreds of people in attendance. Most of those who came spoke in favor of the law, and they represented a wide variety of backgrounds and interests. Those who spoke against the bill were, as the *St. Paul Recorder* described, "small in number but loud in voice." Jack Waite, for example, acknowledged that he had been unable to find enough supporters to form a St. Paul contingent of his Minneapolis group, the Citizen's Emergency Committee, and he focused primarily on linking the NAACP and Urban League to the Communist Party. Over the course of the ensuing months, however, as the city council deliberated and then delayed taking a vote, there was a growing chorus of White individuals and organizations publicly declaring their opposition to the proposed fair housing ordinance. This was evident at a panel discussion in December, hosted by Reverend S. B. O'Leary at the Messiah Episcopal Church in St. Paul's Highland Park neighborhood. One hundred and fifty people attended the forum, which, O'Leary explained, was meant "to find out the facts" in light of the possibility that displaced Black Rondo residents might be pushed into "present all-white" areas, including their own. While at least two panel participants spoke in favor of the legislation, a greater number were against, and they offered a range of objections. St. Paul Home Builders Association executive director John Bohman branded it a "forced occupancy" law, which would "impose the will of the few on the many" and was therefore "un-American." Fred Luft, a St. Paul Board of Realtors representative, said his organization was opposed because it "penalizes" real estate buyers and sellers, and instead they supported "an educational and religious program." Even more blunt, attorney Ward Fleming, from Minneapolis Homeowners Inc., called the proposed ordinance "one of the most dangerous things to property rights in the past 40 years," claiming that it would mean a homeowner could be thrown in jail for refusing to sell their house to "a Negro."[20]

With the campaign in St. Paul delayed again, and a similar effort in Minneapolis blocked by the city attorney's ruling that open-occupancy legislation violated property rights protected by the Fourteenth Amendment, fair housing advocates turned their attention to passing a state law. At the end of December 1958, Minnesota Council for Civil and Human Rights (MCCHR) president Reverend Denzil Carty announced that his group had drafted a bill that would be sponsored by state senator Donald Fraser in the next legislative session. To build support for this, in February, the Twin City Council of Clubs, an association of three dozen civic, social, and business clubs from the Black community, organized a fair housing march and sent one hundred block workers door to door in Minneapolis and St. Paul. Hearings for the bill before the senate judiciary committee began several weeks later, with supporters of the bill presenting their arguments first, including representatives from the MCCHR, the NAACP, the AFL-CIO, the American Civil Liberties Union, as well as Catholic and Protestant groups. Those opposed followed and made what were becoming familiar if convoluted arguments and wily dodges against the idea of government being empowered to enforce equal access to housing. Bohman appeared again on behalf of the St. Paul Home Builders to declare that the bill would put the rights of a person acquiring property above the rights of a person disposing of property, further contending that it might hinder the progress that had already been achieved toward integration. Similarly, St. Paul Rental Property Association representative Leo Sault said the bill would depress property values until landlords

had to sell their buildings at a loss, depriving them of their constitution-
ally protected right to due process. And St. Paul Board of Realtors legislative committee chairman William Dunn simply claimed that there was
no need for a law because there was no problem. Persuaded by these and
other objections, the judiciary committee voted 11 to 7 to not recommend
the bill for passage, effectively killing it.[21]

Still hoping to achieve some kind of legislative remedy, the NAACP
petitioned the St. Paul City Council to consider the proposed municipal open-occupancy ordinance once more. The council agreed to hold
another day of hearings later in April, yet in the end, despite significant community participation and public pressure, the effort was even
less successful than before. The lively session "probably set a record for
length and intensity," according to the *Pioneer Press,* running four hours
and attended by at least 250 people, many of them having to stand in
the chamber. This time, opponents of a fair housing bill spoke first,
throughout the morning, and supporters followed, throughout the afternoon, each making well-rehearsed arguments. In order to avoid taking
an immediate vote, though, council members passed the matter over to
corporation counsel Lawrence P. Sheahan, claiming they needed his
legal opinion first. Two months later, in August, Sheahan reported back.
He echoed the Minneapolis city attorney's objections to the proposed
ordinance and went even further by insisting that the St. Paul City Council had "no lawful authority" to enact such a law. Council members
then voted to accept his report, outraging Leonard Carter. In his public response, he made a point to highlight the lie of Minnesota and the
North being beacons of racial progress. "It seems unbelievable that while
across the nation ordinances are being enacted preventing discrimination in the sale or lease of property," he said, "in St. Paul, a far northern
city, the city attorney and council find legislation in any form to prevent
discrimination is unconstitutional."[22]

Weeks later, as tensions built between residents and public officials,
Rondo erupted. Following police raids on several social clubs for alleged
violations of liquor and gambling laws, officers stepped up their nightly
patrols in the neighborhood and began ordering individuals who were
out late to show their identification. One Friday evening, when White
detectives Robert Morehead and Frank Yost stopped Robert Price, who
was Black, he refused to comply, and a fight ensued. As Morehead grap-
pled with Price and Yost retreated to the squad car to call for assistance, a

crowd began to gather and throw bottles and rocks, continuing the melee as more squad cars and a fire truck arrived. For the next hour, some three hundred people faced off with forty police wielding nightsticks and using police dogs, and the confrontation ended only after firefighters blasted the protesters with water hoses. All told, a half dozen residents were injured, and another half dozen were arrested and jailed. The next day, police chief William Proetz met with Carter and other community leaders, telling them (as if they were unaware) that the "riot" was likely due to "resentment and a misunderstanding of our increased policing." The following Wednesday, Carter called a meeting at the Hallie Q. Brown Community Center that drew a hundred people, including Mayor Dillon and various officials seeking to mollify the angry residents. Carter's patience had waned, however, and he did not mince words when he addressed the audience and placed blame on St. Paul's leaders, not only for the police harassment but also for a long stretch of general government neglect. "They have not helped us," he asserted, and it was time for "every Negro in the city to register and vote and elect officials who will."[23]

Eventually, of course, the state legislature did pass a moderate fair housing law, to go into effect in 1962, but by then the clearance for the interstate highway was complete and the harm to residents and the neighborhood was done. According to interviews with displaced residents conducted by Hamline University sociology professor F. James Davis, nearly all of the White families left Rondo and dispersed widely in the Twin Cities and suburbs, whereas only a handful of Blacks did, and those few relocated in "small pockets in St. Paul." Many Blacks who tried to find housing elsewhere, whether they succeeded or failed, reported encountering discrimination of various kinds, including real estate agents flatly refusing to let them see a house, steering families to poorer quality homes back in the neighborhood, falsely claiming that houses had already been sold, and quoting exceptionally high down payments or selling prices. Ultimately, Davis concluded, the ease Whites had in moving out combined with the impediments African Americans faced in doing the same meant that what had been a "mixed community" became "primarily black." Moreover, construction of the highway required the destruction of not only many of the neighborhood's single- and two-family homes but also of long-established businesses along Rondo and St. Anthony Avenues, as well as other important institutions and amenities. One of the particularly troubling effects, Scott Price remembered, was the closing of McKinley School on Carroll Avenue, which forced its 569 students to go elsewhere. Most of the four remaining public and private elementary schools nearby were already full, however, and many children had to go outside the neighborhood. Similarly, the Union Gospel Mission lost half of the playground used by its Ober Boys Club and Welcome Hall Girls Club members, forcing the organization to cut programs, make heavier use of its gymnasium, and bus children to other recreational areas.[24]

Despite their own awareness of the upheaval caused by the redevelopment and highway projects in the lives of greater Rondo's African American residents, city officials launched yet another urban renewal initiative in the neighborhood at the very end of the 1950s. In the spring of 1959, the St. Paul Housing and Redevelopment Authority prepared a preliminary study for drafting a final plan to address "neglect and decay" in the Selby-Dale area, bounded by Aurora Avenue, Lexington Parkway, Holly Avenue, and Cathedral Place. As the study noted, however, the agency intended to take a different approach than it had before. On the one hand, there would be genuine and ongoing engagement with local citizens to build "strong support" for the final plan, and on the other hand, there would be far more "conservation and rehabilitation" than "clearance and redevelopment," with adequate assistance provided to those few residents who would be displaced. While the SPHRA commissioners involved in this project were still all White men who lacked any personal experience living or working in Rondo, they seemed to have learned something from the authority's past mistakes. "Experience in every part of the country has shown that citizen participation is essential to the success of urban renewal programs of this or any other type," the commission's study declared, and Selby-Dale was being given priority over others "because residents and other interests in the area have expressed and shown a sincere desire for community improvement on a comprehensive scale." Moreover, as chairman Joseph Gabler later explained, the commissioners now believed that their mission was "making available decent affordable housing for citizens affected by urban and other improvement programs that uproot them from their old homes."[25]

As the chairman was well aware, many of the Selby-Dale residents were African Americans who had been removed for the western capitol area clearance or displaced by highway construction but were blocked from leaving Rondo. By the time the SPHRA released its preliminary

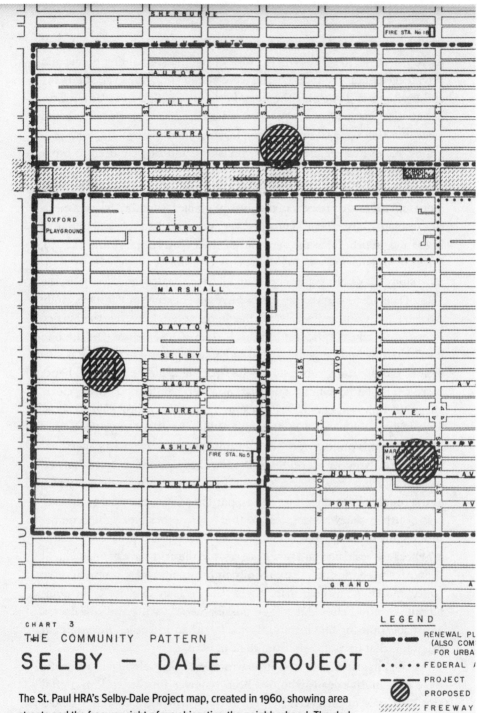

CHART 3

THE COMMUNITY PATTERN

SELBY — DALE PROJECT

The St. Paul HRA's Selby-Dale Project map, created in 1960, showing area
streets and the freeway right-of-way bisecting the neighborhood. The dark
circles show proposed neighborhood centers. The two on the east—the
Hallie Q. Brown Community Center and the Ober Community Center—already
operated, and the other three, marked on top of existing schools, were not built.

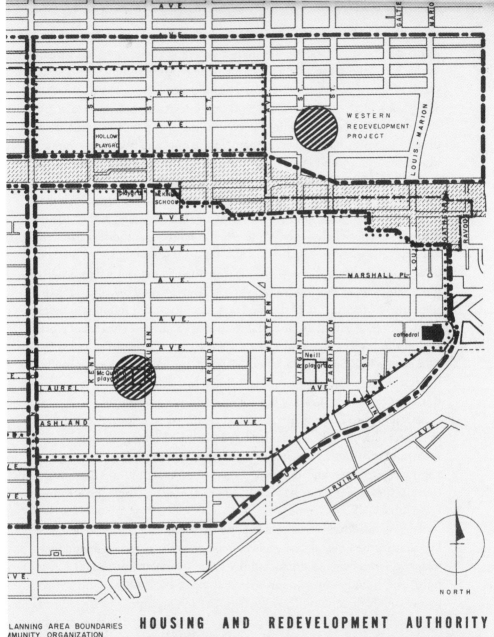

PLANNING AREA BOUNDARIES
MMUNITY ORGANIZATION
AN RENEWAL AREAS)

AID PROJECTS

BOUNDARY

NEIGHBORHOOD CENTER

R.O.W.

HOUSING AND REDEVELOPMENT AUTHORITY

60 EAST FOURTH STREET , SAINT PAUL 1, MINNESOTA

0	500	1000	1500	2000	2500	3000	
							FEET

53 A 19		J.H.S.	
FILE	COMPLETED	PREPARED BY	OFFICIAL REVISIONS

study to the public, nearly all of St. Paul's Black population lived there. Moreover, "non-whites," as the study referred to them, were not spread evenly throughout the area but instead were clustered east of Grotto and south of Iglehart, down to Summit Avenue, a concentration that necessarily coincided with recent changes in the existing housing stock. To accommodate Black relocation as well as natural population increase, property owners had converted many of the one- and two-family homes into three-, four-, and even five-family dwellings, and this section contained the bulk of Selby-Dale's apartment buildings. West of Grotto and north of Carroll, however, the homes were still largely single- and two-family households, with fewer apartment units, and the residents were overwhelmingly White. So, the housing authority observed, although the whole area's density was not excessive relative to the rest of St. Paul, the part where Black residents lived was, with significantly more multifamily dwellings than the city average. Additionally, perhaps indicative of the quality of this housing, the SPHRA's preliminary maps showed that nearly all of the "total clearance" and "spot clearance" work within the project would be done on these blocks, and with the exception of one building near a school site and another near a playground, the rest of the project area was designated for "rehabilitation, conservation (combination)." Besides the matters of disproportionate population density and poor housing quality, the area also "was seriously deficient in open recreational space, organized and equipped play areas, school site areas, and off-site parking space," a deficiency compounded by what the nearby capitol area and highway projects had razed. While there were five playgrounds within the vicinity, there was not a single park within reasonable walking distance.[26]

Seeking to address these problems, with community collaboration as a key feature, the housing and redevelopment authority recommended the formation of a "citizen organization" to complement "municipal direction," one initiated by citizens within the Selby-Dale area but advised by the SPHRA's community organizer. The main purpose of the citizen organization, they said, was "to provide an opportunity for its members to consider together matters of mutual interest and arrange for appropriate action," working toward "community improvement" rather than "protection of the status quo." Once in place, the agency expected that the group would play an important "liaison" role, educating local residents, sustaining their "morale," and directing their participation. In line with the project's emphasis on "rehabilitation," the SPHRA also would rely on the community group to report code violations, neighborhood nuisances, and "other dissatisfactions with the neighborhood environment," as well as assist individual property owners in making voluntary improvements to the exterior and interior of their home or building. Further down the list, recommendation #21 was a vague suggestion that the group "aid in eliminating racial or other minority problems." And that lesser priority, so unspecified, revealed the distance the housing and redevelopment authority still had to go to understanding and confronting the causes of so-called urban blight. Likewise, it might explain at least in part why the proposed citizen organization never came to be and why it was the St. Paul Urban League that ultimately served as the voice of neighborhood residents.[27]

In early March 1959, the Urban League's board of directors approved the Selby-Dale plan and directed its housing committee to determine what needed to be done to implement it. The group arranged a public meeting at the Hallie Q. Brown center, which included the SPHRA community organizer Dorothy Holtz, and following that they sent a petition with one hundred signatures to Mayor Dillon requesting the project's approval by the city council. Several weeks later, more than two hundred residents attended another meeting at Marshall Jr. High School to listen to a panel of city officials. This panel included Dorothy Holtz, Joseph Gabler, and Norton Kent from the housing and redevelopment authority as well as city planning board director Herbert Wieland. In their remarks, the officials stressed the need for "community help and acceptance" in their efforts toward "renewing and rebuilding," and they promised more opportunities for citizens to be heard. A few months after this, when the city attorney ruled the open-occupancy ordinance unconstitutional, and prospects for Black residents ever being able to move out of their increasingly delimited section of St. Paul were dimmed, the *Minneapolis Morning Tribune* reported, "Negro leaders" were even more inclined to look to the SPHRA "for relief with the Selby-Dale project."[28]

Just as formalized community engagement never cohered, however, by the next year the whole initiative was in disarray. Because the capitol redevelopment projects had not yet been completed, the federal Department of Housing and Urban Development (HUD) denied the housing authority's grant application for the Selby-Dale project. Subsequently, in September, when SPHRA executive director Louis Thompson submitted

a revised plan to the city council, the agency had modified it to emphasize urban renewal "by property owners alone instead of as a joint
citizens-and-government effort." For the immediate future, the SPHRA
would limit its role to "a comprehensive study of all structures in the
area to determine what work will be needed and to encourage owners
to proceed with repairs." A few days later, frustrated by long-simmering
tensions with the mayor, Thompson resigned, and Dillon appointed William R. Carter Jr. in his place. Dillon himself was not reelected, though,
and two years later, in April 1962, chairman Joseph Gabler, who had
once been Dillon's campaign manager, also resigned from the housing
authority. This was after he made his own failed bid for mayor with the
support of organized labor, civic organizations, and other community
groups. The winner in the mayoral election, Republican George Vavoulis,
replaced Gabler with the former assistant director of the federal housing
administration in the Twin Cities, Patrick Towle. In the wake of the political shake-up, at another meeting at the Hallie Q. Brown center, this one
attended by three hundred Selby-Dale residents, North Central Community Council president Leroy Lazenberry summed up the inauspicious
situation and discouraging prospects for the neighborhood. The SPHRA
was now "an impotent and supine group," he declared, and meanwhile
all he had heard from Mayor Vavoulis was "double talk."[29]

"Pursuing Some End Based on Bigotry"

In the year before he tendered his resignation from the St. Paul Housing
and Redevelopment Authority, Joseph Gabler and his colleagues were
drawn into a battle with White St. Paul residents opposed to public housing. These residents were part of a newly formed coalition of groups provoked into being by the gathering push for housing integration in the
Twin Cities and the surrounding suburbs. Established in the spring of
1961, the United Citizens League (UCL) was composed of ten smaller
organizations, and cochair William F. Schilling claimed they represented
a total of five thousand members. "We're all for a man of any race or
creed or color building or buying a home wherever he can," he stated,
but "We're against public housing as such because we think 'the more
you give 'em, the worse they get.'" Gabler skewered the coalition for this
barely coded racism and declared that it was "pursuing some end based
on bigotry." The league's response was to appear before the St. Paul City

Council and demand an investigation of the housing and redevelopment authority for mismanagement of its budget as well as for staff "playing too much golf." These accusations gained no traction, though, so the UCL circulated a petition to have a ballot referendum for an ordinance requiring all new housing projects to be submitted to voters for approval. By the early part of 1962, the group supposedly had ten thousand signatures, well over the needed threshold. Corporation counsel Robert J. Swords upended the petition drive, however, with a legal opinion that the proposed ordinance dealt with a matter that was a state rather than a city concern. Despite this second setback, the league and its affiliate groups persisted in their community organizing and vocal opposition, and to avoid drawn-out battles with the coalition, the SPHRA simply stopped proposing more "family" public housing projects. With the exception of expanding the Mount Airy project in the capitol's eastern area in 1967, the only new construction projects undertaken by the authority during the rest of the decade were more politically palatable high-rises for the elderly.[30]

As they had intended, the United Citizens League had effectively blocked low-income Black families in Rondo from finding affordable public housing outside of their shrinking neighborhood. At the same time, African Americans there also discovered that the new open-occupancy law was unlikely to remove impediments to renting apartments and purchasing homes very speedily, even those just on the other side of the area's recognized boundaries. In 1963, the first year that the State Commission Against Discrimination (SCAD) handled housing discrimination cases, it dealt with sixty formal complaints of discrimination, and the next year that number increased to eighty-six. The greatest number of cases involved property owners refusing to rent to prospective tenants, although changing the terms of a rental or sale was a somewhat common violation of the law as well. In one instance, African American Gloria Page answered a newspaper advertisement for an apartment at 1037 Dayton Avenue, owned by Philip Rosenblum, who was White. When she first went to see the place, the caretaker's wife showed it, and the current tenant confirmed that he was moving out. When Page later called Rosenblum, however, he asked if she was a "Negro," and when she said yes, he asked for character references, which SCAD investigators noted was commonly required only for Black prospective tenants "as an obvious attempt to delay." The building owner never called her references, and when Page tracked him down, he told her that the tenant had decided to stay. SCAD investigators determined there was "probable cause," but the Black prospective tenant was still unable to rent the contested apartment.[31]

Ironically, when other areas of the Twin Cities began to open up to Rondo's African American residents, the St. Paul Housing and Redevelopment Authority resumed the Selby-Dale urban renewal project, renaming it the Summit-University project, and the increased property values and higher rents that resulted started pushing Blacks out. The one portion of the original plan the agency had managed to achieve in the early part of the 1960s, before HUD slowed it down, was to clear out forty-eight acres alongside the St. Paul Cathedral to build a technical school, removing rather than rehabilitating the mix of single- and multi-family homes that were in the way. It took several more years, and a lobbying trip to Washington, DC, by local business, labor, and government leaders, to secure federal funding to continue the project. Yet there was still another delay when the city acquired additional federal money by including the area in the Model Cities program, which set up a two-year-long battle between the SPHRA and program staff over control of the project. In the interim, the housing authority tapped Neighborhood Development Program funds to selectively clear housing in the area. Once the two government agencies reached a compromise, at the end of 1970, more displacement, relocation, and clearing followed, and by the end of the decade, the project had cost $32 million. That kind of significant public investment formed the base for extensive gentrification, facilitating improvements that attracted middle-class Whites while increasing the cost of housing that forced out poor and working-class Blacks. By the mid-1980s, urban geographers Judith A. Martin and Antony Goddard observe, this gentrification process was evident in various sections of the neighborhood, where parts of the past lingered next to features of the new present. The Urban League office sat across from the "meticulously restored" Blair House condominiums on Selby Avenue, for instance, and a "tattered" soul food restaurant faced a "nattily restored" Victorian firehouse that had been turned into a fern-bar restaurant. There were remnants of the racially mixed and comparatively tolerant community that Rondo once was, but the neighborhood taking its place was moving ever further from that ideal.[32]

CHAPTER 7

"The First Negro Family on Our Block": A Housing Integration Campaign in Bloomington

BY THE TIME the 1851 treaties of Traverse de Sioux and Mendota stripped the Dakota people of their extensive lands and forced them to the Lower and Upper Sioux Agency reservations, White Christian missionary Gideon Pond had been ministering to the area's native population for nearly two decades. He and his brother Samuel had come to the Minnesota territory in 1833, and over the next ten years they intermittently lived in a house they built near the Mdewakanton village at Bde Maka Ska. When Dakota chief Cloud Man moved the band to make a village closer to the Minnesota River, Gideon Pond followed and established the Oak Grove Mission. In 1855, as White settler-colonists arrived and claimed the land the treaties made available, Pond founded Oak Grove Presbyterian Church and ministered to that growing community as well. Yet even after the federal government moved the Dakota to more distant reservations in 1863 and Pond moved his church to the juncture of Old Shakopee Road and Penn Avenue a year later, the missionary did not give up his work among the Native Americans. A few Dakota families remained in the area, and at least a dozen individuals were members of the Oak Grove congregation. Pond held regular church services and taught Sunday school classes for them in the Dakota language, and he not only married the Native couple John Lawrence and Anna Bluestone but also buried at least ten Dakota in the Bloomington Cemetery. Once he finally retired, in 1873, his son Edward and Edward's wife, Mary, returned from their own missionary service on South Dakota and Nebraska reservations, and they taught Dakota Sunday school classes at Oak Grove too. They did this for another twenty years, but just before the turn of the century the small group of Native people purchased land near the old Lower Sioux Agency and moved there.[1]

Over the next two decades, Bloomington continued to center around Oak Grove Presbyterian Church, as well as an adjacent town hall, and the population grew to more than one thousand residents, most of them farmers. With the exception of African American Walter Harris, a servant in the household of church charter members George and Hana Chadwick, and Black "gun club manager" V. McHenry Nall, his wife Lulu, and their adopted son Clyde Thompson, all of those residents were White. By the 1920s, even Harris and the Nall family were gone, and developers were buying open farmland and turning it into subdivisions. The Yale Realty Company was first, in 1921, selling lots for "Waleswood" on 240 acres that had been part of the Charles Wales estate, located along the Minnesota River bluffs just south of the Old Shakopee Road and Penn Avenue juncture. Ara Berdan was next, with a forty-acre development north of the juncture, on the other side of Nicollet Avenue, in what would become East Bloomington. Subsequently, many more people were drawn to the area, and by the start of World War II the population had increased to more than 3,600. After the war, as Bloomington made its final transformation from rural township to metropolitan suburb, the number of inhabitants swelled to nearly ten thousand. Then, between 1950 and 1960, the population grew fivefold, to more than fifty thousand residents, and it was still a vast White enclave, with fewer than a dozen Black residents. Just as they had done in nearby Edina and Morningside, as well as Brooklyn Center and St. Louis Park, developers, realtors, and homeowners in Bloomington had colluded in all manner of overt and covert ways to prevent Blacks from disturbing the community's racial uniformity, and for a long stretch of years they were overwhelmingly successful.[2]

Looking north on Penn Avenue South at Old Shakopee Road, Bloomington, 1907. On the right is Oak Grove Presbyterian Church, which was moved to this location in 1864.

In the early part of 1962, however, African Americans Charles and Josie Johnson moved into a four-bedroom rambler at 9321 Briar Lane, in West Bloomington, and Josie auspiciously brought with her a wealth of experience as a civil rights activist. She had been born in 1930 and grew up on the west side of Houston, Texas, her parents both college-educated and prominent figures in the community. Her mother, Josie Bell McCullough Robinson, was a tutor and unofficial community caseworker, while her father, Judson Robinson, started a real estate company building public housing and helped to establish the Houston Urban League. The younger Josie went to Fisk University in Nashville and graduated with a degree in sociology in 1951, after which she married Charles "Chuck" Johnson, who had also graduated from Fisk, with an engineering degree. In 1956, he got a job at the Honeywell plant in Minneapolis, becoming the third African American engineer hired there, and the family, which now included their daughter, Patrice, moved to south Minneapolis. The Johnsons soon joined the Minneapolis Urban League and NAACP, and after Josie met Celia Logan, one of Chuck's White colleagues, she got involved with the League of Women Voters (LWV). By 1960, she was an officer on the boards of the NAACP and Minnesota LWV and a community organizer for the Urban League. As the campaign for state fair housing legislation gathered momentum, Josie became chief lobbyist for the effort as well, working out of office space at the Minnesota Fair Employment Practices Commission, provided by her good friend and assistant director Richard Fox. During the spring legislative session of 1961, when the proposed bill got held up in committee, she personally interceded with Republican Governor Elmer Andersen in a meeting at the governor's office, and he declared his unqualified support in a written note to committee members. That got the bill to the floor and passed by the senate, by a one-vote margin, and Andersen signed it, making Minnesota one of the first states in the country to enact a fair housing law.[3]

By 1972, Josie Johnson was on the University of Minnesota's Board of Regents. She is pictured with a Mr. and Mrs. Sandstrom at a meeting in Grand Rapids.

By the time the housing legislation went into effect, and the Johnsons moved into their new home on Briar Lane in West Bloomington, Greater Minneapolis Interfaith Fair Housing Program (GMIFHP) executive director James Tillman and his wife, Mary, bought a house in West Bloomington too, at 3229 West Old Shakopee Road. Tillman had earned a master's degree in sociology from Atlanta University in 1948 and went on to serve as personnel dean and professor at Fisk from 1952 to 1956. He left Nashville the next year and worked as a foreign service officer at the US State Department in Latin America and East Asia until 1959. That summer, after Louise Walker McCannel hired Tillman to run the GMIFHP and he moved his family to Minneapolis, they experienced their own encounter with housing discrimination in the city. At first, they tried working through Unitarians for Equal Opportunity, which maintained a listing of rental and sales properties whose owners pledged not to discriminate, but when the Tillmans went to see one of the houses listed for rent, the White owner gave them various reasons why it was no longer available. Instead, the owner offered to move into the house himself and let the family stay where he was currently living—what Tillman later described as "a dilapidated slum type of house located on the edge of a series of railroad tracks." Following this, Tillman called about rentals listed in the newspaper and found those closed to Blacks too. Only after that frustration, and Black Reverend C. L. Parker's intervention, did Tillman find Jewell Simmons, "a retired Negro hog farmer," who was willing to rent the first floor of his duplex on First Avenue South, one block from the route for Interstate 35W. Not particularly happy with this arrangement, the family moved to the western suburb of Wayzata the following summer, in August 1960, and two years after that they moved to the house on Old Shakopee Road.[4]

In the face of slow and very slight progress toward racial integration, and drawing on Josie Johnson's and James Tillman's activist credentials and tireless initiative, during the spring of 1964 a small group of Bloomington residents began organizing to address the community's exclusive Whiteness. This effort started with discussions among Johnson and local members of the Minnesota League of Women Voters, which had joined several other organizations the year before to establish a Women's Committee on Civil Rights. Those discussions in turn led to a gathering of nearly two dozen people at the home of Barton and Anne Williams, where they formed a "human relations committee" and elected Charlotte

Morse as acting chair. Other than the Johnsons and Tillmans, however, everyone in attendance was White, and the group decided it "needed to spend much time studying the phenomenon of racism before it moved into a serious program of activity." Meeting through the summer, they read and discussed a range of books, viewed films, listened to recordings of lectures, and heard from guest speakers. By September, they felt ready to officially establish the Bloomington Human Relations Committee (BHRC) and elected Charles Lutz as chair, Charlotte Morse as vice chair, and Dorothy Perry as secretary. They also set up several working committees to focus on specific topics, including one on housing chaired by Sue Seymour, one on employment chaired by Robert Burgenstein, and one on neighborhood education chaired by Lynn Taylor.[5]

The BHRC maintained its multiple committees over the next several years, although most of the group's efforts focused on housing integration, which members saw as the key to addressing White prejudice and affecting desegregation more broadly. "The perpetuation of caucasian [*sic*] islands anywhere in America through exclusion of members of any group," one early statement of purpose declared, "is the primary condition behind the shaping of the personality-crippling segregationist mentality." In initial discussions about why racial exclusion was so pervasive and persistent, they gave particular attention to White apprehension about race mixing and interracial sex. A few weeks after the initial gathering at the Williams home, in 1964, the two dozen participants met again and, the minutes noted, several insisted that "one of the underlying problems is the fear of miscegenation, and the group needs to understand this at the outset." They continued to engage the topic at their next meeting a couple of weeks later, with a much longer discussion led by James Tillman. In fact, the Greater Minneapolis Interfaith Fair Housing Program had confirmed the significance of White fears about so-called "miscegenation" earlier that spring in a pilot study led by Donald Irish, a Hamline University sociologist. Commissioned by Tillman, Irish and his interview team surveyed more than two hundred Black and White residents in suburban neighborhoods scattered throughout the Twin Cities metropolitan area. Among the large majority of Whites who objected to living near African Americans, they frequently mentioned the possibility that children would "mingle" and eventually intermarry. "When a [White] child grows up with colored people," one explained, "there is more chance of that barrier being broken."[6]

The other concern the BHRC explored, and which Whites in the Irish study often cited, was that, once allowed, "Negroes would overrun the neighborhood" and "property values would decrease." This idea was built into long-established practices of mortgage lenders and real estate brokers and that is part of the reason it was so widespread among White homeowners. After the federal Home Owners' Loan Corporation's 1938 *Underwriting Manual* introduced color-coded lending risk maps, which closely corresponded to racial demographics, private banks adopted them too. Banks used the maps to avoid mixing "inharmonious races and classes," denying mortgages to Black applicants in highly rated White neighborhoods, assuming that was essential to maintaining existing property values. Similarly, the National Association of Real Estate Boards' 1924 Code of Ethics stated very plainly that a realtor should never introduce "members of any race or nationality, or any individuals whose presence will clearly be detrimental to property values." Decades later, the Minneapolis Board of Realtors was among several state boards that supported removing all references to race (and religion) in the code, but blatant and routine discrimination by brokers continued throughout the Twin Cities and surrounding suburbs. In one case investigated by the State Commission Against Discrimination (SCAD), for example, realtor Eugene Snow distributed a "Home-a-Gram" advertising his services and describing a plan for "neighborhood control." All homes for sale in a particular area would be listed with him, and residents would collude to selectively find buyers "to have the character of their neighborhood preserved and the value of their property maintained." SCAD issued a complaint to Snow, and he claimed that he had dropped the scheme, but he and other brokers were never sanctioned for discrimination and thus were undeterred.[7]

With these considerations in mind, in their pitch to neighbors, school administrators, clergy, and government officials Bloomington Human Relations Committee members fixed on attracting the respectable "Negro family" and, in line with this, emphasized the group's commitment to aiding "stability." They contended that "integrated housing is inevitable" yet insisted that there were ways to avoid or at least lessen the "frictions and fears" that would make the process difficult for and possibly disadvantageous to Whites. With "special efforts," housing committee chair Sue Seymour explained in a presentation to realtors, "stability in both community life and property values ... can be maintained in this transitory period." Still, even this markedly temperate appeal to conventional middle-class values failed to convince many Whites, and into the next decade Bloomington activists made little headway in dismantling racial exclusion. By the end of the 1960s, the population had grown to nearly 82,000 but included just eighteen Black residents, no more than there were in 1962. This failure was a consequence not only of the committee's timidity with Whites but also—despite the roles that Josie Johnson, James Tillman, and other African American advisors played—the result of their disconnect from Blacks. As Sabathani Baptist Church pastor Stanley King declared at the BHRC's May 1966 meeting, "there is still a feeling of superiority among Whites who want to make decisions for Negroes." Having recently become chairman of the Minneapolis All Negro Coalition, composed of Blacks in the NAACP, Urban League, Ministerial Alliance, Fair Employment Practices Committee (FEPC), Mayor's Human Rights Commission, and other groups, he insisted that "Negroes want whites to work *with* them, not for them." Integration had to be a "two-way street," King continued, "and not just a matter of moving Negroes into white areas" or placing Black children in predominantly White schools. This required White liberals to relinquish leadership in civil rights, which was not something committee members and others seemed willing or likely to do.[8]

"A Minimum of Turmoil"

The League of Women Voters cohort that initially proposed the idea of a human relations committee in Bloomington met four times between January and March of 1964 before putting out a general call. After an "enlarged group" met in the first week of April, meeting minutes recorded, residents gathered again at the end of the month, at the home of Charles and Betty Chambers, where they engaged in a wide-ranging discussion about their goals. One participant gave a brief report on the North Suburban Human Relations Committee, which had organized a few months prior and hosted several community-wide workshops, with plans to set up neighborhood discussion groups. This sort of educational outreach appealed to some of those present, while others, not necessarily disagreeing, said "the real problem was to get families of minority races to move into Bloomington." That sparked a debate about the cause of residential segregation. A small number claimed it was due to Blacks' inability to afford homes in the suburbs, and other participants corrected them by noting instances when African Americans did attempt to buy but were refused by sellers or realtors. A few also cited fears of miscegenation, arguing that was the reason why "so many people will go along with equality in almost any field except housing." This returned the discussion to the need for education, one participant musing that "realtors do what the community wants them to [do]." At the end of the meeting, one contingent argued again that "educating the community is not enough—that the best thing would be to help Negroes get homes in Bloomington—integrate, then educate." They proposed submitting an open letter to realtors in the newspaper, followed by letters to the editor. There was no general agreement about any of this, though, and residents resolved to resume the discussion in a couple of weeks.[9]

At the next gathering, on May 5, the continuing division over the group's purpose was on display again, revolving more specifically around the question of whether the council should focus on "study" or "action." "Bloomington will not become integrated in significant numbers in the near future," one member asserted, yet "uprooting racism can be worked on even so." Another countered that "there is more self-education in participating in integrating one family than in discussing racism for two years." They were not suggesting studying racism for two years, the first member responded, but more like two months, to develop a "nucleus of speakers to go out into the community." The back-and-forth continued until James Tillman interceded and declared that the proper purpose of the group was both study and action, which seemed to pacify, if not satisfy, both sides of the debate. Following this, the discussion shifted to a paper Tillman had prepared and circulated beforehand, which asked what was behind the question "Would you want your daughter to marry a Negro?" The question elicited many different answers, including "fear of the unknown," "one is naturally paternal about one's child's marriage," and "sexual competition between Negro and white." Others elaborated, suggesting that the question "had the implication of rape and of the white girl not being virtuous," while someone else pointed out that racism "was not all sexual in origin" and could be due to "fear of economic competition." Perhaps as Tillman intended, no single explanation stood out, yet the discussion had focused members' attention, and they decided to follow up with another conversation about how to respond to a person who asked about miscegenation.[10]

In June, the group developed a general plan of educating themselves about race and racism as well as drafting and discussing a statement of purpose, with continued "guidance of a professional nature" from James Tillman. At the first meeting that month, they hosted African American Calvin Watson, executive director of the Governor's Human Rights Commission, and he acknowledged that "in a community where there are not too many minorities, it is difficult to define the problems and answer the question of what shall we do." To help with this, he reviewed what other human relations committees had already done in places like Duluth, Brooklyn Center, and the St. Paul suburb of White Bear Lake, and he encouraged members to focus on creating a climate that would attract "minority families." The next month, when Sue Seymour presented the statement of purpose she had drafted, Watson's suggestion was prominently featured. Bloomington was "an almost entirely white community," it read, and "efforts are needed to encourage an unprejudiced atmosphere conducive to further integration of housing, in the schools and in employment." Still, the finer question of how to go about that remained unsettled, and more debate followed. In one heated exchange, Joseph Perry insisted that the suburb was ready for integration and the problem was "to get Negroes to move in, rather than getting people to accept them." Charlann Suel disagreed, and at the next meeting, she presented a lengthy statement of her own to explain. "Some members feel that we should actively aid Negroes," she said, while "others, myself included, believe that we will aid the cause of racial justice more by acting indirectly in preparing the ground in our community to accept with a minimum of turmoil the fact of inevitable integration." In her mind, the aim was to make clear how the BHRC could help lessen "friction and discord," and to do this they needed "to convey the impression that our main concern is with the welfare of our community rather than the welfare of the Negro."[11]

As the Bloomington group struggled to find its way, in mid-July Josie Johnson joined three other women on a weeklong trip to Mississippi, where Congress of Racial Equality and Student Nonviolent Coordinating Committee activists were working on the "Freedom Summer" voter registration campaign. Besides Johnson, the interracial and interfaith delegation included Barbara Cunningham, who was White and one of a dozen Brooklyn Center residents who had established their own human relations committee, as well as Mary Kyle, who was Black and from Minneapolis, and Maxine Nathanson, who was White and from St. Paul. They were taking part in the "Wednesdays in Mississippi" initiative, sponsored by the National Council of Negro Women, and because of the dangers there, they were required to travel in segregated pairs in "fast, locked cars." One day, the four women visited a Freedom School in Vicksburg, which was bombed later that same evening, and another day they attended a human rights commission meeting, which had to be held in the federal post office for security reasons. These experiences made the women better understand the difficulties activists faced in the South, and how much safer it was for them to organize in the North. Talking with local White women, they confronted the constraints of patriarchy too, a dimension that was not so pronounced in their efforts in the Twin Cities. "Women involved in human relations work have to lie to their husbands about where they are going and what they are doing," Cunningham explained in a presentation to the Bloomington committee later in September, and even though the League of Women Voters declared their neutrality in that year's elections, "several husbands made their wives withdraw from the group."[12]

At the same September meeting that Cunningham made her presentation, participants also officially established themselves as the Bloomington Human Relations Committee (thereafter they used "committee" and "council" interchangeably). The newly elected officers reflected gender parity, though Charlotte Morse moved from temporary chair to vice chair, and Charles Lutz became the new chair, while Sue Seymour took charge of a housing committee. In the months that followed, residential integration remained the group's main focus, and they hosted several high-profile speakers on the topic, including SCAD chair Kennon Rothchild, SCAD executive director James C. McDonald, and St. Paul Human Rights Commission representative Seth Phillips. Rothchild, who owned a realty and mortgage banking company in St. Paul, joined them at a meeting in mid-December and sanguinely contended that Twin Cities real estate agents were "coming around" to accepting the state's fair housing law. They were realizing that the legislation was "an aid rather than a threat to their business," he said, because it took responsibility for community integration out of their hands, constrained sellers who otherwise might discriminate, and "kept residents from panicking when integration occurs." Likewise, Rothchild assured council members that nothing happened to property values when "a minority group person moves in," yet he stressed the need for the Bloomington group "to calm their neighbors' fears and help them accept integration."[13]

The objections that Whites most often raised in opposing residential integration—declining property values and interracial marriage—were featured prominently in two of the films that council members screened that fall and winter. Both released in 1957, *All the Way Home* and *Crisis in Levittown* had become essential viewing for fair housing activists, each presenting the details of a supposedly typical experience of a Black family moving into an all-White suburb. *All the Way Home* was a composite dramatization, covering a narrative arc from the moment neighbors started calling one another when they heard the news to interactions and meetings where enlightened realtors, bankers, and ministers put the community at ease. Toward the end, the film gave particular emphasis to the idea that home prices go up when a suburb is racially integrated, citing a University of Chicago study, as long as Whites manage not to panic. Similarly, *Crisis in Levittown* put the spotlight on the reaction of White residents, though it was a documentary centered around the real case of African Americans William and Daisy Myers moving into the Levittown, Pennsylvania, suburb. One woman in the film cited her family's prior experience in Washington, DC, as evidence "that property values will immediately go down if [Blacks] are allowed to move in here in any numbers." Moreover, she said, integration in housing "will end up with mixing socially" and "mixed marriages." These and other comments were interspersed, however, with strong counterarguments. "I don't think the Myers have anything to do with property [values] decreasing or increasing," another woman declared. "I think it's purely a White problem, it's not a Negro problem." The narrator also cited several studies, explaining that they showed "among the reasons Negroes have for seeking equal opportunities, intermarriage is the least, and of all the fears that Whites express, this is the greatest."[14]

As BHRC members refined their thinking and purpose through the start of the new year, the neighborhood education committee organized a series of community meetings, held over five Sundays in February and March. Originally proposed by Calvin Watson, the gatherings were advertised as "The First Negro Family on Our Block" coffee parties. "We needed to 'do something,'" the committee report quoted one member saying, "and we did and the sense of taking a first step was rewarding and generated enthusiasm." Twenty different parties were held in as many neighborhoods, with a total of 350 people attending. Each was hosted by a BHRC couple or individual, all of them White, in their own home. Each party also typically involved a featured speaker, a mix of Whites and Blacks, including representatives from SCAD, the Minneapolis Mayor's Commission on Human Rights (one of whom was Josie Johnson), the Anti-Defamation League, and the St. Paul Urban League and NAACP (though, oddly, none from the Minneapolis branches). The speakers and subsequent discussions often emphasized property values and intermarriage in the context of housing integration, directly confronting the most controversial questions. In addition, with weekly coverage in the local and Twin Cities newspapers, the "publicity was excellent and resulted in many people calling to enquire about the BHRC." There were some complaints among the membership that most of those who participated were already committed to the cause, committee chair Lynn Taylor acknowledged, but "hosts and hostesses had learned a great deal about where their own neighbors stood when they issued the initial invitation."[15]

Near the end of March, the housing committee prepared to make presentations at realty companies' weekly sales meetings, and committee chair Sue Seymour developed a draft of what she and others would say. "It may be that some people think the Bloomington Human Relations Council is stirring up trouble," the draft read, but on the contrary they were "trying to do just the opposite," providing "insurance" against trouble. "We believe it is in everybody's interest to promote quiet, rational, regular discussion of racial and minority questions and problems," to avoid the "misunderstanding and fear which harms both human beings and, sometimes, property values." The BHRC could help brokers and realty companies with "grumbling neighbors" who might jeopardize sales or lead to panic selling, offering to talk with them as well as calling in "clergy or professionals" to do the same. Yet, Seymour's draft asserted, realtors had to do their part too. If they are working with a "minority family," brokers should check the council's map showing the location of members and which neighborhoods were "insured," supposedly where they would not encounter prejudiced homeowners. Likewise, they could notify the BHRC if any difficulties arose from a minority family expressing interest in buying a house, let the group know when there was a sale to a minority family, and make the minority family aware that there was a human relations council available to assist them. To test out this pitch, Seymour, Robert Burgenstein, and Ginger Wolner spoke to agents at one of Christy Realty's April sales meetings, and they reported afterward that the talk was "well-received." Encouraged by the favorable reception, the next month they sent letters to all the local companies describing the BHRC and offering help "maintaining stability in integrating neighborhoods" as well as inviting the companies to a presentation that would be attended by SCAD chair and fellow realtor Kennon Rothchild.[16]

In the spring of 1965, the Bloomington council also became (somewhat) involved with the Twin Cities Metropolitan Clearing House Information Center (MCHIC), which was established by the Catholic Interracial Council's Housing Committee the year before. The MCHIC steering committee was made up of representatives from various participating human relations groups, and according to Seymour's description in the BHRC newsletter, its main purpose was to find houses for sale and apartments for rent "on a non-discriminatory basis" and provide that information to "minority group buyers." This caused disagreement among members, however, some of whom questioned the approach. In Seymour's report at the April 6 BHRC meeting, she noted that the primary method of collecting information about nondiscriminatory housing was by residents filling out and returning cards about available housing in their area. A few council members objected, arguing that "it was patronizing to provide a list of houses where one could go despite one's race," and if a seller did not agree with open occupancy that should not stop "minority group families who want to look at a specific house." Another set of members pointed out that "the BHRC aim has always been to encourage good attitudes in the white community rather than to move families into specific houses." In the end, the council's executive committee voted against formally participating in the card-collection efforts, and instead, they mimeographed a hundred copies of a statement about Bloomington (presumably a welcoming one) that the MCHIC could give to Black home buyers. Moreover, they instructed BHRC's representative on the steering committee, Larry Throndson, to report the reason for the council's dissent. Later in July, when the Clearing House again insisted on getting the sale cards, the Bloomington council's executive committee reaffirmed its opposition yet allowed that members could send them individually if they wished. Meanwhile, the MCHIC moved into new office quarters near downtown Minneapolis, the space formerly occupied by the Greater Minneapolis Interfaith Fair Housing Program, which had been discontinued in August.[17]

Despite the persistent hesitancy among council members, that summer the BHRC intervened directly in several local cases of housing discrimination and "stabilization opportunities." In one case, an agent with the Christy Realty Company, whom Seymour had met at the April sales meeting, sold a house to an African American family, became concerned about neighborhood reaction, and contacted the council. Seymour and Charles Lutz met with the agent as well as the seller and urged them "not to hide the fact that a Negro had bought the house but to treat it as the natural occurrence it is." They also advised them "not to stir up trouble by calling a neighborhood meeting," and once Lutz talked to the immediate neighbors himself, "the non-white family later moved in with no apparent discriminatory treatment." In a second case, a salesman from Bell Investment Co., who had attended a different BHRC presentation, called the council after he had shown a house to a Black family and received threats from neighborhood Whites. The agent reported the threats to the State Commission Against Discrimination as well, and the commission asked the BHRC to call on each neighbor. When members did, they found that most were either "sympathetic to integration or neutral," with "only two vocally opposed." Unfortunately, however, the sale did not go through because of a financing problem. In what turned out to be a (slightly) more successful case, an African American man was turned down several times when he tried to find a house for his family to rent, and he filed a complaint with SCAD. To draw publicity to the incident, Sue Seymour arranged for an interview with commission field representative Walter Warfield by the local newspaper, and subsequently, a BHRC member who was leaving the area sold their home to the family.[18]

During the fall, the Bloomington council adopted its first formal constitution and held new elections for officer positions. Charles Lutz remained as chair and Charlotte Morse as vice chair, but several committee chairs changed hands. Phyllis Burpee replaced Sue Seymour as housing committee chair, and she continued the committee's focus on educating realtors. In addition to arranging more talks at realtor sales meetings, Burpee sent letters to every salesman who lived or worked in Bloomington, "telling him about the help we can provide in promoting peaceful integration." In fact, by the summer of 1966, the BHRC stopped holding monthly general meetings and instead did all of its work through the various committees, "each of which takes us into some part of the community." This change was due to dwindling participation, which was

a problem for committee chairs who were "overwhelmed with a pro-
liferation of projects and lack of personnel to carry them out." There
was renewed debate about the council's purpose as well. Some members
suggested that the council should develop closer alliances with other
civil rights groups, "especially those in the Negro area of Minneapolis,"
but most contended that that work should be done by individuals and
that "the goal of the BHRC as an organization should be changing the
attitudes of white Bloomington." A year later, there was still discussion
about this, though changing White attitudes remained the council's primary focus, and despite "increasing opposition and/or lethargy on the
part of most whites," members agreed to redouble their efforts. They recognized once more that their "greatest successes had occurred when we
went out into the community rather than when we invited the community to meet with us," and with that in mind they dedicated themselves to
a speakers program. The housing committee had been a model for this,
yet the council shifted its attention to working with local parent-teacher
associations. The speaker roster was Charles Lutz, John Thomasberg, and
Josie Johnson, the March newsletter explained, and they were "prepared
to talk on many aspects of civil rights, but will emphasize the white problem of prejudice especially as it relates to children."[19]

The BHRC did not completely abandon its work on housing, however,
and in the spring of 1967, the council joined a coordinated lobbying effort
to strengthen Minnesota's fair housing law. There had been attempts to
amend the law in 1965—primarily to extend protection to the purchase
or rental of all single-family dwellings and to those bought or improved
with conventional financing as well as FHA and GI Bill insured loans—
but that campaign ultimately failed. Two years later, the Minnesota Council for Civil and Human Rights tried again with a bill that included the
same amendments, and the Bloomington council's legislation committee worked to mobilize the group in support. The suburb's state senator,
Jerome Blatz, was a member of both the senate civil administration and
judiciary committees, which would first hear the bill, and he had spoken
to the council and solicited their help, encouraging them to write letters
to lawmakers and newspapers and to attend public hearings. "Now is the
time to show our support for [Blatz's] position," noted BHRC legislation
committee chair Allen Kohls, since "he may be fighting a lonely battle
among other suburban legislators." In this round the bill passed, although
the new law still allowed for exceptions, notably "rental of a portion of

a dwelling containing accommodations for two families, one of which is occupied by the owner," and "rental by an owner of a one-family accommodation in which he resides of a room or rooms in such accommodation to another person or persons." Cities and towns could adopt or modify open-occupancy ordinances of their own to remove these exceptions, and St. Paul soon changed its ordinance accordingly, yet when Minneapolis updated its law it retained the provision permitting discrimination in owner-occupied residences for room rentals.[20]

Given the tortured steps toward enacting comprehensive state and local fair housing legislation, decade after decade residential segregation in the Twin Cities metropolitan area was largely unchanged. Tellingly, like in other parts of the country, during the summers of 1966 and 1967 there were uprisings in north Minneapolis Black neighborhoods, and on Labor Day weekend in 1968, the Summit-University Avenue area in St. Paul experienced two days of unrest. Investigations followed, and while they gave much attention to racial inequality and economic disparities as fundamental causes for popular outrage, the reports fixed on "white liberals' paternalistic programs and elitist attitudes" too. This precisely described the siloed and timid approaches of the suburban human relations councils, including the one in Bloomington. Despite the guidance that Josie Johnson, James Tillman, and other African American leaders provided to the group at the outset, and notwithstanding White members' good intentions, the Bloomington Human Relations Council never fully complemented its original aim to study racism with sufficient action to correct it. On the contrary, the council's work was marked by an emphasis on "stability" and "order" and was divorced from Black civil rights activism beyond the suburb. As a result of these shortcomings, even with new fair housing legislation in place, the BHRC struggled to make a demographic impact, and it was not until the next decade that there were any signs of measurable change in Bloomington. Between 1970 and 1980, the community's total population held steady at just below 82,000 residents, but the number of African Americans jumped from eighteen to 702. Even then, although that was a significant increase in absolute terms, Blacks still represented less than one percent of the total population. Moreover, while the city council had established an official human rights commission in the wake of Martin Luther King Jr.'s assassination in 1968 to carry on the BHRC's work, the role that organized White efforts actually played in the increase was arguably limited.[21]

"The Primary Goals of the Group"

One of the other human relations councils working on the outskirts of Minneapolis during the 1960s was located in St. Louis Park, immediately west of Bde Maka Ska and Lake Harriet and north of Edina and Bloomington. Like its neighbors, the suburb grew dramatically after World War II, spurred by federally backed housing construction and home sales. The population increased almost threefold between 1940 and 1950, from 7,737 to 22,644, and then nearly doubled within a decade more, to 43,310. Unlike its neighbors, however, St. Louis Park drew a large number of Jewish families, who were gravitating away from north and south Minneapolis. This migration was initially made possible by a 1919 state law that removed religion as an enforceable category in restrictive housing covenants. "No written instrument hereafter made relating to or affecting real estate," the statute declared, "shall contain any provisions against conveying, mortgaging, encumbering or leasing any real estate to any person or persons of a specified religious faith or creed." Additionally, at the federal and state levels, adjustments in housing policy made FHA and GI Bill loans available to White Jews on the same terms as other Whites. Yet much like the "White flight" of Twin Cities gentiles, Jewish movement from city to suburb was driven by common racial prejudice too. The Minneapolis neighborhoods the transplants left behind were gradually (and not so gradually) filling in with African American residents, often because of "blockbusting" by realtors and "panic selling" among residents. The neighborhoods the Jewish families moved to in St. Louis Park, on the other hand, were almost entirely White. In 1940, the census listed one Black resident in St. Louis Park. A decade later there were just five, and another decade after that, the count was still shy of two dozen, in four different families.[22]

Among the few African Americans who moved to the suburb during its postwar expansion were Woodfin and Virginia Lewis and their two children. The family arrived in St. Louis Park in 1952, after Woodfin was hired at the Minneapolis Honeywell research laboratory, becoming the first African American to hold a professional position there. Prior to the move, the Lewises had been at Fisk University, where they had befriended Chuck and Josie Johnson, and Woodfin went on to Iowa State College to earn a PhD in nuclear physics. Soon after the family came to St. Louis Park, however, the landlord of the house they rented attempted

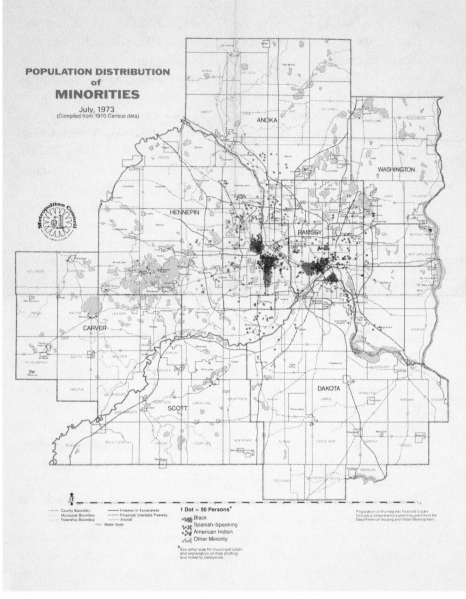

The Metropolitan Council of the Twin Cities Area created this map showing the "Population Distribution of Minorities" in 1973.

to evict them, saying that neighbors had called to object. Some Whites publicly rallied in support of the Lewises, but in the end the landlord allowed the family to stay only six months more, at which point they moved to Minneapolis. Several years later, in 1960, a Black US Army major and his White German Jewish refugee wife bought a home in St. Louis Park and faced constant harassment, including anonymous threatening phone calls, threats to the realtor who sold them the house and banks that gave them loans, and demands to the major's superiors to transfer him. Despite all this, the couple refused to leave. Then, in 1962, veterinarian Robert Lewis and his family moved to the area, provoking a White neighbor to circulate a petition against him, claiming that the family's presence would bring down property values. Only one person signed the petition, though, and Lewis pointed out that he was making significant renovations to his home and the adjacent pet hospital, perhaps winning at least begrudging acceptance that way. Yet another year later, African American Melvin Stone brought his family to the suburb, and on moving day, when a White neighbor knocked on the door and asked them to leave, Stone threatened to shoot them off the porch. "We never had anyone else come," his daughter Debra remembered. "Everybody else was pretty nice to us after that."[23]

In hopes of addressing the deeply rooted and pervasive racism in St. Louis Park, as well as increasing the numbers of African Americans who lived there, a handful of residents organized a human relations council. Several Jewish residents played a critical role in this, and the primary force behind the effort was local obstetrician and Temple Israel member Fred Lyon. He had been born in Berlin in 1928, fled Nazi Germany as a child in 1940, and moved to St. Louis Park with his wife and children in 1959. In June 1964, Lyon called a meeting at city hall, which was attended by a dozen others, and they were advised by Governor's Human Rights Commission executive director Calvin Watson, who emphasized the need for human rights groups in the suburbs. At another meeting the following month, guest speaker Viola Kanatz, the State Commission Against Discrimination assistant director, applauded the group's intention to focus on fair housing. In the first week of August, residents officially established the St. Louis Park Human Relations Council (SLPHRC), with Lyon as president, city councilman James Heltzer as vice president, Dorothy Kelsey as corresponding secretary, and Irene Beatty as recording secretary, all of them White, while African American Robert Lewis was chosen as treasurer. "One of the primary goals of the group," Lyon explained, "would be to prepare the city for the time when more members of minority groups begin to move into the suburbs." Toward that end, over the next several years St. Louis Park council members canvassed in support of open occupancy among their neighbors, organized training sessions for local realtors, and directly intervened in several cases of housing discrimination.[24]

One specific case that the SLPHRC dealt with soon after its founding involved a Black couple who moved to the area when the engineer husband was transferred there for a job. Attempting to find a home near his workplace and close to an elementary school for their two children, the couple contacted a realtor but, the *St. Louis Park Dispatch* reported, immediately encountered "delays, excuses, and rebuffs." The family initially tried to rent a home in the area, and when the realtor told them this was impossible, they decided to buy. The first time the wife went to see a home for sale, however, the woman who came to the door "looked sickened to see her." The realtor later apologized, claiming that he had talked to the woman's husband beforehand and thought they were fine with selling to Black buyers. Eventually, the couple went through three different sales agents, all White, each of whom asked "why they wouldn't move to an area where they'd be happy," the newspaper reported, and each of whom subsequently made "quick disappearing acts." Not sure what else to do, the couple contacted a group of civic leaders, who directed them to the SLPHRC, and the council helped the family find temporary housing until they bought a home in a different suburb. In a second instance, an African American social worker went to look at a home for sale, setting off a wave of White alarm. When a neighbor saw the man walking away from the home, she called others to let them know. They held a meeting "to do something about the situation," the *Dispatch* explained, after which one neighbor was designated as a representative and confronted the seller. "He told him how the neighbors felt, and asked him not to sell to Negroes," and he threatened "that if they did sell to Negroes, their relatives with businesses in the city might feel the effects." Although the homeowner claimed he would not be intimidated and would sell to whomever he chose, and the SLPHRC called in SCAD assistant director Walter Warfield to intervene, in the end the outcry was sufficient to dissuade the Black man from buying the property.[25]

As these and other attempts by African American families to move to St. Louis Park demonstrated, by the mid-1960s increasing numbers of Black middle-class professionals were seeking to live in Minneapolis suburbs, and allowing access to housing there was one of the chief aims of the state fair housing legislation. In the spring of 1968, following Martin Luther King Jr.'s assassination and nationwide riots, the US Congress also passed a federal fair housing bill, first introduced by Minnesota senator Walter Mondale and promptly signed into law by President Lyndon Johnson. Like Minnesota's 1962 law, the 1968 federal legislation exempted owner-occupied family dwellings, which, along with the exclusion of conventionally financed sales, limited its scope to a small portion of the housing market. Yet that same summer, the US Supreme Court ruled in *Jones v. Alfred H. Mayer Co.* that the Civil Rights Act of 1866 already forbid racial discrimination in the sale or rental of property by private individuals even if they received no public funds. This decision, historian Stephen Meyer notes, marked the final victory for the fair housing movement, leaving no written exceptions to the law's coverage. Still, even with that accomplished, as was the case in Bloomington, in the decade to follow demographic impact in St. Louis Park was slight. Between 1970 and 1980, the number of African Americans in St. Louis Park grew from eighty-nine to only 240, among a total population of 42,231. The real population change there and in the suburban population generally would take longer to happen, and the kind of change that took place, representing a new iteration of "White flight," was not in line with "the primary goals" that members of the SLPHRC and the many other human rights councils had organized to achieve.[26]

IN THE EARLY PART OF 1942, as the United States fully committed to war in Europe and Asia, African Americans across the country rallied to the cause under the "Double V" slogan, looking forward to "victory for democracy abroad" and "victory for democracy at home." In the immediate moment, a key part of achieving democracy at home was challenging racial discrimination in war production, which the newly created federal Fair Employment Practices Committee (FEPC) was meant to address. Black union leader and socialist A. Philip Randolph had forced President Franklin Roosevelt to establish the FEPC by threatening a massive "March on Washington," and while the committee's enforcement powers were limited, it could play an important and unprecedented role simply by investigating civil rights violations. Complementing this in Minnesota, in December of 1943 Governor Edward J. Thye established the Governor's Interracial Commission (GIC) to "examine the interracial trends within the state." Working with the understanding that job discrimination was "the more immediately practical problem at the present time," it focused on "racial patterns of employment." Within a little more than a year, the commission released a report, *The Negro Worker in Minnesota,* detailing the "race prejudice" that was "either actively deliberate or calcified in the form of inert custom," not only among employers but also among White workers and their unions. In the final section, it posed a specific question as well, whether or not "constructive change" could happen and long-established prejudices could be "dissolved." "When over 700 Negro soldiers, sailors, and marines return," the GIC rhetorically asked, "must they be denied opportunity for employment or upgrading?" The commission believed that did not have to be the case and called on religious groups, employers' organizations, trade groups, labor unions, schools, women's clubs, veterans' organizations, and state government to make an "organized effort to correct this evil."[1]

After the war, in June 1947, the GIC issued another report, *The Negro and His Home in Minnesota,* and the commission made a point to say that "racial patterns" in housing would be a greater challenge to amend than those in employment. Unlike job discrimination, they observed, housing discrimination was "crystallized" in various legal "instruments" as well as customary practice and would "not yield as readily." One of the legal instruments, of course, was the racial covenant, which the US Supreme Court had sanctioned in a 1926 decision and which the GIC estimated to be attached to at least a quarter of Twin Cities homes. There was also good reason to think that "real estate boards have an agreement or at least an implicit understanding that property in certain areas will not be sold to Negroes." This was besides the "tacit understanding" and considerable latitude real estate companies and individual agents had to hold the line. "If the agent believes in segregation," the report explained, "he can use numerous devices so that the potential seller and the potential buyer will never meet." Still, the commission insisted, behind "all restrictive covenants and policies of real estate boards are the attitudes of many ordinary white persons." While the particular instruments of housing discrimination were part of what made it so difficult to effect change, those instruments were merely the means that Whites used because they were "determined to keep Negroes out of their residential districts." A survey conducted by the GIC in the spring of 1946 found that 60 percent of Minnesota Whites believed that Blacks should not be allowed to move into any neighborhood they wanted to. Likewise, nearly 65 percent said that property values would decrease if a "Negro family" moved into their neighborhood, and those numbers did not notably vary by age, gender, or economic level. The only significant dissimilarity was a marginally higher percentage of urban Whites who opposed residential integration as compared to those in towns and rural areas, perhaps less a reflection of divergent closed-mindedness and more indicative of the actual threat Whites perceived.[2]

As it turned out, the very next year after the commission released its report on housing, the US Supreme Court ruled in *Shelley v. Kramer* that racial covenants were unenforceable, and Minnesota banned new racial covenants in 1953. The other legislative remedies to housing discrimination followed. There were the two laws at the state level, in 1961 and 1967, and the one at the federal level, in 1968. Largely unaddressed by these legal victories, however, and missed in the commission's reports, was the fact that various kinds of discrimination were interconnected, and the long history of job discrimination had made income an additional obstacle for African Americans who wanted to move out of urban "black pockets" to more expensive suburbs. Whites interpreted this in their own way, as an explanation for racial homogeneity, claiming that residential segregation was class segregation rather than racial segregation, the outcome of "free-market meritocracy" rather than "structural racism." Yet for a few years, from the end of 1968 to the end of 1972, federal housing secretary George Romney led a challenge to the economic barriers African Americans faced with attempts to expand affordable housing construction in suburbs around the country. Building on the Fair Housing Act's passage, the secretary launched "Operation Breakthrough," which required localities to waive restrictive requirements in building codes and zoning ordinances. In exchange, they would receive priority for Housing and Urban Development (HUD) assistance, or if that failed to yield cooperation, they could lose HUD funding altogether. Knowing that economic integration also meant racial integration, though, a majority of the localities selected as demonstration sites balked. The most dramatic showdown happened in the spring of 1970 in Warren, Michigan, a working-class suburb of Detroit, which forfeited $20 million in federal urban renewal funds rather than adopt a basic fair housing ordinance. Two years later, when protests against affordable housing flared in the affluent Westchester suburbs outside of New York City, President Richard Nixon announced a moratorium on federally subsidized projects and Romney resigned.[3]

In response to HUD's retreat on suburban racial integration, civil rights leaders protested, including NAACP executive director and former Rondo resident Roy Wilkins. "The big question for the 1970s," he said, "is where shall the Negro live? Will he live in the suburbs?" Fortunately, as the federal initiatives had begun to falter, in the spring of 1970 the recently created Twin Cities Metropolitan Council issued a report pledging to "strengthen the effectiveness of tools ... to provide housing and residential environments for all area residents, including low- and moderate-income people." Six years later, the Metropolitan Land Use Planning Act gave the council authority to set land use planning policy for cities within the seven-county Minneapolis–St. Paul region and required implementation of "fair share housing programs" that would adequately meet the metro area's needs. Similar to Operation Breakthrough, the act also gave the council authority "to tie infrastructure funding to compliance with regional growth plans and affordable housing goals." Subsequently, a large amount of the subsidized housing construction in the region was happening in the Whitest suburban communities, and nearly all parts of the outer metro area saw a noticeable increase in their Black population. Just as the Governor's Interracial Commission had foreseen, however, even with this government intervention, the long history of racial exclusion by Whites against Blacks had left an inveterate legacy that shaped residential patterns in the Twin Cities and elsewhere for decades to come.[4]

In many cases, the rise in the number of African Americans living on the outskirts of Minneapolis and St. Paul happened when Blacks moved outward from the city centers and an even greater number of Whites moved somewhere else. The rise in the proportion of African Americans in different communities also often happened by a contraction of the total population in those places. Given this, suburban demographic change was likely not so much a reflection of racial integration (an intermixing house by house and street by street) as it was evidence of racial succession (a supplanting block by block and section by section). North of Minneapolis, for example, Brooklyn Center had a decrease in its total population between 1980 and 2010, from 31,230 to 30,104, while the Black population increased substantially, from 530 to 7,810, and the White population decreased by half, from 29,984 to 14,788. That is, White flight depopulated the suburb and Whites left in much larger numbers than African Americans arrived. Similarly, the rise in the number of African Americans in St. Louis Park and Bloomington was matched by greater declines in the number of Whites and either a drop in total population or only a nominal increase that was much less than the number of Whites who left. St. Louis Park saw its Black population swell from 240 in 1980 to 3,372 in 2010, but its White population shrank from 42,030 to 37,686, while the total population increased by only 2,319. The number of African American residents in Bloomington went from 530 to 5,957 and the number of Whites dropped from 79,464 to 66,087, with the total population expanding by only 1,002. The same trends could be seen around St. Paul as well, if to a lesser extent. In the Ramsey County portion of White Bear Lake, for instance, the 1970 census recorded 23,205 Whites and a dozen Blacks. Within a decade there were still only 30 African American residents, but the number of Whites had declined to 22,260, and in the next three decades the Black population grew to 577 while the White population contracted still more, to 21,045.[5]

Beyond the Twin Cities metropolitan area, racial exclusion's demographic legacy was manifest in different ways. Some places gained more proportional racial diversity, typically because of significant White flight, while others saw only slow if any undoing of their exclusive Whiteness. In the second half of the twentieth century, Duluth had a steady decline in total population as well as a slight racial reapportionment when a large number of Whites moved away and the number of African Americans noticeably increased, first drawn to the local air force base. There were 100,578 residents in 1970, 98,851 of whom were White and 857 of whom were Black, and by 2010 the total population was only 86,265, counting 77,968 Whites and 1,988 Blacks. In most towns and cities in greater Minnesota, however, there was either decline or stasis in the number of Whites and a much smaller absolute and proportional change in the number of African Americans. In Austin, the White population declined from 1970 to 1980 but held fairly steady thereafter at around 22,000, and the number of Blacks increased from just 14 in 1970 to 27 in 1980 and to 749 in 2010. On the other hand, Red Wing's White population actually grew in those decades, from 10,358 in 1970 to 15,064 in 2010, yet this growth was accompanied by an initial decline in African Americans between 1970 and 1980, from 35 to 30, and then an increase to 312 Black residents over the next three decades.[6]

The persistent effects of White exclusion of African Americans from neighborhoods, suburbs, towns, and cities throughout the state both aligned and diverged with the population histories of other so-called non-White groups. This includes Native Americans, which the Governor's Interracial Commission studied too. Five years after releasing *The Negro and His Home*, the GIC published *The Indian in Minnesota*, detailing the employment, education, and housing of enrolled and non-enrolled Indians. At midcentury, the commission noted, the Indigenous population numbered at least 12,000, the great majority Ojibwe, and that made them the largest "racial minority" in the state. Yet, the report lamented, almost all of the Native people lived on or near one of eight reservations. Driven by an impulse toward forced assimilation, the GIC described this simply as "segregation," and citing the enclaves' "inadequate resources" the commission recommended taking "constructive measures" to abolish them. Three decades later, the reservations remained, yet hundreds of Indigenous people had indeed moved away, mainly to the Twin Cities or Duluth, though some to metropolitan suburbs and other towns or cities. With a couple of exceptions, their population in the latter places was even smaller than the Black population. By 2010, Indigenous people living off the reservations numbered more than twenty thousand, most in particular pockets in Minneapolis and St. Paul, the one counting 7,601 Native American residents and the other 3,016. Except for the marginally larger population in Duluth, however, they were still considerably fewer in number than African Americans in the Twin Cities, and a very small presence in greater Minnesota towns and cities. This was testament to the fact, of course, that the state's Indigenous people had gone through their own long genocidal history at the hands of Whites, one marked by centuries of war, disease, hunger, and removal.[7]

With a somewhat different pattern, the Latino population of Minnesota was another group that the GIC considered in the decade after World War II. A year following publication of *The Indian in Minnesota*, the GIC released a revised version of *The Mexican in Minnesota*, which it had first issued in 1948. In this report, the commission surveyed the lives of the nearly five thousand Mexican nationals and what it called "Texan Mexicans" scattered around the state, most of them recruited for field labor, canning plant jobs, and packinghouse work. As agriculture became more mechanized, though, even more of them found industrial or other manual labor employment, and that brought an ever-increasing number into cities. The greatest concentrations were in West and South St. Paul as well as the West Side of St. Paul, the GIC observed, and Mexicans there typically inhabited some of the poorest housing. In fact, shortly after the report's publication, continued deteriorating conditions on the West Side prompted the St. Paul Housing and Redevelopment Authority to initiate an urban renewal project for the entire four-hundred-acre area. Like the Rondo projects happening at the same time, this project forced from their homes hundreds of families, many of them Mexican, without fair compensation or adequate assistance. Despite that shared experience with African Americans, however, in the decades to follow Mexicans and other Latino groups took a dissimilar demographic path. During the second half of the twentieth century, in most cities and towns throughout the state their number surpassed the number of Black residents, and that trend of greater growth continued over time. In Faribault, for instance, in 1980 there were 77 Hispanic residents (43 of them Mexican) to 18 Blacks, and by 2010 there were 3,026 Hispanics to 1,764 African Americans. To be sure, it took slightly longer for Latinos to surpass Blacks in the suburbs, but it did happen there too. In Richfield, in 1980 there were 208 Latino residents (76 of them Mexican) and 307 Blacks, while three decades later there were 6,436 Latinos and 3,242 African Americans. In both cases, Faribault and Richfield, what were relatively large increases in the Black populations were still not enough to keep up with the Latino populations.[8]

Complementing *The Mexican in Minnesota,* in 1949 the GIC made a report titled *The Oriental in Minnesota,* focusing primarily on Chinese though also giving attention to Filipino and Japanese residents. At the time, the commission counted five hundred Chinese people living in Minneapolis, one hundred in St. Paul, forty in Duluth, fifteen in Mankato, nine in Albert Lea, and four in Austin, along with a few others to make a total population of nearly seven hundred. Most of these families, or in some cases single men, lived in scattered apartment buildings, duplexes, and single dwellings (there were apparently no "Chinatowns" in the Twin Cities or elsewhere). The Chinese did face housing discrimination, the report noted, citing one instance when Whites in a Minneapolis suburb objected to a Chinese family moving into their neighborhood. Yet the commission claimed (however reliably) that Asians in Minnesota never experienced the same degree of discrimination as "other minorities." In the decades following, particularly after federal immigration legislation replaced national origins quotas with a preference system that emphasized family ties, occupational skills, and refugee status, the number of Asians and Asian Americans significantly increased. This was notable in the Twin Cities and their suburbs as well as in cities and towns in greater Minnesota, with new groups like the Hmong and Asian Indians making up a growing share of the population. By 2010, Edina had 2,936 "Asian" residents, compared to 1,446 Blacks and 1,101 Hispanics, and on the edge of St. Paul, Maplewood counted 3,963 Asians, compared to 3,122 African

Americans and 2,342 Hispanic residents. In Rochester, where the Black population had swelled from 375 in 1980 to 6,703 in 2010, and those of "Spanish Origin" had increased from 410 to 5,508, Asians and Asian Americans outnumbered both, with 7,246 residents, many of them probably Mayo Clinic doctors and researchers or IBM employees. Not unlike Hispanics, as a population group they had diverged from African Americans in the amount of their growth, and likewise they showed signs of wide geographic dispersal.[9]

Finally, beyond the shifting demographic figures, one secondary yet critical register of residential segregation's legacy in Minnesota are widely divergent and growing racial disparities in wealth and income as well as related variations in health, education, and incarceration. In 2015, the home ownership rate gap between Whites and African Americans was at least 50 percent, and that in particular impeded Blacks from building equity and accumulating wealth at the same rate as Whites. Compounding this, the state ranked last among all others in terms of the household income rate gap, with an $81,552 median family income for Whites compared to a $33,885 median family income for Blacks. The median family income for African Americans was also $12,000 less than for Latinos, and slightly lower than for Native Americans. With less wealth and lower incomes, many other problems were more likely to plague African Americans than other racial groups as well. As Jonathan M. Rose detailed for the Council on Black Minnesotans, the death rate for African Americans was more than one and a half times higher than for Whites, and the Black infant mortality rate was 16.5 per 1,000 live births (16.2 for Native Americans) and only 6.5 for Whites (7.3 for Hispanics). A differential showed up in obesity and diabetes rates too, with nearly 40 percent of African Americans defined as obese and more than 10 percent diagnosed with diabetes, two times that of Whites in each category. Additionally, Black children were significantly behind Whites in reading proficiencies (and slightly behind Native Americans), and Black high school students were less than half as likely to pursue a college education. And while Blacks in Minnesota represented 7 percent of the state's youth population, they made up 40 percent of those in juvenile detention, compared to Whites, who were 82 percent of the youth population and 38 percent of those in juvenile detention. The difference was even wider for adults, with a 25:1 disparity in Black-to-White imprisonment rates, the highest in the country.[10]

Casting a glance from Minnesota's present into the state's past, it is clear that racial exclusion of African Americans was and is foundational, determining not only residential patterns but also an array of disparities in life circumstances. Various studies have offered theories and explanations for these features of modern American society more generally, ranging from the "culture of poverty" to structural economic change and institutionalized racism, and indeed racial discrimination and disparity are glaring features of the welfare bureaucracy, the labor market, the educational system, as well as the carceral state, both historically and now. Yet Minnesota Whites' largely successful efforts to exclude Blacks from their midst, or contain them in delimited areas, played the formative role in making the current racial order. It is equally important to recognize that Whites had many means at their disposal to accomplish exclusion and containment. This ranged from aid by local, state, and federal governments to collusion by private mortgage lenders and scheming by real estate boards and individual agents. And these policies and practices were not imposed on them. Rather, they were responses to White popular will, and behind the policies and practices was a history of extralegal racial violence and continued threats of it. From decade to decade, the available standard tools evolved, sometimes because African Americans and other Whites challenged their morality and legality, and over time Whites relied less often on community displays of violence and harassment. Once established, however, racial exclusion was fossilized and capable of perpetuating itself through inaction by the White power structure.[11]

Concurrent with effecting exclusive Whiteness in cities, towns, and suburbs, Minnesota Whites also adopted a historical amnesia, which opportunely made them oblivious to how exclusion came to be. They fashioned spurious explanations for the overwhelming Whiteness in their daily lives as well, fictions that absolved them of responsibility for correcting the recurring monumental injustice. The vacuous memory and false discernment were another important part of preserving and perpetuating racial exclusion, keeping the reality of it paradoxically hidden in plain view. Although it can do nothing to change the actual past, *Whiteness in Plain View* is meant to be a counterpoint to this misremembering and misrepresenting, to expose what Minnesota Whites have supposedly forgotten or cunningly occluded. Yet it is important to keep in mind that the state's history is just one set of ghost stories (to return to

Avery Gordon's metaphor), one revelation of how we are haunted as a nation, and one iteration of what we must acknowledge in order to put the many ghosts of racist social violence to rest. Other manifestations in other places have been or need to be methodically chronicled and interpreted too. The expanded historical consciousness that will come from this endeavor is an essential part of a larger collective struggle.[12]

ACKNOWLEDGMENTS

WHITENESS IN PLAIN VIEW was a long time in the making, and it went through many iterations. It started from conversations with the late Jim Loewen, an introduction to Sandy Berman, and an interview with historian Peter Rachleff, all part of preparation to turn the story of Minnesota's racial exclusion into a documentary film. I very quickly realized that a documentary could not do justice to the history, however, and shifted my attention to more conventional archival research for a book. Early on, that work was aided immensely by Debbie Miller at the Minnesota Historical Society, Marci Matson at the Edina Historical Society, and Sue Doocy at the Mower County Historical Society. Later, when I was looking for several elusive sources, I was fortunate to get assistance from Aimee Brown at the University of Minnesota Duluth Special Collections, Ann Mayhew at the James J. Hill Center, and Dana E. Gerber-Margie at the Wisconsin Historical Society. As has been the case with previous books, I also benefited from the gracious competence of interlibrary loan staff at my own university, notably Rose Paton and Deborah Friedman.

Additionally, recovering and understanding critical parts of the racial exclusion history would not have been possible without many other people who lent time, advice, and encouragement to the project. Marion Taylor and Matt Carter both did lengthy interviews, and Barb Sommer provided me with a transcript of her own interview with Matt. Jim Joyce freely offered memories, documents, photographs, and contacts. Bridget Kelleher helped me make sense of the Donald Irish study. Nancy M. Vaillancourt shared materials from her research and writing on Minnesota's Ku Klux Klan. James Curry sent clippings and narratives for the history of racial exclusion in Hastings, part of the "Building Remembrance for Reconciliation" initiative that he, archivist Heidi Langenfeld, and others are doing there. Kirsten Delegard provided both inspiration and insight, grounded in the remarkable and immeasurably important Mapping Prejudice project that she leads. My (former) colleague Elizabeth Herbin-Triant read numerous chapter drafts and greatly aided me in rounds of revision. Likewise, the editorial staff at the *Journal of Urban History* helped me recraft an article about Edina and clarify my account of racial exclusion for that chapter in the book.

I was also very fortunate to have a chance to work with *Minnesota History* editor Laura Weber on another article about Duluth, and she introduced me to staff at the Minnesota Historical Society Press. At the press, both Josh Leventhal and Ann Regan did a full year's worth of labor guiding me in making significant improvements to the *Whiteness* manuscript, chapter by chapter and section by section. That was perhaps the most difficult part of the project, but the book would be a much lesser thing if it were not for their acute observations and consummate patience. Moreover, an anonymous reader offered other useful suggestions for revision, Emily Gurnon performed marvelous feats as a copyeditor (sorry about the commas), and managing editor Shannon Pennefeather skillfully steered *Whiteness* through the final stages of publication.

This book owes a great deal to years of conversations with friends and family as well. Most importantly, Kristen Harol has been my steadfast partner and intellectual companion for a decade now. She has her own career working on affordable housing and racial equity, and while she claims she did not give me the idea for *Whiteness*, she had a lot to do with why and how I wrote it. There were countless mornings, afternoons, and evenings when she was on the project's front lines with me, pondering the sources, connecting the dots, and finding the right words. Thank you for all of that, and more.

NOTES

Notes to Introduction

1. Gordon, *Ghostly Matters*, xvi–xvii, 8, 194.

2. Loewen, *Sundown Towns*, 423.

3. Matthew D. Lassiter and Joseph Crespino, "Introduction: The End of Southern History," in Lassiter and Crespino, eds., *The Myth of Southern Exceptionalism*, 18; Jeanne Theoharis, "Hidden in Plain Sight: The Civil Rights Movement Outside the South," in Lassiter and Crespino, eds., *The Myth of Southern Exceptionalism*, 53; Purnell and Theoharis, eds., *The Strange Career of the Jim Crow North*. See also Cobb, *Away Down South*; Cobb, "An Epitaph for the North."

4. Over the past decade and a half, numerous scholars have given increasing attention to applying race as a category of analysis for understanding the North, much of that work focusing on the deeply rooted racism and militant Black civil rights activism in large urban centers.

Thomas Sugrue's *Sweet Land of Liberty: The Forgotten Struggle for Civil Rights in the North* (New York: Random House, 2008) is a masterful survey with a broad regional scope that highlights New York, Newark, Philadelphia, Detroit, Chicago, and elsewhere. Other books are intentionally narrower studies, including Angela Dillard's *Faith in the City: Preaching Radical Social Change in Detroit* (Ann Arbor: University of Michigan Press, 2007) and Brian Purnell's *Fighting Jim Crow in the County of Kings: The Congress of Racial Equality in Brooklyn* (Lexington: University Press of Kentucky, 2013). See also James Ralph, *Northern Protest: Martin Luther King, Jr., Chicago, and the Civil Rights Movement* (Cambridge, MA: Harvard University Press, 1993); Martha Biondi, *To Stand and Fight: The Struggle for Civil Rights in Postwar New York City* (Cambridge, MA: Harvard University Press, 2003); Robert O. Self, *American Babylon: Race and the Struggle for Postwar Oakland* (Princeton,

NJ: Princeton University Press, 2003); Josh Sides, *LA City Limits: African American Los Angeles from the Great Depression to the Present* (Berkeley: University of California Press, 2003); Jeanne Theoharis and Komozi Woodward, eds., *Freedom North: Black Freedom Struggles Outside the South, 1940–1980* (New York: Palgrave Macmillan, 2003); Matthew Countryman, *Up South: Civil Rights and Black Power in Philadelphia* (Philadelphia: University of Pennsylvania Press, 2006); Clarence Lang, *Grassroots at the Gateway: Class Politics and Black Freedom Struggles in St. Louis, 1936–1975* (Ann Arbor: University of Michigan Press, 2009); and Patrick Jones, *The Selma of the North: Civil Rights Insurgency in Milwaukee* (Cambridge, MA: Harvard University Press, 2009). Similarly, William Green's *A Peculiar Imbalance: The Fall and Rise of Racial Equality in Early Minnesota* (St. Paul: Minnesota Historical Society Press, 2007) and *Degrees of Freedom: The Origins of Civil Rights in Minnesota, 1865–1912* (Minneapolis: University of Minnesota Press, 2015) are mostly concerned with what was happening in Minneapolis, St. Paul, and Duluth.

5.   Early examples of scholarship that examines this forced separation include Douglas Massey and Nancy Denton, *American Apartheid: Segregation and the Making of the Underclass* (Cambridge, MA: Harvard University Press, 1993); Stephen G. Meyer, *As Long as They Don't Move Next Door* (Lanham, MD: Rowman & Littlefield, 2000); Charles Lamb, *Housing Segregation in Suburban America since 1960: Presidential and Judicial Politics* (New York: Cambridge University Press, 2005); David M. P. Freund, *Colored Property: State Policy and White Racial Politics in Suburban America* (Chicago: University of Chicago Press, 2007); and more recently,

Richard Rothstein's *The Color of Law: The Forgotten History of How Our Government Segregated America* (New York: W.W. Norton & Company, 2018).

One book that does not understate or overlook the importance of extralegal White racism in creating and protecting residential segregation in the North is Jeannine Bell, *Hate Thy Neighbor: Move-In Violence and the Persistence of Racial Segregation in American Housing* (New York: New York University Press, 2013). See also Tesa Rigel Hines, "Community Prejudice Is Also to Blame: Significant Causes and Effects of Residential Segregation in St. Louis," *Journal of Urban History* 45, no. 3 (May 2019): 578–94.

6.   "Towns that posted sundown signs implied they were all-white by municipal action. I have confirmed 184 towns in 32 states that displayed sundown signs [enforced by sheriffs and local police]. . . . Towns that sounded whistles or sirens to warn blacks to get out of town at 6pm also implied they were sundown by official action": Loewen, *Sundown Towns*, 104. *The Negro Motorist Greenbook* (1962), 50.

7.   Sun Yung Shin, ed., *A Good Time for the Truth: Race in Minnesota* (St. Paul: Minnesota Historical Society Press, 2016); Walter R. Jacobs, "From Wonderful/Wretched Memories to Sparked Discussion of Racial Dynamics in Minnesota," and Kate Beane, "George Floyd Was Murdered on Dakota Land," in Jacobs, Thompson Taiwo, and August, eds., *Sparked*, x and 185. See also the documentary film *Jim Crow of the North* (Twin Cities Public Television, 2019), which emphasizes the role restrictive housing covenants played in establishing housing segregation in Minneapolis. Additionally, the Mapping Prejudice project has identified every

single one of the Hennepin County deeds that include racial covenants: https://mappingprejudice.umn.edu/.

8. See Kwame Anthony Appiah, "The Case for Capitalizing the *B* in Black," *The Atlantic*, June 18, 2020. See also Nell Irvin Painter, "Why 'White' Should Be Capitalized, Too," *Washington Post*, July 22, 2020. The *New York Times* has not changed its style, stating that white "does not represent shared history and culture": "Why We're Capitalizing Black," *New York Times*, July 5, 2020. The *Washington Post* made the change to universal capitalization in July 2020, however, citing the contrary position. European "ethnicities were eventually assimilated into the collective group that has had its own cultural and historical impact on the nation," their announcement explains, and as such, "White should be represented with a capital W": "*The Washington Post* Announces Writing Style Changes for Racial and Ethnic Identifiers," *Washington Post*, July 29, 2020. "*Star Tribune* to Capitalize Black as Racial, Cultural Identifier," *Star Tribune*, July 1, 2020. Minnesota Public Radio editors also point out that white supremacists have a long-standing practice of capitalizing white, which is true, though as Appiah argues, the point is to undo what they mean by that, to call attention to the construction of all racial categories, and to deny racists the opportunity to use white as a tool of empowerment: "Why We Now Capitalize Black But Continue to Lowercase White," MPR News, August 10, 2020.

9. Daniel Buck, *Indian Outbreaks*, 10–11.

10. Thomas Montgomery to Parents and Brothers, New Orleans, March 23, 1864, folder "Thomas Montgomery Letters, #41–71 [Feb 1864?]–September

1864"; Thomas Montgomery to Father, Oct 6, 1864, Morganzia, Louisiana, folder "Thomas Montgomery Letters, #72–100, September 18, 1864–April 24, 1865"—both box 2, Thomas Montgomery and Family Papers, hereafter cited as "Montgomery Papers." See also Green, *The Children of Lincoln*.

11. *Austin Daily Herald*, July 20, 1922.

12. Chief of Police, John Murphy, interviewed by W. F. Rhinow, Adjutant General, June 23, 1920, roll 1, 5, Duluth (Minnesota) Lynchings of 1920, Selected Materials, Minnesota Historical Society, St. Paul, hereafter cited as "DLM." *New York Times*, June 17, 1920.

13. *St. Paul Recorder*, May 9, 1958.

14. Somali Population, Minnesota Compass: https://www.mncompass.org/topics/demographics/cultural-communities/somali/.

Notes to Chapter 1

"The Master Race of the World Is Caucasian": Punitive Expeditions, Mass Hanging, and Forced Removal

1. Buck, *Indian Outbreaks*, 10–11, 57, 227, 283.

2. Schwalm, *Emancipation's Diaspora*, 116–17; Schwalm, "Overrun with Free Negroes," 152. Henry H. Sibley was born in Detroit in 1811 and came to Minnesota in 1834 to work for a newly expanded American Fur Company. He lived briefly with Alexis Bailly, whose household at the time included Joseph Godfrey and his mother, Courtney. Later, when Sibley set up his own residence, he had a mixed-race cook, an enslaved person named Joe Robinson. Sibley's marriage

to Red Blanket Woman, the daughter of Bad Hail, the chief of the Black Dog band of Mdewakanton Dakota, happened in 1839 or 1840, and their daughter, Helen, was born in 1841. Red Blanket Woman also married a Dakota man but died a couple years later, and when Sibley married Sarah Jane Steele he arranged to have Helen adopted by William Reynolds Brown and his wife, Martha Newman Brown. In 1848, Sibley became an at-large congressional representative for the Minnesota Territory, and from 1858 to 1860, he served as Minnesota's first governor. Meanwhile, his daughter moved with the Browns to St. Paul, allowing her frequent visits with her father until her death during childbirth. See Bachman, *Northern Slave, Black Dakota*, 18; Carroll, "Who Was Jane Lamont?," 192.

3. Green, *A Peculiar Imbalance*, 68; Bachman, *Northern Slave, Black Dakota*, 70; Johnson, *Uncertain Lives*, 16; Osman, "General Sibley's Contraband Teamsters," 62.

4. See Bachman, *Northern Slave, Black Dakota*, 327. Schwalm, *Emancipation's Diaspora*, 177, 182–83; *Chatfield Democrat*, August 19, 1865, as quoted in Green, *A Peculiar Imbalance*, 144.

5. *St. Peter's Indian Agency Handbook* (n.p., 1984), 11; Anderson, *Kinsmen of Another Kind*, 98–100; Anderson and Woolworth, *Through Dakota Eyes*, 8.

6. *St. Peter's Indian Agency Handbook* (n.p., 1984), 28, 30–31. By 1848, Mary Taliaferro had married Warren Woodbury, a soldier at Fort Snelling, and moved with him to West St. Paul. When the Civil War started, he went to join the fighting, leaving her alone. When the US–Dakota War broke out, Mary was visiting some of her Native relations, and she and her children were taken captive, although Little Crow

and other sympathetic Dakota made sure that they survived. Warren was killed at the Battle of Vicksburg in 1863, and Mary continued to live in St. Paul with her children. In 1887 or 1888, they moved to the Santee Indian Reservation in Nebraska, where Mary lived until she died in 1916. See Carroll, "Who Was Jane Lamont?," 184–96.

7. When Harriet and Dred Scott filed separate freedom suits, in 1846, their lawyer was Francis Murdoch, who had read law in Bedford, Pennsylvania, during the same time that Lawrence Taliaferro came and went for his furloughs. In fact, the two men belonged to the same church and were married by the same minister. In such a small town, they must have known each other, and Murdoch might have been aware that Taliaferro eventually hoped to manumit his enslaved people (which he did eventually do). Also, after Murdoch had made his way to St. Louis, he was again acquainted with Harriet through Reverend John R. Anderson, the minister at her church. Anderson had earlier worked for Arthur Lovejoy and was in the print shop on the night when a pro-slavery mob murdered Lovejoy in 1837. Murdoch was then district attorney for Alton, Illinois, and prosecuted the case and likely kept in touch with Anderson afterward. Finally, the other evidence that points to Harriet being from Bedford is that Murdoch filed the case just as Harriet was turning twenty-eight years old, which he would have known was the age for freedom set by Pennsylvania's gradual emancipation law. See Vander Velde and Subramanian, "Mrs. Dred Scott." 1042–47, 1078–88; Bachman, *Northern Slave, Black Dakota*, 3–5.

8. Dred Scott came to Fort Snelling in May 1836 and married Harriet

Robinson shortly after his arrival, when he was forty years old and she was seventeen. They had two sons together, but both died in infancy. They also had two daughters, Eliza and Lizzie. In April 1838 the family left Fort Snelling with Dr. John Emerson, Dred Scott's enslaver, to go to Fort Jesup in Louisiana, then returned a year later to Fort Snelling, where they remained until 1840, when they went with Emerson again to St. Louis. Following Emerson's death, in December 1843, his wife moved to Massachusetts and left the Scotts in the hands of her brother-in-law, Captain Henry Bainbridge, who hired out the couple to Samuel Russell. The Scotts were working for Russell in March 1846, a month before they filed their freedom suits. See Bachman, *Northern Slave, Black Dakota*, 7-10, 33-37; Vander Velde and Subramanian, "Mrs. Dred Scott," 1042-43.

9. Bachman, *Northern Slave, Black Dakota*, 1-5, 29-32.

10. Bachman, *Northern Slave, Black Dakota*, 11, 35-36.

11. Case, *The Relentless Business of Treaties*, 56-60; Wingerd, *North Country*, 109-11, 131, 151, 273; Westerman and White, *Mni Sota Makoce*, 103-7.

12. Samuel Pond was also married in November 1838, to Cordelia Eggleston, at the Lake Harriet mission house. Henry Sibley served as a groomsman, and as Samuel noted in his "Narrative," Dr. John Emerson, Dred Scott's enslaver, was present as well. "A Veteran Departed," S. W. Pond Obituary, *The North Side Chronicle* [Minneapolis], December 26, 1891, roll 2; "Narrative" [1881], vol. 1, p. 46-47, 51-52, 68, 74-75, roll 1, vol. 1; "100th Anniversary," p. 3, roll 2; "A Half Century Since the White Man Came to Town," p. 1-4, roll 2—all Pond Family Papers, Minnesota

Historical Society, St. Paul; Anderson, *Kinsmen of Another Kind*, 165-66.

13. Bachman, *Northern Slave, Black Dakota*, 38, 41-43, 45-46.

14. When Samuel Pond was elected to the 1849 territorial legislature, he called for suffrage to be extended to African American and Indian men: see Williamson, "The Dakota Indian Settlement at the Gideon Pond Farm," 115. Similarly, ten years earlier, in 1839, the Iowa Territorial Legislature passed laws excluding only African American men from voting while barring "Negroes, mulattoes, and Indians" from standing as witness in any court against a White person and limiting public education to Whites only. The next year, the territory also banned interracial marriage, and in 1851, it banned Black settlement. See White, "The Power of Whiteness," 194-95; Green, *A Peculiar Imbalance*, 32, 46-47, 51, 89; Schwalm, "Overrun with Free Negroes," 151; Spangler, *The Negro in Minnesota*; Wingerd, *North Country*, 238-39.

15. Green, *A Peculiar Imbalance*, 50-51; Lieutenant Colonel Edmund B. Alexander replaced Commandant Lee at Fort Ridgley in the early part of 1855 and stayed until 1858. He was from Virginia and personally enslaved Blacks. Among his officers, part of the Tenth Infantry Regiment, at least five kept no fewer than nine enslaved people at the fort during that time. Bachman, *Northern Slave, Black Dakota*, 37, 48-49, 60, 65.

16. "Between 1805 and 1858, a period of fifty-three years," Gwen Westerman and Bruce White explain, "twelve treaties were concluded with the Dakota and the United States.... The negotiation of these treaties was not a clear-cut process or one easily categorized. Collectively these treaties included three great cessions,

comprising the Treaties of 1825, 1837, and 1851. But to call these agreements cessions is to privilege the nonindigenous side of the negotiating table. For the Dakota the word cessions might well be replaced with seizures, because of the stark contrast between the Dakota views of land and that of government negotiators, not to mention the dubious process through which these treaties were written, negotiated, and carried out": Westerman and White, *Mni Sota Makoce*, 134 (quote), 193–94; Case, *The Relentless Business of Treaties*, 149–52.

17. Anderson and Woolworth, *Through Dakota Eyes*, 1; Bachman, *Northern Slave, Black Dakota*, 84–85. For a full and detailed account of the war, see also Anderson, *Massacre in Minnesota*.

18. After the war was over and it was safe to return to the region, New Ulm was repopulated by both prior and new residents. One of the new townspeople was Alexander Berghold. As a young student in Austria, he had read Harriet Beecher Stowe's *Oheim Toms Huette*. He also came across a journal that included a graphic account of the 1862 war, including the attacks on New Ulm. Inspired by these sources, Berghold decided to write a novel of his own, featuring an enslaved girl who ran away and found shelter in New Ulm. He never finished the novel, but after he became a priest he immigrated to the United States and, in 1868, received an assignment to the town. There he published other novels, including *The Indians' Revenge, Prairie Roses,* and *Countries and Their People.* Hoisington, *A German Town*, 24–25, 44–45; Petry, *New Ulm, Minnesota Turnverein*, 5–6.

One of those killed on the conflict's third day was Amos Huggins, the son of Alexander Huggins, who had first sheltered Joseph Godfrey when he ran away from his enslaver. His widow, Josephine Huggins, was saved by a friendly Mdewakanton band. Bachman, *Northern Slave, Black Dakota*, 81–82, 121; Anderson and Woolworth, *Through Dakota Eyes*, 85–86.

19. James Thompson had a daughter too, Sarah Thompson Barnes, who was twenty-four and married to a White man. She did not live on the reservation but was there when the war began, without her husband, probably to collect annuities for herself and her own three young children. She was likewise taken captive. Bachman, *Northern Slave, Black Dakota*, 92–93; Green, *A Peculiar Imbalance*, 49.

20. Westerman and White, *Mni Sota Makoce*, 194; Bachman, *Northern Slave, Black Dakota*, 103, 182; Anderson and Woolworth, *Through Dakota Eyes*, 15; Green, *A Peculiar Imbalance*, 120.

21. Whipple, *Lights and Shadows*, 32, 50–53. President Lincoln initially responded to Bishop Whipple by telling him a bizarre story, one that displayed a casual racism toward African Americans as well as a practical recognition that Native Americans were not well served by the US government. "Bishop," he said, "a man thought that monkeys could pick cotton better than Negroes could because they were quicker and their fingers smaller. He turned a lot of them into his cotton field, but he found that it took two overseers to watch one monkey. It needs more than one honest man to watch an Indian Agent." Whipple, *Lights and Shadows*, 136–39.

22. Moved by the freed slaves making their way into town, Jane Grey Swisshelm decided to stay in DC and work with the National Association for the Relief of Destitute Colored Women and Children: Hoffert, *Jane Grey Swisshelm*, 149–53,

155. Writing to Henry Sibley, *Republican* newspaper editor Thomas M. Newson also showed how liberal thinking about Native Americans and African Americans diverged in the wake of the US–Dakota War: "Of what avail now all the teachings of missionaries?—the parental regard of the national government?,—the false sympathy and partiality of our State in granting them the right of suffrage to the exclusion of the free intelligent black?": Green, *A Peculiar Imbalance,* 120.

23. Bachman, *Northern Slave, Black Dakota,* 124, 131–32, 180.

24. A few days after the Dakota prisoners' arrival at Camp Lincoln, a mob of 150 to 200 Whites came out from Mankato to capture and lynch the doomed men. Soldiers arrested the main conspirators and sent the rest back to town. Bachman, *Northern Slave, Black Dakota,* 228.

25. The bodies were buried, but the cadavers soon went missing, taken for dissection by doctors who included William Mayo, the father of the two physicians who founded the Mayo Clinic: Bachman, *Northern Slave, Black Dakota,* 262, 275; Anderson and Woolworth, *Through Dakota Eyes,* 15.

26. Bachman, *Northern Slave, Black Dakota,* 285, 294, 297, 304, 307, 330, 333; Green, *A Peculiar Imbalance,* 123–24; Wingerd, *North Country,* 328–29, 335–37.

27. Just one week after the contraband camp was established at Fort Snelling, a blackface minstrel troupe, Morris' Minstrels, "an able troupe of Minstrels and Negro Delineators," opened their show at St. Paul's Ingersoll Hall, with a Saturday matinee scheduled for ladies and children: Osman, "General Sibley's Contraband Teamsters," 63, 65.

28. Green, *A Peculiar Imbalance,* 142–43, 145.

29. Green, *A Peculiar Imbalance,* 148, 160, 169, 182; Green, "Minnesota's Long Road to Black Suffrage," 83; Schwalm, *Emancipation's Diaspora,* 176–77, 182–83; Spangler, *The Negro in Minnesota,* 39; Taylor, *African Americans in Minnesota,* 6; Nelson, *Fredrick L. McGhee,* 55–56.

30. Taylor, "Pilgrim's Progress: Black St. Paul and the Making of an Urban Ghetto," 90, 97; Nelson, *Fredrick L. McGhee,* 3–5, 26–27, 29; Taylor, *African Americans in Minnesota,* 25–26. Attesting to the possibility that even prominent Whites might support Black demands for civil rights, one of the other more notable speakers at the 1891 Emancipation Day celebration in St. Paul was Archbishop John Ireland, who condemned discrimination and called for full political and social equality for Blacks: see chapter 6; Nelson, *Fredrick L. McGhee,* 29, 39, 206.

31. The first Pond family reunion was held at Bde Maka Ska, in the 1870s, on the site of the mission house that Gideon and Samuel erected nearly sixty years before: "Pond Celebration," p. 1, roll 2; "Historians Report: 1835 Speaks to 1935," p. 5–6, 8, roll 2—both Pond Family Papers.

32. "Presentation of Memorial Window," [n.d.,] p. 3, roll 2, Pond Family Papers.

Notes to Chapter 2

"They All Must Be Taught Their Duty":
Barbers, Porters, Washerwomen,
and Inmates

1. Thomas Montgomery to Mother, May 2, 1863, folder "Thomas Montgomery Letters, #9–19, April 18–Aug 5, 1863," box 2, Montgomery Papers.

2. Thomas Montgomery to Parents, June 2, 1863; Thomas Montgomery to Mother, June 15, 1863—both folder "Thomas Montgomery Letters, #9-19, April 18-Aug 5, 1863," box 2, Montgomery Papers; Anderson and Woolworth, *Through Dakota Eyes*, 16; Folwell, *A History of Minnesota* 4:279, 297; Wingerd, *North Country*, 344; Westerman and White, *Mni Sota Makoce*, 194-95.

3. Thomas Montgomery to Parents and Brothers, January 23, 1864 Benton Barracks [Missouri], folder "Thomas Montgomery Letters, #21-40, Aug 16, 1863-January 23, 1864"; Thomas Montgomery, no heading, but letter #41; Thomas Montgomery to Parents and Brothers, Benton Barracks, March 8, 1864; Thomas Montgomery to Parents and Brothers, New Orleans, March 23, 1864—all folder "Thomas Montgomery Letters, #41-71 [Feb 1864?]-September 1864"; Thomas Montgomery to Father, October 6, 1864, Morganzia, Louisiana, folder "Thomas Montgomery Letters, #72-100, September 18, 1864-April 24, 1865"—all box 2, Montgomery Papers.

4. Schwalm, "Overrun with Free Negroes," 156-57; Thomas Montgomery to Mother, October 27, 1864; Thomas Montgomery to Brother, November 21, 1864—both Morganzia, Louisiana, folder "Thomas Montgomery Letters, #72-100, September 18, 1864-April 24, 1865," box 2, Montgomery Papers.

5. Thomas Montgomery to Brother, November 27, 1864, Morganzia, Louisiana, folder "Thomas Montgomery Letters, #72-100, September 18, 1864-April 24, 1865," box 2, Montgomery Papers; see also Green, *The Children of Lincoln*, 110-11.

6. Thomas Montgomery to Brother Alexander, January 30, 1866, Baton Rouge, Louisiana, folder "Thomas Montgomery Letters, #101-132, May 1, 1865-May 22, 1866"; June 9, 1907, obituary, unknown newspaper, folder "Thomas Montgomery Biographies and Obituaries"—both box 2, Montgomery Papers.

7. See Green, *Degrees of Freedom*, 61-62. US Census Manuscript and Minnesota Census.

8. In his study of Black migration to Ohio, Indiana, and Illinois, Jack Blocker argues that there was an "age of the village" for African Americans who moved to the North in the decades following the Civil War. Instead of immediately concentrating in the largest cities, he says, they distributed themselves across the "urban hierarchy." Consequently, African Americans were no more "metropolitan" than Whites. By 1890, however, an increasing number of African Americans left the rural villages for metropolitan centers and new migrants from the South bypassed small towns and went directly there as well. Blocker, *A Little More Freedom*, 31, 150. See also Thornbrough, *The Negro in Indiana before 1900*.

9. Spangler, *The Negro in Minnesota*, 40-42, 63-66.

10. Schwalm, *Emancipation's Diaspora*, 2-3.

11. Benjamin Densmore was in the Fourth US Colored Infantry Regiment (USC) and Daniel was in the Sixty-Eighth USC. Three other young White men from Goodhue County also received commissions to command all-Black units by the Bureau of Colored Troops: Fred E. Miller and John G. Gustafson (both in the 112th USC) as well as Elijah Clark (in the 123rd USC). Johnson, *Uncertain Lives*, 19-20; Green, *Degrees of Freedom*, 62-63.

12. Lief, "A Woman of Purpose: Julia B. Nelson," 303-14; Johnson, *Uncertain Lives*, 47-49.

13. Johnson, *Uncertain Lives*, 34, 41; US Census Manuscript and Minnesota Census.

14. US Census Manuscript and Minnesota Census.

15. Black Civil War veterans in Hastings also included George Washington Daniels, who was born enslaved in Georgia, ran away from his enslaver and joined a Union regiment as a horse handler for General William LeDuc, and came to Hastings with the general in 1865 to work on his estate. Additionally, there was Abraham Davenport, who was born enslaved in Raleigh, North Carolina, and joined the Eleventh Regiment US Colored Infantry, as well as Thomas Willis, born enslaved in Mississippi and a soldier in the Eighteenth Regiment US Colored Infantry. US Census Manuscript and Minnesota Census; *Hastings Gazette*, August 24, 1872.

16. *Hastings Gazette*, August 6, 1863, January 2, 1869, January 9, 1875, May 27, 1875.

17. *Hastings Gazette*, November 28, 1891, December 26, 1891, November 22, 1896, November 2, 1907; *Hastings Democrat*, October 31, 1907. Besides helping to purchase the church building, James Curry prospered enough to buy other property as well, which at least some Whites probably did not like to see. He not only worked at the post office but also took jobs as a carpenter, farm laborer, and hotel cook. With saved earnings, Curry bought a lot and built a house, which he later resold, and in 1889 he bought two more lots, built a nine-room home there, and then bought eight adjoining lots that he turned into a farm.

18. US Census Manuscript and Minnesota Census; *Hastings Gazette*, January 24, 1916. Henry Thomas died in 1954, and the *Hastings Gazette* obituary made note of the fact that he was "this city's only Negro resident": *Hastings Gazette*, January 22, 1954.

19. US Census Manuscript and Minnesota Census.

20. US Census Manuscript and Minnesota Census; Johnson, *Uncertain Lives*, 41–43, 47–49, 62.

21. US Census Manuscript and Minnesota Census.

22. Schwalm, *Emancipation's Diaspora*, 138–39, 143.

23. US Census Manuscript and Minnesota Census.

24. Spangler, *The Negro in Minnesota*, 66; Green, *Degrees of Freedom*, 61; Fifteenth Census of the United States: 1930, Census of Agriculture, The Negro Farmer in the United States, 10, 28–30, 33, 35–36, 68.

25. Timothy Ward enlisted in the Union Army in December of 1831, went with his regiment to Tennessee and Mississippi, and in June 1863 was commissioned as an officer in the First Regiment Tennessee Infantry Volunteers of African Descent, later the Fifty-Ninth US Colored Infantry. He and others in the regiment were captured at Ripley, Mississippi, and imprisoned in South Carolina. After being paroled in December 1864, Ward went back to the Fifty-Ninth and was later honorably discharged in the early part of 1866. Pluth, "'A Negro Colony' for Todd County," 312–13, 315–16, 322; see also Green, *Degrees of Freedom*, 64.

26. Spangler, *The Negro in Minnesota*, 66–67; Green, *Degrees of Freedom*, 64–65; US Census Manuscript and Minnesota Census.

27. In November, Joseph Henry Scott pled guilty to first-degree burglary, first-degree robbery, and first-degree

assault "with intent to kill" and was sentenced to thirty years in prison. After the family was expelled, the Jeffersons settled in Minneapolis, Thomas working as a barber, one daughter working as a charwoman, one son employed as a driver, and another daughter caring for the three younger children. See Lehman, "The Contemplation of Our Righteousness," 268–76.

28. Elizabeth Seaquist, "History of St. Peter State Hospital, Folder," 1, 8, "History of St. Peter State Hospital, An Introduction to St. Peter State Hospital, Elizabeth Seaquist, 1961, 1964," St. Peter State Hospital Records, Minnesota Historical Society, St. Paul, hereafter cited as "St. Peter State Hospital Records"; William Erickson, "State Hospital," 20–21, folder "Erickson, Wm. D., The First Decade, 1866–76," St. Peter State Hospital Records.

29. Elizabeth Seaquist, "History of St. Peter State Hospital, Folder," 2, 11–12, "History of St. Peter State Hospital, An Introduction to St. Peter State Hospital, Elizabeth Seaquist, 1961, 1964"; William Erickson, "State Hospital," 29, folder "Erickson, Wm. D., The First Decade, 1866–76"; William Erickson, "This Great Charity," 28–29, 31, folder "This Great Charity: Minnesota's First Mental Hospital at St. Peter: 1866–1991"—all St. Peter State Hospital Records.

30. Marshal [*sic*] Rayford, No. 7, Volume A, Case File Numbers 1–800, May 1864–July 1900, St. Peter State Hospital for the Insane, Statistical Record, St. Peter State Hospital Case Books, 1864–1903, Minnesota Historical Society, St. Paul; US Census Manuscript and Minnesota Census citations.

31. US Census Manuscript and Minnesota Census citations; Elizabeth Bell, No. 16512, St. Peter State Hospital

Patient Registers and Indexes, Vol. 3, St. Peter State Hospital Patient Registers and Indexes—Hospital for Dangerous Insane, 1911–1924, Minnesota Historical Society, St. Paul.

32. "A Summary of Conditions in Minnesota State Hospitals for the Mentally Ill: A Report to Governor Luther W. Youngdahl by the Minnesota Unitarian Conference Committee on Institutions for the Mentally Ill," 2–3, folder "A Summary of Conditions in Minnesota State Hospitals, A Report to Governor Luther W. Youngdahl," St. Peter Hospital Records.

33. Schwalm, *Emancipation's Diaspora*, 3–6, 219, 222.

34. *New Ulm Review*, April 1915; US Census Manuscript and Minnesota Census.

35. US Census Manuscript and Minnesota Census; Johnson, *Uncertain Lives*, 30–32. Thomas Montgomery also died in 1907.

36. Martin, "Letters of a Union Officer," 313–15, 319.

37. Martin, "Letters of a Union Officer," 315, 319; *Minneapolis Journal*, February 1913.

Notes to Chapter 3

Not "a Negro Town": Packinghouse Workers and Whiteness in Austin

1. At some point in the 1920s, the entire Winkels family moved to Austin, including John's father, Frank, who worked as a "maintainer" on the state highways; his mother, Emma, whose parents had been German immigrants; Anthony, his youngest brother, who worked as a laborer at odd jobs; and Margaret, his niece, whose mother

Mary, John's sister, seems to have gone elsewhere since the time they all left Adams. This was in addition to Casper, the brother John worked with at Hormel, five years younger than him. US Census Manuscript and Minnesota Census. *Austin Daily Herald,* July 20, 1922, 1; interview with John Winkels by Roger Horowitz and Rick Halpern, December 4, 1985, audio 1106a, tape 37, side 2; interview with Casper Winkels by Roger Horowitz and Rick Halpern, December 5, 1985, audio 1106a, tape 38, side 2—both at Wisconsin Historical Society, Madison.

2. Among the African Americans living in Austin in 1900 was Alfred Reed, aged sixty-one. He was originally from Alabama and boarded and worked as a general laborer in a hotel. Henry Rogers, aged thirty-four, and his wife, Lulu, aged twenty-nine, both born in Missouri, also lived in Austin, Henry making a living as a "day laborer" and Lulu working as a "washerwoman." Additionally, Adams counted one Black resident, Salomen S. Antoney (as the census taker spelled his name), aged forty, born in Canada, and boarding with James and Annie Dixon, who had four children and were farmers. In 1910, Henry and Lulu Rogers were still living in Austin, but the small group of Black residents included only one other couple, Samuel and Rose Barrett, both born in 1875, along with their two young children. His occupation was listed as a "porter" in a barbershop and hers as "none." The rest were men ranging in age from mid-thirties to mid-sixties and working as porters, housekeepers, and laborers. US Census Manuscript and Minnesota Census.

By 1920, Henry and Lulu Rogers were gone but Samuel and Rose Barrett were still there, with only one young son (the other probably died), and Samuel had become the proprietor of a shoeshine parlor. The other African American couple in town was Isaac and Jennie Bailey, both in their seventies and both originally from Arkansas. Despite his age, Isaac worked as a construction laborer. US Census Manuscript and Minnesota Census.

3. John Winkels interview.

4. Green, *On Strike at Hormel,* 39–40; John Winkels interview.

5. Rachleff, *Hard-Pressed in the Heartland,* 33; *The Unionist,* January 20, 1956, 1.

6. Peter Rachleff, interview by the author, April 28, 2013, recording and transcript in author's possession.

7. Flynn, "The Railroad Shopmen's Strike of 1922," 29–31, 34–35, 67–68; Davis, *Power at Odds,* 83–84.

8. *Austin Daily Herald,* June 6, 1922, 1; July 1, 1922, 1; July 7, 1922, 1; July 8, 1922, 1; July 10, 1922, 1; July 17, 1922, 1.

9. *Austin Daily Herald,* July 21, 1922, 1.

10. *Austin Daily Herald,* July 21, 1922, 1; August 10, 1922, 1; US Census Manuscript and Minnesota Census.

11. *Austin Daily Herald,* July 21, 1922, 1; July 31, 1922, 1.

12. *Austin Daily Herald,* August 8, 1922, 1.

13. *Austin Daily Herald,* September 4, 1922, 1; September 18, 1922, 1.

14. Hatle, *The Ku Klux Klan in Minnesota,* 23, 35.

15. Hatle, *The Ku Klux Klan in Minnesota,* 76–77, 100; Hatle and Vaillancourt, "One Flag, One School, One Language," 363–64.

16. *Call of the North* 1, no. 2 (August 3, 1923): 2.

17. Tolnay, "The African American 'Great Migration' and Beyond," 214–15;

Call of the North 1, no. 2 (August 3, 1923): 3; *Call of the North* 1, no. 7 (September 7, 1923): 3. See also Blocker, *A Little More Freedom*.

18. At the time, nearly 70 percent of Minnesota's population was either foreign-born or the children of foreign-born parents, and "naturalization" allowed the Klan to recruit from among these residents. Probably half of the large Duluth chapter was in this category. Hatle, *The Ku Klux Klan in Minnesota*, 29, 134; *Call of the North* 1, no. 1 (July 27, 1923): 1; *Call of the North* 1, no. 2 (August 3, 1923): 1; *Call of the North* 1, no. 4 (August 17, 1923), 1; *Call of the North* 1, no. 7 (September 7, 1923): 1, 4.

19. *Call of the North* 1, no. 1 (July 27, 1923): 1; *Call of the North* 1, no. 2 (August 3, 1923): 1; *Call of the North* 1, no. 4 (August 17, 1923): 1; *Call of the North* 1, no. 6 (August 31, 1923): 1; *Call of the North* 1, no. 8 (September 14, 1923): 1; *Call of the North* 1, no. 17 (November 21, 1923): 1.

20. *Call of the North* 1, no. 1 (July 27, 1923): 1–2. Getting passed over at the fairgrounds took on another significance for the fact that three years earlier (as the next chapter details) thousands of White Duluth residents lynched three Black circus workers when they passed through town there, claiming they had raped a young White woman behind the tents. Local Klan leaders and readers of *The Call* might have had this in mind as they followed the Austin story. *Call of the North* 1, no. 8 (September 14, 1923): 1.

21. *Call of the North* 1, no. 8 (September 14, 1923): 1; *Call of the North* 1, no. 9 (September 21, 1923): 1.

22. *Call of the North* 1, no. 17 (November 21, 1923): 1; *Minnesota Fiery Cross* 1, no. 30 (February 22, 1924): 1; *Minnesota Fiery Cross* 1, no. 31 (February 29, 1924): 1; Hatle

and Vaillancourt, "One Flag, One School, One Language," 363–64, 367–68.

23. Interview with Sven Godfredsen by Roger Horowitz and Rick Halpern, May 18, 19, 20, 1986, audio 1106a, tape 146, side 2; Rachleff, *Hard-Pressed in the Heartland*, 33.

24. Rachleff, *Hard-Pressed in the Heartland*, 28–30, 32–34, 40–41; Horowitz, *Negro and White, Unite and Fight!*, 36–37; Green, *On Strike at Hormel*, 39–41; Godfredsen interview.

25. Arnesen, "Race, Party, and Packinghouse Exceptionalism," 207; Halpern and Horowitz, *Meatpackers: An Oral History*, 19–20, 25.

26. United Packinghouse Workers of America, "Working agreement between United Packinghouse Workers of America, Local No. 9, CIO, and Geo. A. Hormel & Co., Austin, Minn.: as of Dec. 6, 1940" (Austin, MN, 1940), 2.

27. African Americans were rarely mentioned in the paper during its first decade, from the late 1930s to the late 1940s. Other than a 1942 advertisement for an appearance by Anna Short Harrington, as Aunt Jemima, at a local Red Owl supermarket, the only other reference was in *The Unionist*'s coverage of President Harry Truman's battles with southern Democrats at the 1948 Democratic National Convention over his civil rights program. *The Unionist*, January 9, 1942, 4; February 27, 1948, 4; December 30, 1955, 6; April 6, 1956, 7. The *Austin Daily Herald* also covered Black civil rights this way.

28. *The Unionist*, March 30, 1956, 1.

29. *The Unionist*, June 15, 1956, 1; June 29, 1956, 8.

30. *The Unionist*, September 14, 1956, 1; December 14, 1956, 1; *Austin Daily Herald*, September 12, 1956, 20; "Meetings of

Citizens Committees—Austin," 1–4, folder "FEPC/State Commission Against Discrimination Citizens' Committees, 1959–1963," State Commission Against Discrimination Records, 1951–67, Minnesota Historical Society, St. Paul, hereafter cited as "SCAD Collection." The month after the convention, and a month before the first Human Rights Committee meeting, Local P-9 participated in Austin's July 4 parade and sponsored the "colored" Drum and Bugle Corps from the St. Paul Elks Lodge. They were preceded by a large banner with "Local 9, UPWA-AFL-CIO" printed on it. "The parade route was lined with spectators," *The Unionist* reported, "and the Elks unit received enthusiastic applause all along the route." *The Unionist*, July 13, 1956, 1.

31. "Meetings of Citizens Committees—Austin," 1–4, folder "FEPC/State Commission Against Discrimination Citizens' Committees, 1959–1963," SCAD Collection; *The Unionist*, February 1, 1957, 4.

32. *The Unionist*, March 1, 1957, 1.

33. *The Unionist*, October 11, 1957, 1; October 18, 1957, 1; *Austin Daily Herald*, October 10, 1957, 15; October 12, 1957, 1.

34. *The Unionist*, May 20, 1958, 1.

35. Meeting Report, (Kanatz,) January 8, 1962, Austin, 1–3, folder "State Commission Against Discrimination: Subject Files: Field Reports and Itineraries, 1961–1964," SCAD Collection.

36. "Resume of Helen McMillan," written by Ethel Haase, Austin, in Helen McMillan Papers, Minnesota Historical Society, St. Paul.

37. See Loewen, *Sundown Towns*. *The Negro Motorist Greenbook* (1962), 50; Jim Doughty, interview by author, April 28, 2013, recording and transcript in author's possession; State of Minnesota

Fair Employment Practices Commission, "Population Characteristics in Citizens Committee Areas—1960," William Maupins Papers, Archives and Special Collections, Kathryn A. Martin Library, University of Minnesota Duluth, hereafter cited as "Maupins Papers."

38. In 1979, Local P-9 became part of the United Food and Commercial Workers, formed by a merger of the UPWA, Amalgamated Meat Cutters, and Retail Clerks unions. Rachleff, *Hard-Pressed in the Heartland*, 3; Green, *On Strike at Hormel*, 283.

39. Green, *On Strike at Hormel*, 225–27; Phil Kwik, "Leaders of Hormel Strike Arrested; International Holds Trusteeship Hearing," *Labor Notes*, May 1, 1986.

40. Green, *On Strike at Hormel*, 8, 183, 256–58; Rachleff, *Hard-Pressed in the Heartland*, 85.

41. US Census; Doughty interview. The AFL-CIO did not support the amnesty for undocumented immigrants stipulated by the 1986 Immigration Reform and Control Act until 2000, instead championing restrictive immigration legislation as a way to defend workers' interests. Valdés, *Mexicans in Minnesota*, 78.

Notes to Chapter 4

"In That Very Northern City": Making the Color Line in Duluth

1. See *The Alliance (OH) Review and Leader*, May 26, 1920, May 27, 1920; *South Bend (IN) News-Times*, June 7, 1920, June 8, 1920, in the Papers of the NAACP, Part 7: The Anti-Lynching Campaign, 1912–1955, Series A: Investigative Files, 1912–1953 (Frederick, MD: University

Publications of America), hereafter cited as "NAACP Papers"; *Duluth Herald,* June 16, 1920. One twenty-year veteran of circus work explained to a West Virginia newspaper that circuses were divided between "grifting" and "clean" shows. The "grifting" shows were characterized by gamblers, pickpockets, and burglars, had a "legal adjuster" in charge of the criminal element, and scheduled their shows to move quickly from city to city in order to flee citizen wrath, arrests, and court proceedings. The John Robinson may have been of this sort. See *Fairmont West Virginian,* May 10, 1920; Davis, *The Circus Age Culture.*

2. Fedo, *The Lynchings in Duluth,* 4-5.

3. *Duluth Rip-saw,* June 26, 1920, NAACP Papers; Employer Detective Service Report, cover letter, addressed to Turner, June 28, 1920, St. Paul, 4-5; operative then interviewed Dr. Graham: roll 2, Trial Transcript, Case No. 6785, Max Mason, August 1921 [Dr. David Graham testimony], 219-20, DLM.

4. Dr. Valdo Turner to Mary White Ovington, June 29, 1920, NAACP Papers.

5. *New York Times,* June 17, 1920. Similarly, the *New York Globe* saw the lynching as a challenge to regional distinctions, though suggesting that White "savagery" was not limited to the South because "Negro crime" was not either: "Duluth is not in Georgia, Mississippi, Kentucky, or even Missouri. It is in Minnesota. Yet in Duluth last night a mob of five thousand persons stormed the police station, and, capturing six Negroes, lynched three of them for their alleged attack upon a white girl. . . . The north has criticized the south bitterly for Negro lynchings. Brought in contact with Negro crime, it reaches for rope and tar barrel. The full

implications of this fact have not been comprehended. They go beyond the mere indefensible savagery of the individual incident. They suggest that the Negro problem, so long the south's problem only, is now the nation's. . . . There is that about the Negro and the white which apparently make for savagery like Duluth's regardless of geographical situation and tradition." *New York Globe,* June 16, 1920, in NAACP Papers.

6. Fedo, *The Lynchings in Duluth,* 112, 126, 132-33; *Duluth News Tribune,* June 17, 1920. Transcript of interview with Edward Nichols by David Vassar Taylor, July 17, 1974, 20; transcript of interview with Fred Douglas Bell and Lillian Vina Bell by David Vassar Taylor, Malik Simba, and Musa Foster, July 9, 1975, 24-25— both Minnesota Black History Project, Oral History Interviews, Minnesota Historical Society, St. Paul, hereafter cited as "MBHP." Charles Sumner Smith to James Weldon Johnson, June 21, 1920, 1-2, NAACP Papers.

7. *Duluth Herald,* July 1, 1922; Hatle, *The Ku Klux Klan in Minnesota,* 34-35; *Call of the North* 1, no. 23 (January 2, 1924): 1; US Census 1920, 1930, 1940, 1950.

8. *Duluth Herald Tribune,* August 10, 1967, August 11, 1967, in Unitarian Church, Duluth Records, Archives and Special Collections, Kathryn A. Martin Library, University of Minnesota Duluth, hereafter cited as "Unitarian Church Records."

9. Alanen, *Morgan Park,* xiii-xiv, 21, 113; Fred Douglas Bell and Lillian Vina Bell interview, 1-2, 5.

10. Alanen, *Morgan Park,* 186-87; Nichols interview, 17.

11. Transcript of interview with Charles and Geraldine Stalling by Musa Foster, Malik Simba, and Seitu Jones, July

30, 1975, 23; transcript of interview with Carrie L. Dozier by Musa Foster, Malik Simba, and Seitu Jones, July 30, 1975, 1; transcript of interview with William Maupins by Musa Foster, Malik Simba, and Seitu Jones, July 31, 1975, 10—all MBHP; Herbert Hill [labor director, NAACP] to Wilfred C. Leland [executive director, Minnesota Fair Employment Practices Commission], May 17, 1961, 1; Wilfred Leland to Herbert Hill, July 11, 1961, 1, Maupins Papers.

12. Alanen, *Morgan Park*, 186–87, 198; see also *The Labor World* (Duluth), May 29, 1915, 8; *The Playground* 16, no. 1 (April 1922). "Blackface" minstrel shows continued in Duluth into the 1950s, including annual productions by Trinity Lodge No. 282 at the Shrine Auditorium on East First Street, not far from where the 1920 lynching happened. See "Trinity Lodge No. 282 Minstrel Show Recordings," Archives and Special Collections, Kathryn A. Martin Library, University of Minnesota Duluth. Nichols interview, 18; Turberville, "The Negro Population in Duluth, Minnesota, 1950," 234.

13. Nelson, *Fredrick L. McGhee*, 58–60; *Edward T. Rhone v. Robert N. Loomis*, Records and Briefs in Cases Decided by the Supreme Court of Minnesota, April Term 1898.

14. *Duluth Rip-saw*, September 6, 1919, September 1, 1923. John L. Morrison was born in Iowa in 1863 and grew up on a farm there. After attending Tabor College, he held different jobs, including schoolteacher and traveling salesman. He began writing for newspapers in the late 1880s and came to Duluth sometime during the next decade to be the labor editor for the *Herald*. He eventually founded his own paper, *Citizen*, and started the

Rip-saw in the spring of 1917. *Duluth Rip-saw*, July 12, 1919.

15. *Duluth Rip-saw*, May 19, 1917, July 7, 1917, March 23, 1918, September 21, 1918, February 7, 1920.

16. *Duluth Herald*, September 5, 1919; *Duluth Rip-saw*, September 6, 1919, September 20, 1919.

17. *Duluth Herald*, September 5, 1919. When the cases of those arrested went to court, the Black women involved either were sentenced to sixty days in jail or failed to show up, forfeited their bail money, and left town, and the men, all Finnish and Swedish immigrants, pleaded guilty to charges of disorderly conduct and received suspended sentences. *Duluth Rip-saw*, September 20, 1919, October 4, 1919, October 18, 1919.

18. *Duluth Rip-saw*, June 26, 1920, roll 1, DLM. There is a large gap in the *Rip-saw* issues available at the Minnesota Historical Society. Most of those missing are from the spring to fall of 1920, which would include Morrison's coverage of the lynching and subsequent trials as well as the arrest of the chief of police. However, the "Duluth Lynching Materials" collection as well as the "Papers of the NAACP, Part 7: The Anti-Lynching Campaign, 1912–1955, Series A: Investigative Files, 1912–1953" both have some relevant articles interspersed with organizational correspondence, investigation reports, and trial records.

19. H. J. Carling [Employers Detective Service general manager] to Dr. Valdo Turner [St. Paul NAACP president], June 28, 1920, 3–4, roll 1, DLM. Operative Morgan did not interview James Sullivan, however, because Sullivan had left town after the lynchings, and nobody could tell Morgan where he was or when he would return. Trial Transcript, Case No. 6785,

Max Mason, August 1921, Irene Tusken testimony, 8–10, Dr. David Graham testimony, 219–20—both roll 2, DLM. Irene Tusken's "virtue" was called into question again when Dr. W. A. Coventry examined her for a gonorrhea infection, on July 10, although it's not clear why he knew to do this. Her infection was confirmed by a smear specimen as well as profuse vaginal discharge, which he said indicated that her case was quite recent. The doctor also tested James Sullivan on July 12 or 13 and determined he had no venereal infection. In court, Coventry explained that gonorrhea manifests two to ten days after contact, yet despite the fact the alleged rape happened on June 14, nearly a month before, Coventry also had Dr. M. A. Nicholson test the circus workers in jail. Nicholson testified that Max Mason had an active case, though the latter claimed that his only infection happened in the middle of December 1919, before he joined the circus, and that he was treated by a doctor for it in Louisville, Kentucky, with no signs of gonorrhea since then. Nevertheless, this was used as critical evidence to convict him of rape, and he served five years at Stillwater prison. See County Attorney Warren Greene to Governor Joseph Burnquist, December 14, 1920, and Report—both roll 1; Trial Transcript, Case No. 6785, Max Mason, August 1921, Dr. William A. Coventry testimony, 223–26, Dr. M. A. Nicholson testimony, 227–37, Max Mason testimony, 366–67—all roll 2, DLM.

20. Valdo Turner to James Weldon Johnson [NAACP executive secretary], June 21, 1920, and Louis Ervin report enclosed with letter, 1, NAACP Papers. The only part of Ervin's investigation made public was a brief article in *The Crisis*, drawing from the letter he sent to

Turner. The journal explained that the investigator had determined it was not certain that any of the lynched men was guilty of rape, that "it was not even certain that the girl was assaulted," and that all of the men he interviewed "protests his innocence" and "none of them saw the crime committed, if one was committed." Curiously, the article also included Ervin's explanation for why he thought the jailed workers were credible. "These men are extremely ignorant," he had condescendingly written to Turner, and *The Crisis* article quoted, "and I do not believe they could tell a lie so consistently that I could not catch them in it." *The Crisis* 20, no. 4 (August 1920): 179, roll 1, DLM. Nate Graves Statement, Clarence Green Statement, Lonnie Williams Statement, Louis Hayes Statement, W. M. Miller Statement, and Frank Spicer Statement, Louis Ervin Report, NAACP Papers. Like Mason, Miller was also tried for rape, but he was acquitted by the jury.

21. *Duluth Herald*, July 8, 1920, July 21, 1920; *Duluth Rip-saw*, November 27, 1920; Witness Testimony, Chief of Police John Murphy, interviewed by Adjutant General W. F. Rhinow, June 23, 1920, 2–5, roll 1, DLM. The *Herald* also noted that interest in the case was increased by the fact that Frank Bradley "has been particularly active in bringing to justice offenders against liquor laws," suggesting that he was using his authority to maintain his own group's control of the illicit trade: *Duluth Herald*, July 9, 1920.

22. Lucas, "Rape, Race, and Redemption," 176, 205, 214; *Duluth Herald*, August 9, 1920; US Census 1880, 1900, 1910, 1920; Minnesota Death Index.

23. *Duluth News Tribune*, June 18, 1920; Grand Jury Statement to Judge Cant, 10–11—both NAACP Papers.

24. In the winter after his release from prison, in 1923, Carl Hammerberg and a friend hopped a freight train to Minneapolis looking for work, but finding none, they took another train home, choosing a car warmed with charcoal burners to keep the cargo from freezing, and both suffocated to death. Fred Davis ("special policeman") testimony, 1–3; Carl Hammerberg testimony, 46–62; Charge of the Court (judge's instructions), 63–72, 81–85—all Inmate Case File, No. 5148, Carl John Alfred Hammerberg, Trial Transcript, June 1921, District Court Case No. 5723, Minnesota State Reformatory for Men, Inmate Case Files, 1889–1978, roll 1, DLM.

25. Herbert J. O'Brien testimony, 17; Oscar Olson testimony, 13; Judge William Cant, Sentence, 88; Francis McHugh testimony, 42; Carl Hammerberg testimony, 49–50—all Carl John Alfred Hammerberg, Trial Transcript, June 1921, roll 1, DLM.

26. More than a few of Minnesota's African American leaders were veterans of the Spanish-American War and even more were members of the all-Black Sixteenth Battalion in the Minnesota Home Guard, a volunteer organization formed in April 1917 to replace the National Guard, which had been federalized. DeCarlo, "Loyalty within Racism," 209–10. Schneider, *"We Return Fighting,"* 109. Charles Sumner Smith to James Weldon Johnson, June 21, 1920, 2; Charles Sumner Smith to James Weldon Johnson, June 29, 1920, 1; Charles Sumner Smith to James Weldon Johnson, July 22, 1920, 2—all NAACP Papers. The legal team included Ferdinand Lee Barnett of Chicago (Ida B. Wells Barnett's husband), R. C. McCullough of Duluth, and Charles Scrutchins of Bemidji.

27. Alanen, *Morgan Park*, 225.

Defending Steelworkers Local 1028's commitment to "tolerance," at the end of World War II, recording secretary Ronald Carson contributed a letter to the *Duluth News Tribune* rhetorically asking, "how many organizations allow Negroes as members and allow them to be officers?" The local "not only allows them to be members," he said, "but they are elected to office." In a June 1945 picture, however, all of the local board officers are White. *Duluth News Tribune*, n.d. [but other items in the collection are dated 1945], and picture, June 1945, folder "United Steelworkers of America Local Union No. 1028 (Duluth, Minn.), records," United Steelworkers of America, Local Union No. 1028 (Duluth, Minn.), Records, Minnesota Historical Society, St. Paul. Richard K. Fox, Jr., to William Maupins, May 2, 1960, 1; Wilfred Leland to Herbert Hill (NAACP Labor Secretary), July 11, 1961, 1—both Maupins Papers; Maupins interview, 5. In the 1950 study, one respondent said he was refused a manufacturing job because "there were no separate washrooms available for Negroes," another explained that he was refused work at a construction site because "they never hire colored bricklayers," a third said that the barber's union "wouldn't give me a job in a white shop," and a fourth said he "had to give up with the railroad because I could not join the brotherhood." Turberville, "The Negro Population in Duluth, Minnesota, 1950," 233–34.

28. Turberville, "The Negro Population in Duluth, Minnesota, 1950," 231–34.

29. Turberville, "The Negro Population in Duluth, Minnesota, 1950," 235–36; "B'Nai Brith Minstrel Women's minstrel show at the covenant club in Duluth, Minnesota," c. 1940–1949, Nathan and Theresa Berman Upper Midwest Jewish

Archives, University of Minnesota Libraries, Minneapolis. In 1953, Senator Hubert Humphrey gave a speech at the club on humanitarianism, declaring, "we must recognize the threat inherent for all of us in the oppression of any minority. . . . Hatred breeds hatred, and blinds the world to the reality of man's brotherhood under God." Hubert Humphrey, "Humanity in a Free World," September 22, 1953, 3, Minnesota Historical Society, St. Paul; "Trinity Lodge No. 282 Minstrel Show Recordings," Archives and Special Collections, Kathryn A. Martin Library, University of Minnesota Duluth.

30. Correspondence makes the actual date when Bill Maupins took over from Lee Wiley a bit unclear, because some state and national NAACP leaders were addressing inquiries to the latter rather than the former, although Maupins would then reply as president. See, for example, the exchange in which Maupins learned that the national office was threatening to revoke the Duluth branch charter: Leonard Carter (field secretary, NAACP) to Lee Wiley, September 9, 1960; William F. Maupins to Leonard Carter, September 21, 1960—both Maupins Papers. In the interview Maupins did for the Minnesota Black History Project, however, the interviewers say that he served from 1958 to 1969: see Maupins interview, 1–4, 9, 19–20. There is also other correspondence which suggest the 1958 date: see William Maupins to Benjamin Sigler, September 24, 1963, Maupins Papers.

31. See Housing and Redevelopment Authority of the City of St. Paul, "The Proposed Selby-Dale Renewal Plan: A Study of and Recommendations for Community Rehabilitation and Conservation," March 1960, 33–38, Minnesota Historical Society, St. Paul; Davis, "The Effects of a Freeway Displacement," 209–15; William Maupins to Rep. Arne C. Wanvick [state representative], March 21, 1961; Report of the Duluth Fair Employment Practices Commission to the City Council of Duluth, June 1961; Duluth Fair Employment Practices Commission Meeting Minutes, May 15, 1962, and November 27, 1962—all Maupins Papers. See Louise W. McCannel, "Statement Concerning Fair Housing Legislation" and "Minnesota Has a New Housing Law," and folder "Legislation—undated; 1953–Feb 1959," box 15, Greater Minneapolis Interfaith Fair Housing Program, Records, 1946–1989, Minnesota Historical Society, St. Paul, hereafter cited "GMIFHP Collection."

32. Matt Carter was born in Laurel, Mississippi, in 1926 and went to Chicago at the end of World War II, when his cousin encouraged Matt to join him on a lake freighter galley crew. Matt met Helen when his cousin went back to Mississippi to get married. Matt was the best man, and Helen was also in the bridal party. She was born in Columbus in 1921, attended Rust College to become a teacher, and became involved in an NAACP voter registration project after graduating. Helen married and had a child as well, but the marriage did not last, and she was single when she met Matt. They married in 1953 and she moved with him to Chicago, and they had their own first child after they moved to Duluth. Matthew Carter, interview by author, October 29, 2017, recording and transcript in author's possession. And see *Lake Meadows, Designed for Modern Living on Chicago's New Southside Lake Front* (Chicago: New York Life Insurance Company, 1952), 1–8; "A Second Transformation Awaits Lake Meadows," *Chicago Tribune*, March 23, 1997. Report of the

Duluth Fair Employment Practices Commission to the City Council of Duluth, June 1961, Maupins Papers; *Duluth Herald Tribune*, March 7, 1963, Unitarian Church Records.

33. Carter interview.

34. Minutes of Public Hearings and of the Meeting of the City Planning Commission, March 5, 1963, 3, Maupins Papers; Carter interview.

This is the full list of the residents who signed the petition: Gertrude Klippen 4540 London Road, Ruby Allenfall 4610 London Road, Mr. and Mrs. Irvin Dutcher 4619 Cambridge Street, Mr. and Mrs. Robert Jones 4602 Cambridge Street, Mr. and Mrs. E. M. Spearin 4550 London Road, Mr. and Mrs. Edmond Hebert 4623 London Road, Mr. and Mrs. Allan B. Christiansen 4615 Cambridge Street, D. P. Kelso 4631 London Road, Mr. and Mrs. M. G. Braden 4605 Cambridge Street, Mr. and Mrs. William Frey [no address], Mr. and Mes. [*sic*] James V. Achesen 4432 Cambridge Street, Mr. and Mrs. J. J. Voloshik 4424 Cambridge Street, Mr. and Mrs. Walter Arseneau 4414 Cambridge Street, Mr. and Mrs. Oscar B. Strom 4431 Cambridge Street, Mr. and Mrs. Stanley Gottlieb 305 45th Avenue East, Mr. and Mrs. William Dunbar 4340 London Road, Mr. and Mrs. John M. Swain 4520 London Road, Mr. and Mrs. Ernest D. Oakes 4619 London Road, Mr. and Mrs. N. A. Hewitt 4627 London Road, Mr. and Mrs. E. F. Hensch 4614 London Road, Lois K. McKibbin 4611 London Road, Mr. and Mrs. Allan N. Winters 4541 London Road, Mr. and Mrs. L. G. Brown 4532 London Road, Mr. Geo. L. Gross 4530 London Road, Marion Johnson 4632 London Road, Mr. and Mrs. R. R. Asplund 4419 Luverne Street, Mrs. Thomas M. Starkey 4407 Luverne Street, Mr. J. R. Marshall 4402 Luverne Street, Charles H. Lindberg 4403 Luverne Street, Mr. and Mrs. A. Setterquist 4402 Gilliat Street, Dorothy Hornby 4500 London Road, Thomas W. Starkey 4407 Luverne Street, Mr. and Mrs. S. M. Johnson (?) Jr. 4730 London Road, Mr. and Mrs. R. E. Myers 4824 London Road, Axel R. Holmgren 4800 London Road, Mrs. Axel R. Holmgren 4800 London Road, Henning N. Orrfal 4731 Robinson Street, Mrs. L. D. Rawn 4401 Gilliat Street, Walter L. Swanson 406 Gilliat Street, Mrs. Walter L. Swanson 4406 Gilliat Street, W. C. Dunlop 4512 London Road. Petition to City Planning Commission, Duluth, Minnesota, March 1, 1963, Maupins Papers.

35. Viola May Kanatz (assistant director, State Commission Against Discrimination) to William Maupins, January 16, 1963; Donald Lewis (president, Minnesota-Dakota NAACP State Conference) to William Maupins, March 6, 1963; Minutes of Public Hearings and of the Meeting of the City Planning Commission, March 5, 1963, 4–5; Newton S. Friedman to City Planning Commission, City of Duluth, May 29, 1963—all Maupins Papers. *Duluth Herald Tribune*, March 6, 1963, March 7, 1963, Unitarian Church Papers.

36. Carter interview; Duluth Fair Employment Practices Commission, Annual Meeting Minutes, June 5, 1963, Maupins Papers.

37. *Duluth Herald Tribune*, October 6, 1963, Unitarian Church Papers.

38. *Duluth Herald Tribune*, October 21, 1966, November 2, 1966, Unitarian Church Papers.

39. *Duluth Herald Tribune*, August 10, 1967, August 11, 1967, Unitarian Church Papers; Carter interview.

40. Carter interview.

41. Duluth Fair Employment

Practices Commission Meeting Minutes, May 6, 1959, Maupins Papers; Memo, Joseph Byrne to Frank C. Kent (Commissioner, Department of Human Rights), folder "Duluth: Duluth General Correspondence, 1960–72"; "A Preliminary Analysis of Minority Group Housing and Employment in Duluth, Minnesota," 9, 10, folder "Minnesota State Commission Against Discrimination: Employment, Housing Analysis (Duluth, Minnesota)"— both Minnesota Human Rights Department Records: 1947–2010, Minnesota Historical Society, St. Paul, hereafter cited as MHRD. Department of Research and Planning, Community Improvement Division, Community Renewal Program: Minority Profile, Duluth, Minnesota (1969), 40.

42.   *New York Times*, December 5, 2003.

Notes to Chapter 5

"A Bigoted, Prejudiced, Hateful Little Area": Racial Exclusion in Edina

1.   *The Crier*, May 1938, 1, Edina (Minnesota) Historical Society; US Census 1920, 1930. There is a rich literature on minstrel shows in the nineteenth century but very little written about their persistence in the twentieth century and nothing at all about blackface in the new, middle-class suburbs. See Lott, *Love & Theft*, as well as the chapter "White Skins, Black Masks: Minstrelsy and White Working Class Formation Before the Civil War," in Roediger, *The Wages of Whiteness*.

2.   For specific examples of this see Stahl, *The High School Minstrel Book* and *The Varsity Minstrels*. At some point, another Minneapolis publisher, T. S. Denison and

Company, acquired the rights to Stahl's books, adding them to their vast "line of minstrel books and scripts, staging accessories, advertising cuts, and make-up": *Denison's Minstrel and Song Catalogue*. The postmark on the back of the catalog in the Boston Public Library collection is September 1, 1951. See also *Step Lively: Minstrel Vod'Ville Review*.

3.   Alden R. Grimes "Descendants of Jonathan Taylor Grimes: Pre-Publication Manuscript Excerpt, The Grimes Family, Vol. II, 1988," 4, Minnesota Historical Society, St. Paul; Grimes, *The Grimes Family*, 19. Johnson, *Suburban Dawn*, 44; "Biographical Sketch," 2, box 1, Coates Preston Bull and Family Papers, 1865–1939, Minnesota Historical Society, St. Paul; Holcombe and Bingham, eds., *Compendium of History and Biography of Minneapolis and Hennepin County*, 532–33. See January 5, February 11, March 4, and March 24, 1883, in Sarah Baird Diary, Vol. 2 (1883), Sarah G. Baird and George W. Baird, Diaries, Account Books, and Memorabilia, 1883, 1886–1918, Minnesota Historical Society, St. Paul; March 7, 1879, March 21, 1879, April 4, 1879, Minnehaha Grange Hall Association Secretary's Book 1879–1907, Minnesota Historical Society, St. Paul; August 7, 1875, December 4, 1875, July 19, 1876, December 2, 1876, Minute Book, folder "Minute Books, Dec 9, 1873– Jan 7. 1881," box 1, Minnehaha Grange No. 398 (Edina, MN), Minnesota State Grange, Minnehaha Juvenile Grange No. 2, Grange Records, 1873–1985, Minnesota Historical Society, St. Paul, hereafter cited as "Minnehaha Grange Records."

4.   Thorpe Bros., *Country Club District*, 3; Document No. 1324919, Deed Restriction for The Country Club District of Edina, 4524 Casco Avenue, Minnesota, Book 1054 Deeds, p. 560.

5. Hesterman, *The History of Edina, Minnesota*, 3–4; Dunwiddie, "The Six Flouring Mills on Minnehaha Creek," 167; Johnson, *Suburban Dawn*, 49–50; Scott and Hess, *History and Architecture of Edina, Minnesota*, 9.

6. Holcombe and Bingham, eds., *Compendium of History and Biography of Minneapolis and Hennepin County, Minnesota*, 532–33.

7. Shutter, ed., *Progressive Men of Minnesota*, 193; *National Cyclopedia of American Biography*, 16:57; Dunwiddie, "The Six Flouring Mills on Minnehaha Creek," 286; Morse-Kahn, *Edina: Chapters in the City History*, 40.

8. US Census Manuscripts 1850, 1860, 1870; Minnesota Territorial and State Census Manuscripts, 1849–1905; SAM 296, Roll 120 (1893); SAM 87, Roll 53 (1899)—both Hennepin County Auditor Tax Lists, 1860–1895, Minnesota Historical Society, St. Paul; Richfield Assessment Roll, 1882, box 11, Hennepin County, Minnesota, Assessment Books, 1858– , Minnesota Historical Society, St. Paul; "Histories and Stories of Morningside," folder 70.3.11, Edina (Minnesota) Historical Society.

9. July 19, 1876, December 2, 1876, December 19, 1879, January 2, 1880, January 16, 1880, folder "Minute Books, Dec 9, 1873–Jan 7. 1881," box 1; Mrs. Elvira H. Vinson, "The Grange Hall," 3–4, folder "Historical Record and Background Information, 1874, 1927–ca., 1976," box 3—all Minnehaha Grange Records; E. J. Woodward (President), Edina Mills, Richfield, March 7, 1879; E. J. Woodward (Secretary), Edina Mills, Richfield, March 21, 1879; E. J. Woodward (Secretary), Edina Mills, Richfield, April 4, 1879; Edina Mills, Aug. 29, 1879; Edina Mills, October 7, 1879—all Minnehaha Grange Hall Association Secretary's Book 1879–1907; Morse-Kahn, *Edina: Chapters in the City History*, 61.

10. White concern about interracial marriage was persistent in the nineteenth and twentieth centuries. At the opening meeting of the Social Service Club for the year 1909, for example, University of Minnesota sociology professor Albert E. Jenks spoke in warning that "amalgamation is going on rapidly." Jenks made clear he did not like the idea and rhetorically asked, "Are any of you women open to proposals of marriage from negroes?" Four years later, the Minnesota state legislature considered a bill prohibiting interracial marriage. It was introduced by Representative Frank E. Nimrocks of Minneapolis, and he advised his colleagues that similar laws had already been adopted in twenty-seven states. After Black leaders lobbied against the bill, however, the judiciary committee did not send it out for a vote, even though Governor A. O. Eberhart was likely to sign it. See *Minneapolis Tribune*, October 21, 1909; *Twin City Star*, January 18, 1913, February 8, 1913, April 25, 1913; US Census Manuscript 1870, 1880, 1900, 1910; September 19, 1908, March 16, 1909, December 21, 1912, and folder "Minute Books, April 7, 1906–March 20, 1915," box 1; October 5, 1918, folder "Minute Books, April 3, 1915–Sept. 12, 1919," box 1—all Minnehaha Grange Records; Morse-Kahn, *Edina: Chapters in the City History*, 56–62; Sullivan, "Edina's Pioneer Black Farmers Left a Legacy of Civic Involvement," 6–13.

11. October 31, 1905, Day Book, box 2, 41, Coates and Preston Bull Family Papers; December 2, 1905, March 6, 1915, March 20, 1915, folder "Minute Books, July 1, 1899–Jan. 6, 1906," box 1, Minnehaha Grange Records.

12. Johnson, *Suburban Dawn*, 79, 81, 131–32; Martin, *The Life and Professional Career of Emma Abbott*, 188; SAM 87, Roll 53 (1899); SAM 88, Roll 3 (1910); SAM 90, Roll 20 (1920)—all Hennepin County Auditor Tax Lists, 1860–1895; Hesterman, *The History of Edina, Minnesota*. Charles altered his name slightly, to Bruce C. Yancey, after the embezzlement scandal, and the family moved to Twenty-Eighth Avenue South, in Minneapolis, renting a house. The children, Beryl (twenty-three), Edgar (twenty-one), and Helen (thirteen), were still with them. Charles worked as an "abstractor" in title insurance, Helen as a music teacher, and Beryl as a schoolteacher. US Census Manuscript 1930.

13. US Census Manuscript 1920; SAM 88, Roll 3 (1910); SAM 90, Roll 20 (1920)—both Hennepin County Auditor Tax Lists, 1860–1895; Johnson, *Suburban Dawn*, 79–81, 117–20, 131; Scott and Hess, *History and Architecture of Edina*, 10–11; Thorpe Bros., *Country Club District*, 2, 3, 10; Thorpe Bros., flyer, n.d., Edina (Minnesota) Historical Society.

14. US Census Manuscripts 1910, 1920, 1930, 1940; *Edina City Directory*, 1949, 1960.

15. Johnson, *Suburban Dawn*, 122; US Census Manuscripts 1930, 1940.

16. *New York Age*, June 3, 1909; *Minneapolis Messenger*, October 28, 1922; *Northwest Bulletin*, December 20, 1924; *Minneapolis Tribune*, July 15, 1931; *Twin City Herald*, July 16, 1931; September 17, 1932, September 24, 1932.

17. *Twin City Herald*, June 11, 1932.

18. Federal Housing Administration, *Underwriting Manual* (1938), 980; Bell, *Hate Thy Neighbor*, 23, 25. See also Federal Housing Administration, *Underwriting Manual* (1947). The award-winning documentary film *Jim Crow of the North*

examines the ways racially restrictive covenants aided Minnesota's White residents in establishing and maintaining exclusive communities: https://www.tpt.org/minnesota-experience/video/jim-crow-of-the-north-stijws/. The Mapping Prejudice project (https://mappingprejudice.umn.edu/) has actually identified all of the properties in Hennepin County with racially restrictive covenants in their titles.

19. Katznelson and Mettler, "On Race and Policy History," 519–37; Frydl, *The GI Bill*, 31, 222, 237. See also "White Veterans Only," in Katznelson, *When Affirmative Action Was White*, 113–41.

20. Robert C. Weaver, Administrator, Housing and Home Finance Agency, "Equal Opportunity in Housing," February 8, 1963, Smith College, 8–9, folder "Citizens' Committee on Discrimination in Housing," box 8; "History of Events Leading Up to the Establishment of Interfaith Fair Housing Project," 1, folder "Background Materials and History," box 1; Charles A. Sawyer, City Attorney, "To the Standing Committee on Ordinances and Legislation," February 17, 1958, folder "Legislation—undated; 1953–Feb 1959," box 15; "Editorial—If Not a Law, What?," *Minneapolis Tribune*, July 28, 1958, folder "Citizens' Committee on Discrimination in Housing," box 8; Report of the Legislative Interim Commission on Housing Discrimination and Segregation Practices to the Legislature of the State of Minnesota (1959), 25, 27, folder "Legislation—undated; 1953–Feb 1959," box 15; F. Gordon Wright [34th District, Minnesota House of Representatives] to Rev. Richard E. Sykes [assistant minister, First Unitarian Society, Minneapolis], August 8, 1958; Newsletter From Your Legislator, F. Gordon Wright, March 10, 1958—both

in folder "Legislation—undated; 1953–Feb 1959," box 15—all GMIFHP Collection. Those opposed also included representative and building contractor Marvin Anderson, who asserted that discrimination was a "small matter" and "nothing drastic to worry about" while also admitting he did not accept Blacks in his developments. Representative Franklin P. Kroehler acknowledged that "there is a problem" of housing discrimination, yet insisted that "we are able to make better progress through education and most of all our church efforts than we can through a law." *St. Paul Recorder,* August 1, 1958.

21. In 1962, the *Minneapolis Realtor* pointed to recent court cases that declared open-occupancy laws in other parts of the country unconstitutional, which indicated that "so-called 'fair housing' legislation" was doomed, and soon it would become unnecessary to abide by Minnesota's law. Louise W. McCannel to Mrs. John Gruner, May 8, 1962, 1; *Minneapolis Realtor,* 5—both folder "Minneapolis Urban League, Cr. & Mis, Jan–Mar 1963," box 4, GMIFHP Collection. St. Paul Board of Realtors, St. Paul Rental Property Association, Minnesota Home Owners, United Citizens League, Memo To the Honorable Committeemen and Legislators of the State of Minnesota, n.d., folder "SCAD Minutes and Memoranda, June 1962–June 1963," Minnesota Human Rights Department, SCAD Collection. Starting in the 1920s, real estate brokers nationwide had been professionalizing their trade, setting themselves apart with a claim to particular knowledge, recognized standards, and exclusive organization, all of which enabled them to effectively perpetuate segregated housing. The 1924 Realtors Code of Ethics even spelled

out the ethical imperative to practice discrimination, warning against introducing "members of a race or nationality" whose presence "will clearly be detrimental to property values." And, as late as 1957, the National Association of Real Estate Boards teaching manual advised against introducing "undesirable influences" like "a colored man of means who was giving his children a college education and thought they were entitled to live among whites." Hornstein, *A Nation of Realtors,* 14–16, 107.

22. The six "pocket areas" in Minneapolis were Humboldt Heights, Glenwood-Grant-Harrison, Riverside–Seven Corners, South Central and part of Central Parkway, Snelling Avenue south of Lake Street, and the Franklin Avenue area. With the exception of the Humboldt Heights area and a few blocks north and south of the boundary between South Central and Central Parkway, Robert L. Williams also explained in his testimony, "the 'pockets' to which Negroes have been limited are located in areas which the Minneapolis Housing and Redevelopment Authority has designated as areas of blight." Census Track Tables, folder "Census Figures, Minneapolis," box 8; Statement of Robert L. Williams [executive director, Minneapolis Urban League] to the Civil Administration Committee, House of Representatives, Minnesota State Legislature, March 24, 1959, 1, folder "Undated; 1958–Sept. 1961," box 27; "Program Prospectus, 1963," 1–3, folder "Minneapolis Urban League, Cr. & Mis, Jan–Mar 1963," box 4; Statement of Shelton B. Granger [executive secretary, Minneapolis Urban League] to the General Legislation Committee, House of Representatives, Minnesota State Legislature, 1959, 1, folder "Legislation—undated; 1953–Feb

1959," box 15—all GMIFHP Collection; Tillman, *Not By Prayer Alone*, 33, 37, 39.

23. Marion G. Taylor to Mr. Walter F. Mondale [State Attorney General], November 10, 1960, 1, folder "Taylor, Marion G.," box 26; James A. Tillman, "Schedules for Study of Integration Processes Involving Pioneer Families and Their New Neighborhoods," folder "Interview Schedule I, nos 1–7," box 33—both GMIFHP Collection; Marion Taylor, interview by author, May 9, 2014, recording and transcript in author's possession; Case # 3-ER-63, Mrs. Marion Taylor vs. Heldwood Nursing Home (January 29, 1959), S.A.; Case # 5-GR-125, Mr. Marion G. Taylor vs. Veterans Administration Chemistry Lab Services, Dismissed, NPC, June 15, 1964—both folder "Journal of Cases, 1955–1964, Including Case Statistics," SCAD Collection.

24. *Minneapolis Tribune*, January 5, 1960; *Edina Courier*, January 7, 1960; "Jan. 1960 Petition" and Marion G. Taylor to Mayor Kenneth Joyce, June 19, 1960—both folder "Taylor, Marion G.," box 26, GMIFHP Collection. The village had owned the lot until 1955, when Minneapolis developer R. L. Lindquist purchased it and shortly after sold it to contractor James C. Hildreth, who sold it to Marion Taylor in December 1955. Tillman, *Not By Prayer Alone*, 139; *Minneapolis Tribune*, January 5, 1960. Donald Irish, "Greater Minneapolis Interfaith Housing Program, Pilot Study, 1963–64" (carbon copy), folder "Irish, Donald P.," box 13, GMIFHP Collection; Al White to Morning Village Council Mpls [*sic*], St. Paul, Jan 20 160 [*sic*], 1, Edina (Minnesota) Historical Society.

25. "City of Minneapolis, Voluntary Committee on Housing, Meeting of September 25, 1958, Minutes"; "Minutes of the Voluntary Housing Committee, December 16, 1958"; "Citizens Committee on Discrimination and Housing, March 3, 1959, Minutes"—all folder "Citizens Committee on Discrimination and Housing," box 8; "History of Events Leading Up to the Establishment of Interfaith Fair Housing Project," 1–2; "Resume, James Tillman," 1–2—both folder "Background Materials and History," box 1—all GMIFHP Collection; Tillman, *Not By Prayer Alone*, 29–31.

26. Tillman, *Not By Prayer Alone*, 138; *Minneapolis Tribune*, January 19, 1960; *Minneapolis Star*, January 19, 1960; *Edina Courier*, January 14, 1960, January 21, 1960; *New York Times*, January 31, 1960; "Jan. 1960 Petition"; James A. Tillman to Mr. Sherman S. Hasbrouck [4246 Scott Terrace], February 15, 1960; Merrill Beale to James Tillman, Jan. 12, 1960; Mayor James Joyce, "A Matter of No Prejudice," January 18, 1960—all folder "Taylor, Marion G.," box 26, GMIFHP Collection.

27. *Edina Courier*, January 21, 1960; Marion G. Taylor to Mr. John deLaittre [president, Farmers & Mechanics Savings Bank], July 2, 1960; Mr. Marion G. Taylor to Mr. Walter F. Mondale [State Attorney General], November 10, 1960—both folder "Taylor, Marion G.," box 26, GMIFHP Collection; Taylor interview; Jim Joyce, interview by author, April 27, 2013, recording and transcript in author's possession; Al Siftar, interview by author, June 25, 2015, recording and transcript in author's possession.

28. Irish, "Greater Minneapolis Interfaith Housing Program, Pilot Study, 1963–64"; Taylor interview; Joyce interview; Siftar interview; Edina-East High School, *Whigrean* (yearbook) 22 (1972): 224–25, Edina (Minnesota) Historical Society.

29. Minnesota SCAD, July 1967–December 1968 Annual Report, 14, folder "State Commission Against Discrimination," MHRD; Negro Sample By Neighborhood, n.d. [c. 1967], folder "Minnesota State Commission Against Discrimination: Fair Housing Compliance Survey," Minnesota Human Rights Department, SCAD Collection; Sandy Berman, interview by author, April 27, 2013, recording and transcript in author's possession.

30. Edina-East High School, *Whigrean* (yearbook) 23 (1973); *Zephyrus* (Edina High School newspaper), October 5, 1982—both at Edina (Minnesota) Historical Society.

Notes to Chapter 6

"This Vicious Vice":
Black Removal in St. Paul

1. St. Paul began as "Pig's Eye," named for French Canadian fur trader and tavern owner Pierre "Pig's Eye" Parrant, who had lost one of his eyes. It was renamed in the mid-1840s and designated the territorial capital in 1849. In the decades to follow, it grew with the increase in Mississippi River traffic and wave after wave of migrants. Lindeke, *St. Paul*, 16–19. Nelson, *Fredrick L. McGhee*, 29, 39, 41.

2. "The Church's Work for the Negro Race," *Sacred Heart Review* 44, no. 10 (August 27, 1910): 6–7; "The Catholic Negro," *The Crisis* 11, no. 6 (April 1916): 317–18; Adams, *To Work for the Whole People*, 124–25.

3. Taylor, *African Americans in Minnesota*, 25–27; Wilkins, *Standing Fast*, 34–36; Nelson, *Fredrick L. McGhee*, 147, 206.

4. Jan Price in Zielinski, ed., *Children of Rondo*, 72. Sonny Lewis ran an upholstery business at 502 University Avenue, not far from where Fredrick McGhee and his family had lived. Gloria Jeanne Lindstrom Lewis in Cavett, ed., *Voices of Rondo*, 112–14, 121. "One thing I liked about the neighborhood was that we were multi-cultured," Lewis's niece also remembered. "Native Americans, Caucasians, Black families. They all just got along really well." Estelle Hartshorn Jones in Zielinski, ed., *Children of Rondo*, 4.

5. Nieeta Laurene Neal Presley lived at 622½ Rondo Avenue, near the Dale Street intersection. Nieeta Laurene Neal Presley in Zielinski, ed., *Children of Rondo*, 59–60.

6. St. Paul's first African American resident was James Thompson, who had been purchased and freed from slavery by White Methodist missionary Alfred Brunson, to help the latter in his work at Kaposia. Thompson was married to the daughter of Dakota leader Cloud Man and fluent in the Dakota language. He soon joined another missionary endeavor but left that work in 1839. After living for a few years in a nearby settlement called Rumtown, where he participated in the whiskey trade, Thompson moved to St. Paul, where he ran the Mississippi River ferry. Decades later, when the US-Dakota War broke out, he was at the Lower Sioux Agency, making a living as a barber and musician, and Dakota fighters killed him. Bachman, *Northern Slave, Black Dakota*, 35–36. Taylor, *African Americans in Minnesota*, 14, 32–33; Taylor, "Pilgrim's Progress: Black St. Paul and the Making of an Urban Ghetto," 48–49, 51; Wilkins, *Standing Fast*, 27–28; Benjamin Louis Alexander Senior in Cavett, ed., *Voices of Rondo*, 30; Nieeta Laurene

Neal Presley in Zielinski, ed., *Children of Rondo*, 60.

7. Kathryn Corman Gagnon in Cavett, ed., *Voices of Rondo*, 170; Anisah Hanifah Dawan in Cavett, ed., *Voices of Rondo*, 43. Dawan's parents, Albert and Martha Payne, adopted her in 1922 and named her Elizabeth; she later changed her name after converting to Islam. "Union Gospel Mission Annual Meeting, Feb. 26, 1962" program, 5–8, folder "Historical and Background Information About U.G.M., undated," box 2, Union Gospel Mission Records, 1902–1992, Minnesota Historical Society, St. Paul, hereafter cited as "UGM Records."

8. William "Billy" L. Collins Jr. in Cavett, ed., *Voices of Rondo*, 288–89.

9. *St. Paul Pioneer Press*, December 6, 1951, February 7, 1952; *Minnesota Municipalities* (March 1952): n.p.—all roll 1, St. Paul Housing and Redevelopment Authority, Clippings, Scrapbooks and Loose Clippings, 1951–1977, Minnesota Historical Society, St. Paul, hereafter cited as "SPHRA Clippings Collection."

10. *St. Paul Pioneer Press*, February 6, 1952, February 7, 1952; *Minnesota Municipalities* (March 1952): n.p.—all roll 1, SPHRA Clippings Collection.

11. *St. Paul Pioneer Press*, February 25, 1952, March 7, 1952; *Minnesota Municipalities* (March 1952)—all roll 1, SPHRA Clippings Collection. See also Martin O. Weddington vita (n.d.) and biography (October 31, 1979), folder "General information and vitas, 1975–2000," box 1, Martin O. Weddington Papers, Minnesota Historical Society, St. Paul.

12. *St. Paul Dispatch*, May 16, 1956, July 18, 1956, August 15, 1956, September 28, 1956, roll 1, SPHRA Clippings Collection; Nathanial Abdul Khaliq in Cavett, ed., *Voices of Rondo*, 221–22, 224–25, 228.

13. "Summary Relocation Report, Eastern and Western Redevelopment Projects, Saint Paul, Minnesota, March 13, 1958," 1–4, folder "Relocation Report for Eastern and Western Redevelopment Projects, March 1958," St. Paul Housing and Redevelopment Authority, Redevelopment Project Files, 1953–1969, Minnesota Historical Society, St. Paul, hereafter cited as "SPHRA Project Files Collection." In different official reports as well as newspaper and magazine articles, the demographic details of the populations affected by the redevelopment projects varied, although not by much. The numbers cited in the SPHRA relocation report were derived from an actual census of the population. *St. Paul Pioneer Press*, June 27, 1954, November 8, 1957; *Minnesota Municipalities* (March 1952): n.p.—all roll 1, SPHRA Clippings Collection.

14. *St. Paul Dispatch*, August 7, 1957, August 8, 1957, August 17, 1957, May 27, 1958; *St. Paul Pioneer Press*, November 9, 1957, April 16, 1958, November 18, 1958—all roll 1, SPHRA Clippings Collection; Davis, "The Effects of a Freeway Displacement," 210.

15. *St. Paul Pioneer Press*, September 29, 1955; *St. Paul Dispatch*, May 22, 1956; *Minneapolis Tribune*, January 12, 1959—all roll 1, SPHRA Clippings Collection; Cavanaugh, *Politics and Freeways*, 14–15.

16. Cavanaugh, *Politics and Freeways*, 15–16; *St. Paul Dispatch*, February 4, 1957, roll 1, SPHRA Clippings Collection.

17. Cavanaugh, *Politics and Freeways*, 16; *St. Paul Pioneer Press*, June 24, 1957, roll 1, SPHRA Clippings Collection; *St. Paul Recorder*, April 4, 1958, April 18, 1958, May 2, 1958, May 9, 1958. The newspaper cited several cases that the state appealed and listed the court-appointed appraisers' amount and the state appraisers'

offer, revealing the wide gap. For example: Mollie Peyre ($9,000/$6,700); Cordelia Clay ($9,500/$7,500); Florence Gaylord ($8,500/$5,900); John Patton ($12,000/$8,500); Hazel Wiseman ($14,500/$10,000); Harry Peterson ($13,000/$10,000); and others. In the end, largely because it was too burdensome and costly to contest the state appraisers' offers, all residents accepted those lower awards.

18. *St. Paul Recorder,* March 14, 1958; *St. Paul Pioneer Press,* March 14, 1958—both roll 1, SPHRA Clippings Collection; Teresina "Willow" Carter Frelix in Cavett, ed., *Voices of Rondo,* 280–82.

19. *St. Paul Recorder,* April 11, 1958, April 18, 1958; *St. Paul Dispatch,* March 29, 1956, August 24, 1956; *St. Paul Pioneer Press,* April 14, 1958, June 6, 1958, July 23, 1958—all roll 1, SPHRA Clippings Collection; *St. Paul Recorder,* July 25, 1958.

20. *St. Paul Recorder,* August 29, 1958. *St. Paul Pioneer Press,* December 3, 1958; *St. Paul Dispatch,* December 4, 1958—both roll 1, SPHRA Clippings Collection.

21. *St. Paul Pioneer Press,* December 25, 1958, February 4, 1959, March 24, 1959; *Minneapolis Tribune,* February 17, 1959, April 9, 1959—all roll 1, SPHRA Clippings Collection.

22. *St. Paul Pioneer Press,* May 17, 1959, May 22, 1959; *Minneapolis Tribune,* August 5, 1959—all roll 1, SPHRA Clippings Collection.

23. *St. Paul Recorder,* January 31, 1958, February 7, 1958; *St. Paul Pioneer Press,* August 20, 1959—all roll 1, SPHRA Clippings Collection.

24. Davis, "The Effects of a Freeway Displacement," 211–15; Davis and Onque, *Freeway Exodus,* 16; Scott Price in Zielinski, ed., *Children of Rondo,* 121. The other elementary schools were Hill, Marshall, Maxfield, and Webster. See Housing and Redevelopment Authority of the City of St. Paul (HRA St. Paul), "The Proposed Selby-Dale Renewal Plan," 20; "Memorandum Re: Union Gospel Mission Ober Club Condemnation," 2, folder "Ober Boys Club—Condemnation: Legal Memos, undated and 1963–64," box 4, UGM Records.

25. In 1960 the SPHRA commissioners included Joseph F. Gabler (chairman), Clayton G. Rein (vice-chairman), Harold J. Moriarty (secretary), Jerome L. Loberg (assistant-secretary), and Frank H. Delaney (treasurer), and the executive director was Louis J. Thompson. HRA St. Paul, "The Proposed Selby-Dale Renewal Plan," vii, 1–2, 13, 26; *Pittsburgh Catholic,* October 8, 1961.

26. HRA St. Paul, "The Proposed Selby-Dale Renewal Plan," 2, 14, 17, 20, 41; HRA St. Paul, *Selby-Dale Renewal Area* (December 1959), 1, 8, 10–12, 34, Minnesota Historical Society, St. Paul.

27. HRA St. Paul, "The Proposed Selby-Dale Renewal Plan," 21–23, 26–27, 31.

28. *St. Paul Pioneer Press,* March 11, 1959, March 16, 1959; *Your Neighbor,* April 8, 1959; *Minneapolis Morning Tribune,* September 7, 1959—all roll 1, SPHRA Clippings Collection.

29. *St. Paul Pioneer Press,* September 23, 1960, July 31, 1962—both roll 1, SPHRA Clippings Collection. In June 1962, Joseph Gabler was confirmed to head the Federal Housing Administration for Minnesota. *St. Paul Pioneer Press,* April 26, 1962; *St. Paul Dispatch,* June 19, 1962; see also *St. Paul Pioneer Press,* September 16, 1961, roll 1, SPHRA Clippings Collection.

30. The United Citizens League groups included the Minnesota Home Owners Association, North End Civic and

Betterment Club, Mar-Dale Improvement Club, Selby Hill Boosters Club, West Side Citizens, Inc., East Side Citizens, Inc., Rental Property Owners Association, and St. Paul Home Builders Association, beside two that Soderberg and Schilling left unspecified. *St. Paul Pioneer Press*, August 5, 1961; *St. Paul Dispatch*, August 10, 1961, January 19, 1962, February 9, 1962—all roll 1, SPHRA Clippings Collection; Martin and Goddard, *Past Choices/ Present Landscapes*, 19–20.

31. The number of formal complaints to the State Commission Against Discrimination increased to ninety-eight in 1965, with refusing to rent and changing the terms or conditions of rental or sale still the main types of discrimination. SCAD, 9th Annual Report, 1964, 7, folder "State Commission Against Discrimination," MHRD. FEP Form #6, Exhibit IV, May 27, 1963, Case #4-OAR-H12"; FEP Form #6, Exhibit VIII, May 27, 1963, Case #4-OR-H19—both folder "SCAD Minutes and Memoranda, June 1962-June 1963," SCAD Collection.

32. Model Cities was a Great Society program that broke with traditional urban renewal efforts by attempting a comprehensive approach to solving urban problems, addressing both physical aspects of urban decay and related social disorder. The Neighborhood Development Program was similar but established later by the US Fair Housing Act of 1968. At the time HUD gave its approval to the Summit-University project in 1969, it was the largest neighborhood redevelopment project in the country, encompassing 1,035 acres and 21,700 residents. Martin and Goddard, *Past Choices/Present Landscapes*, 19, 104–8.

Notes to Chapter 7

"The First Negro Family on Our Block": A Housing Integration Campaign in Bloomington

1. "Narrative" [1881], 56–57, vol. 1, roll 1; "100th Anniversary," 5, roll 2—both Pond Family Papers. In 1880 there were four Dakota households containing a total of nineteen persons living in and around Bloomington, in 1883 there were twenty individuals, and in 1890 there were two households with eight people between them. Those who remained after the US-Dakota War, however, faced considerable hostility from the White residents. Gideon Pond recalled one spring day in 1863, for example, talking to a friend visiting from a neighboring village who, after he spied an "Indian woman" pass by, asked if they were allowed to be there. The minister admitted that they were not but came anyway, and the friend insisted that "if we should see one of them in our streets, we would shoot her." Williamson, "The Dakota Indian Settlement at the Gideon Pond Farm," 115–19. In 1889, an incomplete census by government agent Robert Henton counted 264 Mdewakanton families scattered among several settlements and camps. A census done a year later by US Indian inspector James McLaughlin recorded 903 Dakota people. See Westerman and White, *Mni Sota Makoce*, 202–3.

2. The 1870 census manuscript lists one Black resident of Bloomington, Dan Ebens, born in Alabama about 1855, and the 1900 census manuscript lists only Walter Harris. He is not in the 1905 Minnesota census or 1910 federal census, but those both include V. McHenry and Lulu Nall, and the federal census manuscript records Clyde Thompson. Johnson,

Suburban Dawn, 128, 144, 148, 195; *Minneapolis Star,* December 14, 1961; US Census 1940, 1960.

3.   Bloomington Human Relations Committee (BHRC), April 6, 1964, Meeting Attendees, folder "Membership and Mailing Lists, 1964–1965," Bloomington Human Relations Council, Organization Records, 1964–1968, Minnesota Historical Society, hereafter cited as "BHRC Records." Mary C. Pruitt, "Racial Justice in Minnesota: The Activism of Mary Toliver Jones and Josie Robinson Johnson," in Vaz, ed., *Black Women in America*, 71–72, 83–84, 86–88, 91. The first Black engineer hired at Honeywell was Woodfin Lewis, whom Josie and Charles Johnson knew, along with his wife, Virginia, from Fisk University. The second Black engineer at Honeywell was Luther Prince, whom Charles knew from when they were graduate students at MIT. Johnson, Little, and Holbrook, *Hope in the Struggle*, 39–40, 44–48, 53–55.

4.   BHRC, April 6, 1964, Meeting Attendees, folder "Membership and Mailing Lists, 1964–1965," BHRC Records; "History of Events Leading Up to the Establishment of Interfaith Fair Housing Project," 1–2; "Resume, James Tillman," 1–2—both folder "Background Materials and History," box 1, GMIFHP Collection; Tillman, *Not By Prayer Alone*, 29–32, 40–41.

5.   BHRC, "Bloomington Human Relations Council: A Quick History for New Members, April 1964 to September 1965," 1, folder "Background and History, 1964–65," BHRC Records.

6.   BHRC, "About the Bloomington Human Relations Council (Committee, Group?)—(tentative)," 1, folder "Background and History, 1964–65"; Meeting Minutes, April 27, 1964, 2; May 5, 1964, 2—both folder "Minutes and Agendas,

April 1964–March 1966,"—all BHRC Records; "Majority Group Comments," n.p., in Irish, "Greater Minneapolis Interfaith Housing Program, Pilot Study, 1963–64."

7.   "Majority Group Comments," n.p., in Irish, "Greater Minneapolis Interfaith Housing Program, Pilot Study, 1963–64"; Hornstein, *A Nation of Realtors,* 17; Report of the Legislative Interim Commission on Housing Discrimination and Segregation Practices to the Legislature of the State of Minnesota (1959), 14; State Commission Against Discrimination vs. Eugene V. Snow, FEP Form #6, Exhibit IV, January 8, 1963, Case #4-A-H3, folder "SCAD Minutes and Memoranda, June 1962–June 1963," Minnesota Human Rights Department, SCAD Collection; SCAD, 8th Annual Report, 1963, 17, folder "State Commission Against Discrimination," MHRD.

8.   "First Draft: Suggested Presentation to Realtors, March 30, 1965," 1, folder "Minutes and Agendas, April 1964–March 1966"; "Bloomington Human Relations Council, Newsletter, May 1966," 2, folder "Newsletters, April 1965– June 1967"— both BHRC Records; US Decennial Census 1970.

9.   Meeting Minutes, April 6, 1964, 1–2; April 27, 1964, 1–2—both folder "Minutes and Agendas, April 1964–March 1966," BHRC Records.

10.   Meeting Minutes, May 5, 1964, 1–2, folder "Minutes and Agendas, April 1964–March 1966," BHRC Records.

11.   BHRC, "Quick History for New Members, April 1964 to September 1965," 1; "Draft of Human Relations Committee Meeting Minutes, June 2, 1964," 1; "Human Relations Committee, Bloomington, Minn., July 1964 Draft," 1; Minutes of Steering Committee Meeting,

July 21, 1964, 1; Meeting Minutes, July 28, 1964, 1—all folder "Minutes and Agendas, April 1964–March 1966"—all BHRC Records.

12. Barbara Cunningham also provided a brief history of the Brooklyn Center human relations committee, which she and a dozen other residents had established the previous October. Their group was made up of both White and Black members, but unlike the Bloomington committee, they decided not to focus on discrimination against African Americans. Rather, they intentionally avoided using the terms "race" and "rights" and instead referred to "background, color, origin, and religion." Additionally, their work in the community was limited to an organized "Listening Post," with one family on each block "keeping aware of human relations problems," as well as exchanging information with government and civic groups. Meeting Minutes, September 8, 1964, 1–2, folder "Minutes and Agendas, April 1964–March 1966," BHRC Records; Pruitt, "Racial Justice in Minnesota," 72.

13. Meeting Minutes, September 8, 1964, 1, folder "Minutes and Agendas, April 1964–March 1966," BHRC Records; *Minnesota Tribune*, December 16, 1964; BHRC, "Quick History for New Members, April 1964 to September 1965," 1.

14. "Meeting Minutes, September 22, 1964," 1, folder "Minutes and Agendas, April 1964–March 1966," BHRC Records; *All the Way Home* (Dynamic Films, 1957) and *Crisis in Levitto*wn (Dynamic Films, 1957).

15. "Human Relations Council, Bloomington, Minnesota, 'The Family Next Door' Coffee Party Committee Report," 1–2, folder "Minutes and Agendas, April 1964–March 1966"; BHRC,

"Quick History for New Members, April 1964 to September 1965," 2; BHRC, "Bloomington Human Relations Council, Newsletter, April, 1965," 3, folder "Newsletters, April 1965–June 1967"—all BHRC Records.

16. BHRC, "First Draft: Suggested Presentation to Realtors, March 30, 1965," 1–2; "Human Relations Committee, Bloomington, Minn., Report of Executive Comm. meeting, March 30, 1965," 3—both folder "Minutes and Agendas, April 1964–March 1966"; "Bloomington Human Relations Council, Newsletter, April, 1965," 3; "Bloomington Human Relations Council, Newsletter, May, 1965," 2—both folder "Newsletters, April 1965–June 1967"—all BHRC Records. The St. Louis Park Human Relations Council (SLPHRC) was doing work similar to the Bloomington Human Relations Committee during this time. SCAD chair and realtor Kennon Rothchild led a training session for members at Aldersgate Methodist church, and the group sent letters to forty realty companies located in the Minneapolis suburb or who did business there. "Realtors who favor open occupancy will be asked to allow a Council member to speak to their agents at a sales meeting," chair Fred Lyon told the *St. Louis Park Dispatch,* and they will be "asked to make their acceptance public." However, Gordon Peterson, the head of the Hennepin County Board of Realtors and president of Calhoun Realty, made it clear that he believed brokers "are strictly the agents of their customers and that home sellers—not the realtors—are responsible for making the decision to sell or not to sell to minority groups." In mid-June 1965, when the SLPHRC contacted four dozen local realty companies about adding their names to a newspaper advertisement

endorsing open occupancy, one that the BHRC had given their support to as well, only five were willing to do so. *St. Louis Park Dispatch*, May 13, 1965, June 17, 1965.

17. "Bloomington Human Relations Council, Newsletter, August-September, 1965," 3-4, folder "Newsletters, April 1965-June 1967"; BHRC, "Human Relations Committee, Bloomington, Minn., Report of Executive Comm. meeting, March 30, 1965," 2, folder "Minutes and Agendas, April 1964-March 1966"; "Bloomington Human Relations Council, Newsletter, July, 1965," 3; "Bloomington Human Relations Council, Newsletter, October, 1965," 3—both folder "Newsletters, April 1965-June 1967"—all BHRC Records.

18. BHRC, "Quick History for New Members, April 1964 to September 1965," 2; "Bloomington Human Relations Council, Newsletter, June, 1965," 3; "Bloomington Human Relations Council, Newsletter, July, 1965," 3; "Bloomington Human Relations Council, Newsletter, May, 1966," 3—all folder "Newsletters, April 1965-June 1967"—all BHRC Records.

19. The new executive committee also included Bonnie Hutchens (secretary-treasurer), Ann Williams (publicity), Judy Boris (library-publications), Evelyn Carter (liaison), Robert Wilson (schools), James Wego (legislation), Bob Burgenstein (employment), and Lynn Taylor (neighborhood education). BHRC, "Quick History for New Members, April 1964 to September 1965," 2. "Bloomington Human Relations Council, Newsletter, October, 1965," 2; "Bloomington Human Relations Council, Newsletter, November, 1965," 1; "Bloomington Human Relations Council, Newsletter, January, 1966," 2; "Bloomington Human Relations Council, Newsletter, February, 1966," 2—all folder

"Newsletters, April 1965-June 1967," BHRC Records.

John Thomasberg and his wife, Vonnie, had been involved with the BHRC since the spring of 1965. Soon after they joined, John met with a local school principal (unnamed) about a blackface program the school (also unnamed) was organizing. "The principal asked a number of Negroes if they would be offended," according to the group's April meeting minutes, and "when they replied affirmatively, he agreed to drop the black face." In the discussion that followed during the council meeting, members decided to write a letter to the principal to commend him for his action and noted that "further work with the schools was necessary and should include Indian stereotypes." "Bloomington Human Relations Council, Minutes, April, 1965," 2, folder "Minutes and Agendas, April 1964-March 1966"; "Bloomington Human Relations Council, Newsletter, June, 1966," 1; "Bloomington Human Relations Council, Newsletter, March, 1967," 4—both folder "Newsletters, April 1965-June 1967"—all BHRC Records.

20. In January 1965, state attorney general Walter Mondale called for a "united front" of state civil rights organizations to modify the law with these additions and to give SCAD the power to issue binding orders enforceable in a court of law after notice and a hearing and to obtain a temporary injunction to halt the sale or rental of a property while a discrimination complaint was pending. Office of the Attorney General, Press Release, January 21, 1965, 1, folder "Legislation, 1962-1964," box 15, GMIFHP Collection; Meeting Minutes, January 5, 1965, 1, folder "Minutes and Agendas, April 1964-March 1966," BHRC Records.

"BHRC Annual Report, 1965-1966," 2, folder "Newsletters, April 1965-June 1967"; "Bloomington Human Relations Council, Newsletter," June 1966, 2; "Bloomington Human Relations Council, Newsletter," April 1967, 2-3—both folder "Newsletters, April 1965-June 1967"—all BHRC Records; Auerbach, "The 1967 Amendments to the Minnesota State Act against Discrimination and the Uniform Law Commissioners' Model Anti-Discrimination Act," 259-61.

21. Delton, *Making Minnesota Liberal*, 167-69; US Decennial Census 1980.

22. Star-Lack, "Close to Home," 15, 17-18, 23; Governor's Interracial Commission, *The Negro and His Home in Minnesota* (1947), 65; US Decennial Census 1940, 1950, 1960, 1970.

23. Johnson, Little, and Holbrook, *Hope in the Struggle*, 39-40; Star-Lack, "Close to Home," 1-2, 27.

24. *St. Louis Park Dispatch*, June 4, 1964, July 16, 1964, August 6, 1964, September 3, 1964.

25. *St. Louis Park Dispatch*, January 28, 1965, October 7, 1965.

26. The precedent for the federal fair housing law was Executive Order 11063, which had been signed by President John F. Kennedy in November 1962. The order directed federal agencies "to take all action necessary" to prevent discrimination in the sale or rental of property owned or operated by the federal government or provided with the aid of federal loans or grants. Meyer, *As Long as They Don't Move Next Door*, 169, 209; US Decennial Census 1970 and 1980.

Notes to Epilogue

1. The Governor's Interracial Commission became the Governor's Human Rights Commission in 1956. Governor's Interracial Commission of Minnesota, *The Negro Worker in Minnesota* (March 1945), 25, 48-49.

2. Governor's Interracial Commission of Minnesota, *The Negro and His Home in Minnesota* (1947), 50-52, 61, 66, 69, 71.

3. Lassiter, *The Silent Majority*, 1-2; Lamb, *Housing Segregation in Suburban America since 1960*, 63-64. George Romney had been chairman and president of the American Motors Corporation, from 1954 to 1962, and governor of Michigan, from 1963 to 1969. Lassiter, *The Silent Majority*, 307.

4. Lassiter, *The Silent Majority*, 307; "Housing in the Comprehensive Plan: Study Results of the Twin Cities Metropolitan Council, Final Report I" (March 1970), 5; Goetz, Chapple, and Lukerman, "Enabling Exclusion," 213-14; Myron Orfield, "Integration and Neo-Segregation in Minnesota, Draft Report" (University of Minnesota Law School, December 2018), 1-2; US Decennial Census 1970, 1980; *Minnesota: 2010 Summary of Population and Housing Characteristics* (Washington, DC: US Department of Commerce, 2012).

5. In Golden Valley, the Black population increased from 340 in 1980 to 1,441 in 2010, yet the White population there plummeted, from 22,026 to 17,390, and the total population fell from 22,775 to 20,371. US Decennial Census 1970, 1980; *Minnesota: 2010 Summary of Population and Housing Characteristics*. See also Meyer, *As Long as They Don't Move Next Door*, 212-14.

6. In Albert Lea, another packinghouse city near Austin, the White

population dropped from 19,288 to 16,213 between 1970 and 2010, while African Americans increased from 40 to 204. In New Ulm, the number of Whites was fairly fixed, at just over 13,000 from 1970 to 2010, and the increase in the number of Blacks was even more miniscule than in Albert Lea, from 4 to 42. US Decennial Census 1970, 1980; *Minnesota: 2010 Summary of Population and Housing Characteristics*.

7. The introduction to the Governor's Interracial Commission report *The Indian in Minnesota* included an explanation of how the GIC defined an Indian: "An Indian is a person enrolled in an Indian Agency or recognized as an Indian in the community. An enrolled Indian is one whose name is found on the census rolls of any Indian agency in 1950. A non-enrolled Indian is one who was not enrolled in any Indian agency in 1950." Governor's Interracial Commission of Minnesota, *The Indian in Minnesota* (1952), 7, 25, 33, 50, 77. US Decennial Census 1970, 1980; *Minnesota: 2010 Summary of Population and Housing Characteristics*.

8. Governor's Interracial Commission of Minnesota, *The Mexican in Minnesota* (1953), 79–80. In the 1920s, the St. Paul Urban League studied the living conditions of Black migrants who moved to the West Side, most of them coming directly from Kansas City, Omaha, Chicago, and "other cities of the Central West" but originally from the "Far South." The fifty or so families living there faced a "severe housing shortage," the study explained, and what housing they did find was "not only deplorable but a menace to the health and well being of the entire city." *Northwestern Bulletin* (St. Paul), November 17, 1923. As the St. Paul Housing and Redevelopment

Authority undertook redevelopment projects in the 1950s that would displace many Mexican families living on the West Side, Whites who had formed the United Citizens League successfully pressured the city council to turn down all nine of the proposed sites for new public housing there. *St. Paul Dispatch*, August 9, 1957, September 28, 1960; *St. Paul Pioneer Press*, September 16, 1961—all roll 1, SPHRA Clippings Collection. Like Rondo, the West Side was ethnically diverse, including not only Mexicans but also Russian Jews, Chinese, Italians, and others. Urban reformers had long had their eye on the area, however, with the aim of developing an industrial zone that would take advantage of rail and river transportation. This would increase St. Paul's industrial tax base and lower city tax rates. And, in the end, the land clearance and construction of the River Industrial Park made the area unrecognizable. See Lindeke, *St. Paul*, 109–12. US Decennial Census 1980; *Minnesota: 2010 Summary of Population and Housing Characteristics*.

9. The GIC's report on *The Oriental in Minnesota* noted that the Minnesota general census did not list Filipinos as a separate group, but community leaders estimated that the number of individuals with some Filipino heritage was between three hundred and five hundred in 1949. The largest portion was in Minneapolis, followed by St. Paul, with smaller populations in Owatonna, LeSueur, Duluth, and Albert Lea. With only eight "native Filipino" women counted in the state, 90 percent of the Filipino men were married to White women. The GIC also estimated that 40 percent of Filipinos were homeowners and claimed they "have not reported any difficulty in buying homes in a part of the Twin Cities where they

have desired to do so." Additionally, according to a 1948 community survey, there were about 150 Japanese-born residents and five hundred Japanese Americans in Minnesota. Like the Chinese, they did face discrimination when attempting to buy or rent homes, though supposedly "not frequently." Governor's Interracial Commission of Minnesota, *The Oriental in Minnesota* (1949), 14–15, 33, 43. *Minnesota: 2010 Summary of Population and Housing Characteristics*.

10. Christopher Magan, "Minnesota's Worsening Racial Disparity: Why It Matters to Everyone," *St. Paul Pioneer Press*, May 16, 2010; "Racial Disparities and Equity," https://minnesotago.org/application/files/7214/5825/5846/Racial_Inequality_Public_Final.pdf; Metropolitan Council, "Diving Deeper: Understanding Dis-

parities between Black and White Residents in the Twin Cities Region," 5–6, https://metrocouncil.org/Data-and-Maps/Publications-And-Resources/MetroStats/Census-and-Population/Diving-Deeper-Understanding-Disparities-Between-B.aspx. See also Amy August, "Coloring in the Progressive Illusion: An Introduction to Racial Dynamics in Minnesota," in Jacobs, Thompson Taiwo, and August, eds., *Sparked*, 1–14; Jonathan M. Rose, "Disparity Analysis: A Review of Disparities Between White Minnesotans and Other Racial Groups," Council on Black Minnesotans (2013), 4–15.

11. Massey and Denton, *American Apartheid*, 2–3, 7–8; Meyer, *As Long as They Don't Move Next Door*, 7–8.

12. Gordon, *Ghostly Matters*.

BIBLIOGRAPHY

Primary Sources

Repositories

Edina (Minnesota) Historical Society

Kathryn A. Martin Library, University of Minnesota Duluth

William Maupins Papers.
Unitarian Church Duluth Records.

Minnesota Historical Society, St. Paul

Bloomington Human Relations Council, Organization Records, 1964-1968.
Coates Preston Bull and Family Papers, 1865-1939.
Duluth (Minnesota) Lynchings of 1920, Selected Materials.
Greater Minneapolis Interfaith Fair Housing Program Records, 1946-1989.
Helen McMillan Papers.
Minnesota Black History Project, Oral History Interviews.
Minnesota Human Rights Department Records, 1947-2010.
Minnesota State Grange, Minnehaha Juvenile Grange No. 2, Grange Records,
    1873-1985.
Thomas Montgomery and Family Papers.
Pond Family Papers.
St. Paul Housing and Redevelopment Authority, Clippings, Scrapbooks and Loose
    Clippings, 1951-1977.

St. Paul Housing and Redevelopment Authority, Redevelopment Project Files, 1953-1969.

St. Peter State Hospital Case Books, 1864-1903.

St. Peter State Hospital Patient Registers and Indexes—Hospital for Dangerous Insane, 1911-1924.

St. Peter State Hospital Records.

State Commission Against Discrimination Records, 1951-67.

Union Gospel Mission Records, 1902-1992.

United Steelworkers of America, Local Union No. 1028 (Duluth, Minn.) Records.

Martin O. Weddington Papers.

University of Minnesota Libraries, Minneapolis

Nathan and Theresa Berman Upper Midwest Jewish Archives.

Newspapers

Austin Daily Herald
Bloomington Sun
The Call of the North (St. Paul)
The Crier (Edina)
Duluth Herald
The Duluth Rip-saw
Edina Courier
Edina-Morningside Courier
The Labor World (Duluth)
Minneapolis Messenger
Minneapolis Spokesman
Minneapolis Star
Minneapolis Tribune
The Minnesota Fiery Cross
The National Advocate
New Ulm Review
New York Age
Northwest Bulletin (Minneapolis)
St. Louis Park Dispatch
St. Paul Dispatch
St. Paul Echo
St. Paul Pioneer Press
St. Paul Recorder
South Bend News-Times
Twin City Herald
Twin City Star
The Unionist (Austin)

Secondary Sources

Adams, Mary Christine. *To Work for the Whole People: John Ireland's Seminary in St. Paul*. New York: Paulist Press, 2002.

Alanen, Arnold R. *Morgan Park: Duluth, U.S. Steel, and the Forging of a Company Town*. Minneapolis: University of Minnesota Press, 2015.

Anderson, Gary Clayton. *Kinsmen of Another Kind: Dakota-White Relations in the Upper Mississippi Valley, 1650-1862*. Lincoln: University of Nebraska Press, 1984.

———. *Massacre in Minnesota: The Dakota War of 1862: The Most Violent Ethnic Conflict in American History*. Norman: University of Oklahoma Press, 2019.

Anderson, Gary Clayton, and Alan R. Woolworth. *Through Dakota Eyes: Narrative Accounts of the Minnesota Indian Wars of 1862*. St. Paul: Minnesota Historical Society Press, 1988.

Arnesen, Eric. "Race, Party, and Packinghouse Exceptionalism." *Labor History* 40, no. 2 (May 1999): 207-11.

Auerbach, Carl A. "The 1967 Amendments to the Minnesota State Act against Discrimination and the Uniform Law Commissioners' Model Anti-Discrimination Act: A Comparative Analysis and Evaluation." *Minnesota Law Review* 949 (1967): 231-435.

Bachman, Walt. *Northern Slave, Black Dakota: The Life and Times of Joseph Godfrey*. Bloomington, MN: Pond Dakota Press, 2013.

Bell, Jeannine. *Hate Thy Neighbor: Move-In Violence and the Persistence of Racial Segregation in American Housing*. New York: New York University Press, 2013.

Blocker, Jack Jr. *A Little More Freedom: African Americans Enter the Urban Midwest, 1860-1930*. Columbus: Ohio State University Press, 2008.

Buck, Daniel. *Indian Outbreaks*. 1904; Minneapolis, MN: Ross & Haines, 1965.

Carroll, Jane Lamm. "'Who Was Jane Lamont?': Anglo-Dakota Daughters in Early Minnesota." *Minnesota History* 59, no. 5 (Spring 2005): 184-96.

Case, Martin. *The Relentless Business of Treaties: How Indigenous Land Became US Property*. St. Paul: Minnesota Historical Society Press, 2018.

Cavanaugh, Patricia. *Politics and Freeways: Building the Twin Cities Interstate System*. Prepared for the Center for Urban and Regional Affairs and the Center for Transportation Studies, University of Minnesota, 2006.

Cavett, Kateleen Jill Hope, ed. *Voices of Rondo: Oral Histories of Saint Paul's Historic Black Community*. Minneapolis, MN: Syren Book Company, 2005.

Cobb, James C. *Away Down South: A History of Southern Identity*. New York: Oxford University Press, 2005.

———. "An Epitaph for the North: Reflections on the Politics of Regional and National Identity at the Millennium." *Journal of Southern History* (February 2000): 3-24.

Davis, Colin J. *Power at Odds: The 1922 National Railroad Shopmen's Strike*. Urbana: University of Illinois Press, 1997.

Davis, F. James. "The Effects of a Freeway Displacement on Racial Housing Segregation in a Northern City." *Phylon* 26, no. 3 (Fall 1965): 209-15.

Davis, F. James, and Alice Onque. *Freeway Exodus; Experiences in Finding Housing as a Result of the St. Anthony-Rondo Freeway Displacement from Western to Lexington Avenues in St. Paul: A Research Report*. St. Paul, MN: Hamline University, 1962.

Davis, Janet M. *The Circus Age Culture and Society under the American Big Top*. Chapel Hill: University of North Carolina Press, 2002.

DeCarlo, Peter J. "Loyalty within Racism: The Segregated Sixteenth Battalion of the Minnesota Home Guard during World War I." *Minnesota History* 65, no. 6 (2017): 208-19.

Delton, Jennifer. *Making Minnesota Liberal: Civil Rights and the Transformation of the Democratic Party*. Minneapolis: University of Minnesota Press, 2002.

Denison's Minstrel and Song Catalogue. Minneapolis, MN: T. S. Denison and Company, n.d.

Dunwiddie, Foster W. "The Six Flouring Mills on Minnehaha Creek." *Minnesota History* 44, no. 5 (April 1975): 162-74.

Federal Housing Administration. *Underwriting Manual*. Washington, DC: Government Printing Office, 1938.

Federal Housing Administration. *Underwriting Manual*. Washington, DC: Government Printing Office, 1947.

Fedo, Michael. *The Lynchings in Duluth*. 1979; St. Paul: Minnesota Historical Society Press, 2000.

Flynn, James R. "The Railroad Shopmen's Strike of 1922 on the Industry, Company, and Community Levels." PhD diss., Northern Illinois University, 1993.

Folwell, William Watts. *A History of Minnesota*. 4 vols. St. Paul: Minnesota Historical Society, 1924.

Frydl, Kathleen J. *The GI Bill*. New York: Cambridge University Press, 2009.

Goetz, Edward G., Karen Chapple, and Barbara Lukerman. "Enabling Exclusion: The Retreat from Regional Fair Share Housing in the Implementation of the Minnesota Land Use Planning Act." *Journal of Planning Education and Research* 22, no. 3 (2003): 213-25.

Gordon, Avery F. *Ghostly Matters: Haunting and the Sociological Imagination*. 1997; Minneapolis: University of Minnesota Press, 2008.

Green, Hardy. *On Strike at Hormel: The Struggle for a Democratic Labor Movement*. Philadelphia: Temple University Press, 1990.

Green, William. *The Children of Lincoln: White Paternalism and the Limits of Black Opportunity in Minnesota, 1860-1876*. Minneapolis: University of Minnesota Press, 2018.

———. *Degrees of Freedom: The Origins of Civil Rights in Minnesota, 1865-1912*. Minneapolis: University of Minnesota Press, 2015.

———. "Minnesota's Long Road to Black Suffrage, 1849-1868." *Minnesota History* 56, no. 2 (Summer 1998): 68-84.

———. *A Peculiar Imbalance: The Fall and Rise of Racial Equality in Early Minnesota*. St. Paul: Minnesota Historical Society Press, 2007.

Grimes, Mary A. *The Grimes Family*. Minneapolis, MN: n.p., 1946.

Halpern, Rick, and Roger Horowitz. *Meatpackers: An Oral History of Black Packinghouse Workers and Their Struggle for Racial and Economic Equality*. New York: Twayne Publishers, 1996.

Hatle, Elizabeth Dorsey. *The Ku Klux Klan in Minnesota*. New York: History Press, 2013.

Hatle, Elizabeth Dorsey, and Nancy M. Vaillancourt. "One Flag, One School, One

Language: Minnesota's Ku Klux Klan in the 1920s." *Minnesota History* 61, no. 8 (Winter 2009-10): 360-71.

Hesterman, Paul Donald. *The History of Edina, Minnesota: From Settlement to Suburb*. Edina, MN: Burgess Publishing, Edina Historical Society, 1988.

Hoffert, Sylvia D. *Jane Grey Swisshelm: An Unconventional Life, 1815-1884*. Chapel Hill: University of North Carolina Press, 2004.

Hoisington, Daniel John. *A German Town: A History of New Ulm, Minnesota*. New Ulm, MN: City of New Ulm, 2004.

Holcombe, R. I., and William Bingham, eds. *Compendium of History and Biography of Minneapolis and Hennepin County, Minnesota*. Chicago: Taylor Company, 1914.

Hornstein, Jeffrey M. *A Nation of Realtors: A Cultural History of the Twentieth-Century American Middle Class*. Durham, NC: Duke University Press, 2005.

Horowitz, Roger. *Negro and White, Unite and Fight!: A Social History of Industrial Unionism in Meatpacking, 1930-90*. Urbana: University of Illinois Press, 1997.

Jacobs, Walter R., Wendy Thompson Taiwo, and Amy August, eds. *Sparked: George Floyd, Racism, and the Progressive Illusion*. St. Paul: Minnesota Historical Society Press, 2021.

Johnson, Frederick. *Suburban Dawn: The Emergence of Richfield, Edina, and Bloomington*. Richfield, MN: Richfield Historical Society, 2009.

———. *Uncertain Lives: African Americans and Their First 150 Years in the Red Wing, Minnesota Area*. Red Wing, MN: Goodhue County Historical Society Press, 2005.

Johnson, Josie, Arleta Little, and Carolyn Holbrook. *Hope in the Struggle: A Memoir*. Minneapolis: University of Minnesota Press, 2019.

Katznelson, Ira. *When Affirmative Action Was White*. New York: W. W. Norton & Company, 2005.

Katznelson, Ira, and Suzanne Mettler. "On Race and Policy History: A Dialogue about the G.I. Bill." *Perspectives on Politics* 6, no. 3 (September 2008): 519-37.

Lamb, Charles. *Housing Segregation in Suburban America since 1960: Presidential and Judicial Politics*. New York: Cambridge University Press, 2005.

Lassiter, Matthew. *The Silent Majority: Suburban Politics in the Sunbelt South*. Princeton, NJ: Princeton University Press, 2006.

Lassiter, Matthew D., and Joseph Crespino, eds. *The Myth of Southern Exceptionalism*. Oxford: Oxford University Press, 2010.

Lehman, Christopher P. "'The Contemplation of Our Righteousness': Vigilante Acts Against African Americans in Southwest Minnesota, 1903." *Minnesota History* 64, no. 7 (Fall 2015): 268-76.

Lief, Julia Wiech. "A Woman of Purpose: Julia B. Nelson." *Minnesota History* 47, no. 8 (Winter 1981): 302-14.

Lindeke, Bill. *St. Paul: An Urban Biography*. St. Paul: Minnesota Historical Society Press, 2021.

Loewen, James W. *Sundown Towns: A Hidden Dimension of American Racism*. New York: Simon & Schuster, 2005.

Lott, Eric. *Love & Theft: Blackface Minstrelsy and the American Working Class*. 1995; New York: Oxford University Press, 2013.

Lucas, Cassandra Lynn. "Rape, Race, and Redemption: A Northern Translation of the

Southern Script in the 1920 Duluth Lynching." PhD diss., University of Minnesota, 2006.

Martin, Judith A., and Antony Goddard. *Past Choices/Present Landscapes: The Impact of Urban Renewal on the Twin Cities*. Minneapolis, MN: Center for Urban and Regional Affairs, 1989.

Martin, N. B. "Letters of a Union Officer: L. F. Hubbard and the Civil War." *Minnesota History* 35, no. 7 (September 1957): 313–19.

Martin, Sadie. *The Life and Professional Career of Emma Abbott*. Minneapolis, MN: L. Kimball Printing, 1891.

Massey, Douglas, and Nancy Denton. *American Apartheid: Segregation and the Making of the Underclass*. Cambridge, MA: Harvard University Press, 1993.

Meyer, Stephen G. *As Long as They Don't Move Next Door: Segregation and Racial Conflict in American Neighborhoods*. Lanham, MD: Rowman & Littlefield, 2000.

Morse-Kahn, Deborah. *Edina: Chapters in the City History*. Edina, MN: City of Edina, 1998.

The National Cyclopedia of American Biography. Vol. 16. New York: James T. White & Company, 1918.

Nelson, Paul. *Fredrick L. McGhee: A Life on the Color Line, 1861–1912*. St. Paul: Minnesota Historical Society Press, 2002.

Osman, Stephen. "General Sibley's Contraband Teamsters." *Minnesota Heritage* 7 (January 2013): 54–74.

Petry, Eduard. *New Ulm, Minnesota Turnverein, 1856–1906*. Ed. Dr. Frederic R. Steinhauser. Trans. August G. Kent. 1906; Minneapolis, MN: General College University, 1979.

Pluth, Edward J. "'A Negro Colony' for Todd County." *Minnesota History* 61, no. 7 (Fall 2009): 312–24.

Purnell, Brian, and Jeanne Theoharis, eds., with Komozi Woodward. *The Strange Career of the Jim Crow North*. New York: New York University Press, 2019.

Rachleff, Peter. *Hard-Pressed in the Heartland: The Hormel Strike and the Future of the Labor Movement*. Boston: South End Press, 1993.

Roediger, David. *The Wages of Whiteness: Race and the Making of the American Working Class*. 1991; New York: Verso, 2013.

Schneider, Mark Robert. *"We Return Fighting": The Civil Rights Movement in the Jazz Age*. Boston: Northeastern University Press, 2002.

Schwalm, Leslie A. *Emancipation's Diaspora: Race and Reconstruction in the Upper Midwest*. Chapel Hill: University of North Carolina Press, 2009.

———. "'Overrun with Free Negroes': Emancipation and Wartime Migration in the Upper Midwest," *Civil War History* 50, no. 2 (March 2004): 145–74.

Scott, William W., and Jeffrey Hess. *History and Architecture of Edina, Minnesota*. Edina, MN: City of Edina, 1981.

Shutter, Marion D., ed. *Progressive Men of Minnesota: Biographical Sketches and Portraits of the Leaders in Business, Politics and the Professions; Together with an Historical and Descriptive Sketch of the State*. Minneapolis, MN: Minneapolis Journal, 1897.

Spangler, Earl. *The Negro in Minnesota*. Minneapolis, MN: T. S. Denison and Company, 1961.

Stahl, LeRoy. *The High School Minstrel Book: Suitable Material for High School Presentation*. Minneapolis, MN: Northwestern Press, 1938.

———. *The Varsity Minstrels*. Minneapolis, MN: T. S. Denison and Company, n.d.

Star-Lack, Russell. "Close to Home: Suburbanization, Residential Segregation, and Jewish-Black Relations, in St. Louis Park and North Minneapolis, MN." BA thesis, Carleton College, 2020.

Step Lively: Minstrel Vod'Ville Review: A Rollicking Mixture of Fun, Songs, and Dances: For the Benefit of Charity Fund, Metropolitan Opera House . . . St. Paul Lodge No. 59 B.P.O. Elks. St. Paul, MN: n.p., 1922.

Sullivan, Joe. "Edina's Pioneer Black Farmers Left a Legacy of Civic Involvement." *About Town: Official Magazine of the City of Edina* (Autumn 2006): 6–13.

Taylor, David Vassar. *African Americans in Minnesota*. St. Paul: Minnesota Historical Society Press, 2002.

———. "Pilgrim's Progress: Black St. Paul and the Making of an Urban Ghetto." PhD diss., University of Minnesota, 1977.

Thornbrough, Emma Lou. *The Negro in Indiana before 1900: A Study of a Minority*. 1957; Bloomington: Indiana University Press, 1993.

Thorpe Bros. *Country Club District*. Minneapolis, MN: Thorpe Bros., 1924.

Tillman, James A. *Not By Prayer Alone: A Report on the Greater Minneapolis Interfaith Fair Housing Program*. Philadelphia: United Church Press, 1964.

Tolnay, Stewart. "The African American 'Great Migration' and Beyond." *Annual Review of Sociology* 29, no. 8 (2003): 209–32.

Turberville, Gus. "The Negro Population in Duluth, Minnesota, 1950." *Sociology and Social Research* 36, no. 4 (March–April 1952): 231–38.

Valdés, Dionicio. *Mexicans in Minnesota*. St. Paul: Minnesota Historical Society Press, 2005.

Vander Velde, Lea, and Sandhya Subramanian. "Mrs. Dred Scott." *Yale Law Journal* 106 (December–January 1997): 1033–1122.

Vaz, Kim Marie, ed. *Black Women in America*. Los Angeles: SAGE Publications, 1994.

Westerman, Gwen, and Bruce White. *Mni Sota Makoce: The Land of the Dakota*. St. Paul: Minnesota Historical Society Press, 2012.

Whipple, Henry Benjamin. *Lights and Shadows of a Long Episcopate, Being Reminiscences and Recollections of the Right Reverend Henry Benjamin Whipple, D.D., L.L.D., Bishop of Minnesota*. New York: Macmillan, 1912.

White, Bruce M. "The Power of Whiteness, or The Life and Times of Joseph Rolette Jr." *Minnesota History* 56, no. 4 (Winter 1998): 178–97.

Wilkins, Roy. *Standing Fast: The Autobiography of Roy Wilkins*. New York: Viking Press, 1982.

Williamson, Jeffrey. "The Dakota Indian Settlement at the Gideon Pond Farm, 1863–1891." *Minnesota's Heritage* 2 (July 2010): 114–20.

Wingerd, Mary Lethert. *North Country: The Making of Minnesota*. Minneapolis: University of Minnesota Press, 2010.

Zielinski, Kimberly, ed. *Children of Rondo: Transcriptions of Rondo Oral History Interviews*. St. Paul, MN: Hamline University Press, 2006.

INDEX

Page numbers in *italics* indicate illustrations.

Abbott, Seth, 132
Adams, John Quincy, 37
Adams family, 51
Adelhelm family, 152
African Americans: in armed services, 223n26; Civil War veterans, 215n15; "contrabands," 19, 20, 35, 63; decrease in number rural areas, 54, 55, 56; diabetes and obesity, 202; early arrivals, 19; early interactions between Whites, Native Americans, and, 7; education, 109; and farming, 3, 10, 43, 55-56; federal legislation granting rights to, 37; and gentrification process, 172; "Great Migration," 74; home ownership rate gap with Whites, 202; housing segregation and discrimination in employment, 197; incarceration, 49, 202; income, 109, 119, 120, 202; infant mortality, 202; as inferior to Whites, 19-20; institutionalization of, 49, 57-60; legal racial equality, 37; measures to bar, from settling in Minnesota, 20, 21, 26-27; racism toward, as natural, 33; stereotypes of, in Bloomington schools, 237n19; as strikebreakers, 66, 70; suffrage, 21, 26, 27, 36, 37, 50, 211n14; and union membership, 109, 223n27; in UPWA, 80; Whites' attitude toward and treatment of, post Civil War, 36, 61, 213n27; World War II "Double V" slogan, 195. *See also* employment; housing segregation; lynchings; violence against African Americans
African Americans: population: Albert Lea (1970-2010), 238n6; Austin (1900-1930), 66-67, 217n2; Austin (1970-2010), 199; Austin (1990-2010), 89; Austin (eve of World War II), 67; Bloomington (1870-1910), 234n2; Bloomington (1941-1960), 174; Bloomington (1969), 180; Bloomington (1980-2010), 189, 199; Brooklyn Center (1980-2010), 198; Duluth

249

Whiteness in Plain View: A History of Racial Exclusion in Minnesota
was designed and set in type by Judy Gilats in St. Paul, Minnesota.
The text typeface is Clifford and the display face is Proxima Nova Condensed.